An Intelligent Person's Guide to Classics

An Intelligent Person's
Guide to Classics

PETER JONES

Duckworth

First published in 1999 by
Gerald Duckworth & Co. Ltd.
61 Frith Street
London W1V 5TA
Tel: 0171 434 4242
Fax: 0171 434 4420
Email: enquiries@duckworth-publishers.co.uk

A catalogue record for this book is available
from the British Library

ISBN 0 7156 2866 6

Illustrations

The author and publisher are very grateful to Nicholas Wood
for permission to reproduce his reconstruction from p. 21 of
The House of the Tragic Poet (London, 1996) and to Thames and
Hudson Ltd, London, for the reconstruction painting
by William Suddaby from *Roman Art and
Architecture* by Mortimer Wheeler.

Typeset by Ray Davies
Printed in Great Britain by
Biddles Ltd, Guildford & King's Lynn

Contents

Plates between pages 32 and 33

Preface

This is the only book ever published whose author may well agree with the critic who says he should have written a different one. But I probably could not have written it.

Its aim is three-fold: first, to outline the history of the period covered by Classics (roughly 700 BC – AD 500); second, to indicate briefly how the literature and remains of the ancient world have been preserved and revealed; and finally to discuss certain aspects of Greeks and Roman life and thought that I hope will strike the Intelligent Person as interesting. It says little about classical literature *qua* literature since I have said what I want to say about that in my *Classics in Translation* (Duckworth).

Angela Lambert read four chapters of some early drafts and completely reconstructed them, to their very considerable benefit. My colleagues of many years around the Sunday evening snooker table, Alan Beale and Adrian Spooner, improved much of the rest, remaining icily calm among the balls as they did so. My best thanks too to Andrew Morley for the illustrations.

I dedicate this book, on her instructions, to my daughter Phoe.

July 1999   Peter Jones
Newcastle upon Tyne

Reading List

Classical Literature
Penguin's 'Ancient Classics' series, Oxford's 'World's Classics' series and Wordsworth Classics provide a wide range of inexpensive translations of mainstream authors.

The Loeb Classical Library (Heinemann-Harvard) publishes texts and facing-page translations of virtually all classical literature.

The latest editions of the multi-volume *Cambridge Ancient History* remain essential reading for those who want up-to-date, detailed scholarship.

General Introductions
Paul Cartledge (ed.), *Ancient Greece* (Cambridge 1998).
K.J. Dover, *Greek Popular Morality* (Blackwell 1974).
S. Hornblower and A. Spawforth (edd.), *The Oxford Classical Dictionary* (third edition, Oxford 1996).
JACT, *The World of Athens* (Cambridge 1984).
Peter Jones and Keith Sidwell (edd.), *The World of Rome* (Cambridge 1997).
Peter Jones, *Ancient & Modern* (Duckworth 1999).
Jo-Ann Shelton, *As the Romans Did* (Oxford 1988).

The Languages
Peter Jones, *Learn Latin* (Duckworth, 1997).
Peter Jones, *Learn Ancient Greek* (Duckworth, 1998).

The Classical Heritage
R.R. Bolgar, *The Classical Heritage and its Beneficiaries* (Cambridge 1954).
M.I. Finley (ed.), *The Legacy of Greece* (Oxford 1981).
Richard Jenkyns (ed.), *The Legacy of Rome* (Oxford 1992).
Oliver Taplin, *Greek Fire* (Jonathan Cape 1989).

Textual Transmission
L.D. Reynolds and N.G. Wilson, *Scribes and Scholars* (second edition, Oxford 1974).
N.G. Wilson, *Scholars of Byzantium* (Duckworth 1983).
N.G. Wilson, *From Byzantium to Italy* (Duckworth 1992).

1

Greeks in a Roman World

We are in ancient Asia Minor (modern Turkey), an area under Roman rule, and the date is around AD 100. Greeks, who started inhabiting this region over a thousand years earlier, have now for some 200 years been living under a Roman provincial governor and paying taxes to Rome. The glory that was classical Athens – the golden age of Pericles and Socrates, Greek tragedy and the Parthenon – is over five hundred years in the past: from our perspective at the dawn of a new millennium, it would be like looking back on Columbus.

It is mid-summer, but the morning dawns as chilly as autumn and, as our narrator Dio, the Greek orator, essayist and public servant, tells us in his *Discourse* 52, he is not feeling particularly well. So he gets up, does the necessary, offers a prayer and goes for a spin in his chariot. After that he takes a stroll, lies down for a little, has a bath and eats. What now? Dio decides to spend the day reading classical Greek tragedy. He selects as his topic the story of the Greek mythic hero Philoctetes, as told by the fifth-century BC Athenian tragedians Aeschylus, Sophocles, and Euripides.

The outline of the story was well known. Philoctetes helped Heracles commit suicide, and Heracles rewarded him by giving him his invincible bow. Philoctetes took the bow to Troy, but was bitten in the foot by a snake. The wound refused to heal, and the stench of it, combined with Philoctetes' cries of agony, made life for the army intolerable. Odysseus therefore persuaded the Greeks to ditch him, with his bow as his only life-line, on the nearby island of Lemnos. Some years later, however, the Greeks received an oracle that Troy would not be taken without the help of Philoctetes and his bow, and Odysseus was commanded to bring him back. But the years of abandonment had soured Philoctetes against the Greeks in general and Odysseus in particular.

Dio tells us he is thrilled at the prospect of his day's employment. Greek tragedies, he remembers, were staged in competition against each at the two major dramatic festivals in fifth-century BC Athens (the Lenaea in January and Dionysia in March-April), with three playwrights battling it out for the prize. But, Dio reflects, while Aeschylus on occasion competed on the same bill with Sophocles, and Sophocles with Euripides, because of the age difference all three of them were never on the same bill together.

So Dio sees that he is able to do something that no Athenian of the time could have done – to judge plays by the three greatest Greek tragedians, all in one swoop. Moreover, he realises, the plays are on the same theme too, surely a rare occurrence in fifth-century Athens. And so he settles down.

Dio's words are for us purest gold. We know from various sources (e.g. records of ancient *Lives*, ancient encyclopaedia entries and lists) that Aeschylus wrote between seventy and ninety plays, but we possess only six in full, plus the almost certainly unAeschylean *Prometheus Bound*. Sophocles wrote more than one hundred and twenty plays; we have but seven. Euripides wrote about ninety plays, of which we possess eighteen, plus *Rhesus*, probably not by Euripides. So of the *c.* 300 plays written by these master playwrights, we possess only thirty-one in full, plus two probably by other hands. Parts of many more plays by the three tragedians survive, of course, some retrieved from the desert sands, most quoted in the works of other ancient Greek authors – but the amount we can glean from these varies enormously.[1] We have, for example, only about a dozen lines of Aeschylus' and fewer than forty lines of Euripides' versions of *Philoctetes*, and they give us virtually no clue as to how their responses to the myth were shaped. So Dio's golden words (he was nicknamed Chrysostom, *chrusostomos*, 'golden-mouthed') enable us to get some sort of grip on their versions.

The results are fascinating. In Sophocles, as we know, the young, idealistic Neoptolemus (son of Achilles) is brought by Odysseus to trick Philoctetes into returning to Troy. Odysseus, being hated by Philoctetes, stays well out of sight. The chorus consists of Neoptolemus' shipmates. But Neoptolemus, overcome by pity for the helpless old man (who is utterly alone on the island), is unable to maintain the deception, reveals all and wrecks the scheme. Indeed, he is even about to leave for Greece (not Troy) with the outcast, and Philoctetes is willing to use the bow against the Greeks who will certainly come after them, when Heracles intervenes and straightens everything out.

In Aeschylus, Odysseus acts on his own. The chorus consists of people of Lemnos. Odysseus is not recognised by Philoctetes because Philoctetes is at the end of his tether. Philoctetes tells the chorus his story, and Odysseus persuades him to return to Troy by arguing deceitfully that the Greeks have suffered numerous defeats, Agamemnon is dead, Odysseus is on a charge, and the whole expedition has gone to pot.

In Euripides, Odysseus has been disguised by Athene and arrives with the Greek hero Diomedes. The chorus consists of Lemnians, and there is a Lemnian Aktor, who has known Philoctetes for some time. Odysseus reveals that he has heard that an embassy of Trojans is about to arrive to beg Philoctetes to become their king: with his bow, they will easily repel the Greek invaders. The Trojans duly arrive, a series of debates ensues (Euripides adores debates), and Odysseus wins out.

So much, then, for the partial survival of the otherwise lost Aeschylean and Euripidean versions of *Philoctetes*. The classical texts that fully survive do so mostly in medieval manuscripts, the end-product of copying over hundreds, in some cases, thousands, of years (not one of our manuscripts is an autograph). For example, our earliest manuscript of fifth-century BC Sophocles dates to about AD 950 and the next earliest to about 1150 (and is an indirect descendant of the first). In all there are about one hundred and fifty such medieval manuscripts of Sophocles in various libraries around Europe (Florence, Venice, Vienna, Paris, the Vatican, Milan, and so on), and one of the jobs of textual scholars is to show whether and how they relate to each other. Our earliest manuscripts of Greek literature date from the tenth century AD, and of Latin literature from the fifth century AD. Every ancient author who survived in manuscript till the fourteenth century and the printing revolution still survives – though we know of some manuscripts that were available in the tenth century but still, infuriatingly, did not make it to the fourteenth and are lost for ever. When, for example, the Franks sacked Athens during the Fourth Crusade in 1205, they destroyed the last manuscript of most of the poetry of Callimachus.

Dio survives in medieval manuscript form and, as we have seen, is a marvellous indirect source for two Greek tragedies that did not make it into the middle ages. Sources like Dio are, in fact, extremely important, in some cases the rule rather than the exception. For example, there is no manuscript tradition of Greek lyric poetry. All that we possess survives in quotation in other authors or in papyrus finds (see below). A major source of quotation from many otherwise lost ancient works is the unlikely figure of Athenaeus. His wonderfully lunatic fifteen-book *Deipnosophistai* ('Intellectuals at Dinner'), written *c.* AD 200, is a discussion of the sorts of topics that intellectuals debate at table, covering everything from philosophy, literature, law, and medicine to whores, cooking and sex, and cites some 1,250 authors, gives the titles of over a thousand plays and quotes more than ten thousand lines of verse.[2]

Then take Photius. Around AD 855, this future patriarch of Constantinople was invited to join a dangerous diplomatic mission to the Arabs. Before he left, his brother Tarasios asked him to make a summary of all the books he had read. The result is Photius' *Bibliotheca*, 'library' (first published in 1601), a series of summaries and comments on two hundred and eighty books by a huge number of Greek, Roman and Byzantine author prose authors (no poets), half of them now lost. For example, out of the thirty-three historians Photius summarises, twenty do not otherwise survive.[3] Then take Isidore, seventh-century AD bishop of Seville, who wrote the equivalent of a classical encyclopedia called *Etymologiae*; or Hesychius, fifth-century AD author of a lexicon of rare words; or Stobaeus, a contemporary of Hesychius, who wrote an anthology of excerpts from poets and prose authors to instruct his son Septimius. They all preserve for us quotations from or summaries of texts that would otherwise be lost.[4]

One obvious question emerges from Dio's *Discourse*: could he have chosen for comparison any of the three hundred-odd plays of the three tragedians? The answer to that is 'yes', given a handy library. Quotations and references in contemporary authors make it clear that virtually the complete corpus of classical Latin and Greek literature was available till about the fourth century AD.[5] Increasingly after that time, education was in the hands of the Church. Consequently, though there is almost no evidence of book-burning or institutionalised suppression, the corpus was no longer routinely copied – through lack of general interest (as Christianity blossomed) and concentration only on specific authors, for strictly educational purposes.[6] Papyrus, the basic ancient paper,[7] probably did not last longer than about a hundred years in normal use anyway: so texts on papyrus needed copying every century or so to survive (though the doctor Galen talks of handling a roll three hundred years old). Parchment (usually sheep or goat skin, treated, cleaned, stretched and smoothed) lasts a very long time indeed but is very expensive. So parchment carrying 'useless' classical texts was from this time frequently scrubbed or scraped almost clean and more relevant texts, usually scriptural, written over them. Indeed, from such parchments, known as palimpsests, vital ancient texts have been recovered with the help of magnifying glasses and bright lights in the past and multi-spectral imaging now.[8] The text of Cicero's *de republica*, for example, survives only in this form, composed by Cicero in the first century BC, copied onto the parchment we now possess in the fifth century AD, and overwritten with Augustine's thoughts on the psalms in the seventh.[9]

So educational choice largely controlled what was copied and therefore what we now possess. But chance, in the shape of papyrus fragments, has played its part too.[10] The hot, dry desert is the only environment where papyrus and its ink survive unaided, and our earliest scraps from that source date to the fourth century BC. Aristotle's *Constitution of Athens* emerged from Egyptian sands in 1891, causing a sensation and giving the search for papyri a tremendous boost; our store of Greek lyric poets like Sappho would be much diminished without such finds; our knowledge of the wildly popular Greek 'drawing-room' comic poet Menander depends almost entirely on papyrus discoveries. But one must dismiss 'Indiana Jones' images of this activity. The fact is that any 'new find' will have been lying in a university or museum for years, waiting to be deciphered – for the depressing fact is that there are not enough papyrologists to go round.[11] Even as I write, for example, a papyrus found and read many years ago has been looked at again, this time with a computer programmed to search for matches between any text, however fragmentary, and the rest of surviving Greek literature. It now appears that it records long extracts from the fifth-century BC Greek philosopher Empedocles – previously known only from disembodied quotations in other authors. Empedocles is enormously important in the history of thought (e.g. for his theory that earth, air, fire and water are the four basic forms of perceptible matter).

Even less Indiana Jonesian is the fact that most of the Greek papyri found in the desert are not texts of Aeschylus but less romantic documents relating to life in Egypt – official correspondence, edicts, petitions, complaints, legal contracts, lists, receipts, letters and private papers of every description. So life in Egypt under the Greeks and the Romans is pretty well documented. Latin papyri are far less common, Greek being the main language of the eastern Mediterranean where conditions permit papyrus to survive. Most of those that have been recovered are – surprise, surprise – military documents.

The main sources of papyrus texts have now been mostly worked out. There is one other remaining, most unexpected source of further possible papyrus finds – mummy cases. These are made out of layers of papyrus, sometimes reinforced with linen cloth, covered with plaster and painted. Where the case-makers pillaged written papyrus for their construction, the papyrus can be removed and read. In the early twentieth century this was done crudely by removing the layers by hand. Now modern enzyme technology is used to unglue the layers. Important finds have been made this way (lost extracts from Euripides and Menander), but since museums are loath to see their precious cases destroyed, more could be awaiting discovery.[12]

The great prize, however, is Herculaneum, one of the towns buried by Vesuvius in AD 79. Here a complete ancient library belonging to Philodemus, tutor to Virgil, came to light in 1752. One level of the library has been investigated. There are two more currently sealed off. The papyrus rolls in them survived through being carbonised at 325°C (a little hotter and they would have gone up in flames, a little cooler and they would not have been preserved). Those that have come out are the devil to unroll and read. They include Lucretius, Ennius and a comedy by Caecilius Statius, as well as works by Philodemus. But what else is in this library? And when will it be recovered?[13] That said, it must be emphasised that, even if the rolls can be read, it will take centuries to read them – unless there is a huge increase in the number of papyrologists.

All this makes it clear why Dio's *Discourse* 52 is so valuable – another grain of 'lost' knowledge added to the precious heap that survives from 1200 years of Graeco-Roman culture, beginning (in literary terms) in the Greek world with Homer (*c.* 720 BC) and ending (let us say) around AD 500. The crucial point is that in Dio's day, whatever else has happened over the five hundred years since the 'classical age' of Athens, and however much the Greek world may have changed (especially with the imposition of Roman rule in the second century BC), the cultural achievements of fifth/fourth-century BC Athens still dominated the intellectual horizon of both Greeks and Romans.

Take, for example, the Greek essayist Plutarch. A contemporary of Dio, he devotes one whole dialogue to a discussion of what Plato must have meant by saying that 'God is always doing geometry'. The parties start by agreeing that this saying is not found anywhere in Plato but still insist is utterly Platonic.[14] Plato, remember, had been dead nearly five hundred years. The various analyses centre around Plato's views about perfection (geometry being as near perfection as one can get) and world control (whether control of mankind, that men must receive their dues in geometric proportion, or of matter, that, being in principle infinite, needs confining and structuring, a job for the geometer).

It is very doubtful whether we would know much about ancient Greeks at all if the Romans had not taken on board their ideas wholesale and put them at the heart of their own culture and educational system. The Romans, whatever one may make of their military and imperial record, were not slow to recognise that, when it came to things of the mind, they had to bow to the Greeks.

But it is now time to put all this in context. The next chapter gives a brief description of what is meant by the classical world.

2

The Classical Period:
700 BC – AD 500

In traditional Classics, language and literature reign supreme. So the Greeks come before the Romans because Greek literature antedates Roman by about five hundred years. This is the first Great Truth of classical education. Greek literature – indeed, *western* literature – begins with Homer's unmatched epics the *Iliad* and *Odyssey*, produced somewhere on or off the coast of western Turkey, usually dated to *c.* 720 BC or later. It flowers through the archaic age (700-500 BC, with early philosophers like Thales and lyric poets like Sappho); through the classical period (500-323 BC, with all the great names like Aeschylus, Sophocles, Euripides, Aristophanes, Herodotus, Thucydides, Plato and Aristotle); and from then on in a continuous tradition down to the present.

Roman literature, however, does not become a potent force for us till the second century BC with the comic playwright Plautus; and even then pickings are pretty thin until the Roman classical period, the 'golden' first century BC during Republican times (Lucretius, Catullus, Caesar, Horace, Virgil, Livy, Cicero) and 'silver' first century AD when the empire had begun (Ovid, Pliny, Seneca, Martial, Tacitus, Juvenal).

What most people today still mean by 'Classics' is learning the language and studying the literature of classical Greece in the fifth and, to a lesser extent, fourth century BC (with eighth-century Homer) and of classical Rome in the first century BC and, to a lesser extent, first century AD. The reason is that Classics, like any discipline, is a matter of human choice ('a cultural construct' is a grander way of putting it), and what we know as classical Greek and Latin literature consists largely of what the *ancients themselves* thought were the best bits. Obviously, what they thought was good had a serious chance of surviving.

So: first the Greeks, and then the Romans. The second Great Truth of a classical education is that Roman literature – indeed, most of Roman high culture – was developed out of Greek. While Greeks, one way and another, had had a presence in Italy from the eighth century BC, Romans had had little to do with them till the third century BC. The cultural transformation in the Roman world was then dramatic. An outline historical account of the Greeks and Romans in the Mediterranean is now in order.

Greek speakers probably entered the Greek mainland during the third millennium BC; and about 1100 BC, some migrated from the mainland east to the Aegean islands and west coast of Turkey (i.e. when 'palace' civilisation – the heroic strongholds like Mycenae and Pylos referred to by Homer – collapsed). Then in the eighth century BC colonisation from the Greek mainland spread Greek speakers westwards: first to Corcyra (Corfu), then on to the south of Italy starting around Naples and down to Sicily. Later, this whole area was known as Magna Graecia. About 630 BC Greeks went to Cyrene in North Africa, and from 600 BC onwards to Marseille and Emporion ('Tradersville') in northern Spain. Slightly later, existing Greek settlements in Turkey sent out colonies further east along the coast of Turkey to Byzantium and on to the Black Sea (e.g. Crimea in the north and Trebizond in the south). So by 580 BC, there were Greek speakers all round the Mediterranean and Black Sea, 'like frogs around a pond', in Plato's vivid phrase.

During this period, the foundations of the Greek intellectual, artistic and literary achievement were laid – not on the Greek mainland so much as on the Greek-occupied islands off, and the coast of, modern Turkey. It cannot be insignificant that the great civilisations of the Near East were on the doorstep of these Greeks (see Chapter 4). Indeed, in the eighth century BC the Greeks developed their writing system and the world's first alphabet from the Phoenicians (roughly modern Lebanon).

It is important to emphasise that at this period Greece was never a political unity: the individual city states that developed out of the eighth century BC like Athens, Sparta, Corinth, etc. were free, proud, autonomous, competitive and rarely stopped squabbling. They were united only in that they all spoke various dialects of Greek. Again, what we know specifically as 'classical Greece' is in fact not Greece at all, but the city state of Athens. Athens was the home of the great fifth-century cultural leap, a creative and refining development of the work of earlier Greek thinkers and artists to the east. But whatever its ultimate explanation, this 'leap' was surely given impetus by the Athenian Cleisthenes' invention of radical democracy in 507 BC (see Chapter 5) and the defeat of the invading Persians (in the Persian Wars) in 490-479 BC, in which Athens played a leading part – an event whose cultural significance has been likened to the defeat of the Spanish Armada.

But the glory years were not to last. Thucydides' magnificent *History of the Peloponnesian War* describes Athens' defeat at the hands of Sparta in 404 BC after a stupendous 27-year conflict. Then, in 338 BC, Macedon to the north, which had been encroaching south for twenty years under King Philip II, defeated the free Greek states to become master of the Greek mainland. Philip was assassinated shortly after, and his son Alexander the Great became king. Determined to show how Greek he was, he famously set out to avenge Greeks on the Persians for the Persian Wars one hundred and fifty years earlier. Sweeping all before him eastwards across Turkey,

Iraq, and Iran, he planted Greek cities as he went and took Greek culture as far as India.

It was a short-lived triumph. Alexander died in Babylon in 323 BC (the end of the 'classical' age and start of the 'Hellenistic' age). The Macedonian generals he had left in charge of conquered areas abandoned the link with Macedon and turned themselves into autonomous Greek kings. For example, Ptolemaios (=Ptolemy), Alexander's regent in Egypt, became king Ptolemy I of Egypt, and Ptolemies ruled Egypt till it became a Roman province, after the victory in 31 BC of Octavian – soon to be the first Roman emperor Augustus – over Antony and his Greek consort Cleopatra. She was the last Ptolemy, queen of Egypt. This event heralds the end of the 'Hellenistic' age.

But Greeks did not stop being Greeks merely because of various political upheavals: they did not stop building or writing or thinking. Enormously influential philosophies were invented. In Athens, for example, Stoicism was invented by Zeno (d. 263 BC) and Epicureanism by Epicurus (d. 270 BC) (see Chapter 13). The Ptolemies turned Alexandria into a cultural centre to rival Athens, luring the best Greek literary, scientific and medical researchers in the Mediterranean with their cash and facilities to work at the magnificent Museum.

This *Mouseion*, literally a temple to the muses, goddesses of culture, was established *c.* 280 BC and became the ancient world's greatest research centre. Its Library was reputed to contain anything from 200,000-490,000 books, i.e. papyrus rolls. In this Library great scholars like Aristophanes from Byzantium (d. 180 BC – not the Athenian comic poet) and Aristarchus (d. 144 BC) produced the first definitive texts of all classical Greek literature, from which ours descend today. The scientific research centre offered its facilities to an astonishing range of inventive geniuses like Archimedes, Euclid, the geographer Eratosthenes, Apollonius (conic sections), Ctesibius (ballistics), Heron (steam-engine). This added up to a post-classical 'Hellenistic' age, as it is called, of considerable cultural significance.

But while much of this was going on, Rome remained just another little Italian hill-town. The Etruscans were the main power in Italy in the eighth century BC, spreading from Salerno (south of Rome) northwards almost as far as the Alps. This people had rich commercial and cultural links with the Greeks who had planted colonies in Italy from the eighth century onwards. Rome's rise to power began when they threw out the Etruscan kings in 509 BC and founded the republic after, as tradition has it, Sextus Tarquinius, son of king Tarquin, raped the Roman noblewoman Lucretia.[1] From now on, Rome began aggressively to expand its power outwards, south and north, making alliances with or mopping up local tribes as it went, till by 295 BC it was the dominant power in Italy, and Latin, the language of Latium (modern Lazio, the region where Romans lived), became the *lingua franca* of the whole mainland.

In 280 BC Tarentum, a Greek colony deep in south-eastern Italy, called in Greek King Pyrrhus from north-west Greece over the water to help fight Roman expansion. Pyrrhus enjoyed some success, but after one too many Pyrrhic victories (with victories like these, he lamented, who needs defeats?), he retired back to Greece. This sent out a signal out that Rome was a formidable new power. The international stage beckoned.

Rome now fought the Punic wars against Carthage in North Africa. Carthage was a colony founded by Phoenicians in the ninth century BC. The wars are 'Punic', because *Punici* was the best Romans could do with *Phoinikes*, the Greek for 'Phoenicians'. The first war was fought over possession of Sicily and won by Rome in 241 BC, Sicily becoming its first province. The second began in 218 BC when Hannibal, bent on revenge, established a base in Spain and famously took his army, complete with elephants, over the Alps and down into Italy from the north. His aim was to destroy Roman power by encouraging the Italian tribes to shake off the yoke of Rome. But he could not drive home his initial stunning successes at battles such as Trasimene (217 BC) and Cannae (216 BC). Publius Cornelius Scipio 'Africanus' then took the battle first to Spain and in 205 BC to Africa. Hannibal was forced to return and was defeated at Zama in 202 BC. In 197 BC, Spain was divided into two more Roman provinces.

Rome looked back on the defeat of Hannibal as their 'finest hour'. Rome also learned the lesson of Hannibal. It had fielded massive citizen armies to keep Hannibal at bay, and it maintained those armies from now on as it began its rise to absolute dominance in the Mediterranean.[2] Its first target after Zama was – Greece. The Greek king Philip V, believing that Hannibal would defeat the Romans, had foolishly allied himself with Carthage. Rome decided to bring him to heel. A prolonged period of political jousting and occasionally military engagement ensued. Embassies, including senators, went back and forth. Roman traders and businessmen began to appear in Greece. Greeks, especially slaves, began to appear in Rome. Greek envoys came on missions; foreign hostages were taken.[3] Romans and Greeks started becoming seriously acquainted.[4] At the political level, however, Rome eventually lost patience and in 146 BC Greece was turned into a province, soon to be followed by Asia (i.e. western Turkey). Meanwhile, after the Elder Cato's repeated demand *Carthago delenda est*, Carthage was razed to the ground in 149 BC.

Greeks and Romans had now encountered each other seriously for the first time. The effect on Rome was earth-shaking. On this critical period, the Roman poet Horace rightly commented *Graecia capta ferum victorem cepit et artes / intulit agresti Latio* ('Captured Greece captured its wild conqueror, and brought culture to savage Latium').[5]

To summarise, then, in two columns:

Greece	Rome
1600-1100 BC	
Mycenean (bronze age) Greece.	
1100	
Mycenaean culture collapses. Many	**1000 BC**
Greeks migrate to Aegean islands and	Continuous occupation of Rome.
western Turkey.	
800-580	
Greeks establish colonies all round	**753**
the Mediterranean and Black Sea.	Traditional date for founding of Rome.
507-400	**509**
Cleisthenes invents democracy 507;	Rape of Lucretia; Tarquins expelled.
Persian Wars 490-479; 'golden age' of	Foundation of the Roman republic.
Athenian culture.	Rome's rise to power begins.
338-146	
Philip of Macedon controls Greece	
(assassinated 336); Alexander the	
Great takes Greek culture as far east	
as India; after his death in 323 (the	**295**
start of the **Hellenistic** period),	Rome dominant force in Italy
territories he conquered taken over by	**264-202**
the men he left in charge, e.g. Ptolemy	Two Punic wars; Carthage defeated.
in Egypt, Philip V in Macedon, etc.	Sicily and Spain become provinces.
146	**146**
Greece becomes a province of Rome	Rome makes Greece a province.

Rome was now at the centre not just of a political but also of a cultural empire. It was to remain this way throughout the Republican period and the empire (which began with the accession of the first emperor Augustus in 31 BC: see Chapter 8). But as with the earlier conquest of Greece by Philip and Alexander from distant Macedon, Greek cultural activity did not cease because Greeks now had Roman masters. From its provinces Rome demanded tribute and compliance in foreign policy, and that essentially was all. But as Horace pointed out, Romans took on Greek culture with an enthusiasm that made it look as if Greece was the master, not Rome.

For example, the Greek philosopher Panaetius (c. 185-109 BC) joined the intellectual circle of the Roman general Scipio Aemilianus, as did the great Greek historian and statesman Polybius (c. 200-118 BC), who accompanied him all over the Mediterranean. Polybius watched the destruction of Carthage and helped negotiate the settlement of Greece, all the while writing his superb history of the rise of Roman power in the Mediterranean. The Roman poet Plautus, whose comedies were Roman adaptations of Greek originals, the epic poet Ennius and the first Roman historian

Quintus Fabius Pictor, all working at about this time, instigated the first truly Roman literature – and they worked throughout with Greek models, which they fashioned to Roman ends.[6]

There is a telling story in Polybius' histories. His patron, Scipio Aemilianus, was besotted with all things Greek, and admitted to Polybius that his reputation suffered: he was considered to be lacking typical Roman energy and drive. Yet he had a brilliant career; and as he supervised the final destruction of Carthage in 149 BC, he quoted, from Homer's *Iliad*, the Trojan champion Hector's vision of what would happen to his own city: 'A day will come when sacred Troy shall perish and Priam and its people be slain.' The Romans saw themselves as descendants of Troy. Scipio continued: 'A glorious moment, Polybius; but I have a terrible fear that some day someone else will pronounce the same fate for my own country.'

For some time Romans nurtured forebodings about their power and its implications. Nor were they wholly reconciled to their admiration for Greek culture. The stern old Roman Cato the Elder (234-149 BC), who urged the destruction of Carthage, wrote to his son:

> The results of my own experience in Athens are that it is a good idea to dip into Greek literature, but not to become too immersed in it ... they are a most iniquitous and intractable people, and you may take my word as the word of a prophet – if that people shall ever bestow its literature upon us, it will corrupt everything.
>
> Pliny, *Natural History* 29.13

Naturally, what remains of Cato's work demonstrates a deep knowledge of Greek literature.

But whatever Cato's concerns, in the course of the second century BC Greek literature and Greek-inspired Roman literature became firmly established in Roman life, and by the first century BC, they were a central feature of the Roman cultural and educational scene.[7] Élite Romans like Caesar and Cicero went to Greece to get educated in the real thing; the first emperor Augustus (31 BC – AD 14) went out of his way to present a cultivated, Greek side to his otherwise all-Roman image; and educated Greeks flocked to Rome to make their fortunes in the education-and-culture business.[8] Private libraries flourished – the politician and philosopher Cicero built up a huge collection – and Rome's first public library was founded in 39 BC.

The text-copying industry (by hand) was now in full swing in Rome too, though copying papyrus rolls and selling them were hazardous, and errors could be corrected only by hand and word of mouth. Thus Cicero's friend Atticus, who saw to the publication of Cicero's work, was informed by Cicero (in a letter) that in his *de republica* he (Cicero) had called the inhabitants of Phlius *Phliuntii*, when it should have been *Phliasii*. Doubtless Atticus corrected what texts he could, but it made no difference – the sole surviving manuscript of *de republica* has *Phliuntii*. Nevertheless, the work of guarding and transmitting texts was now firmly in train. Public and private libraries flourished from the first century AD onwards. Roman education became standardised throughout the Roman world and Latin became the official language of the Roman West.

While all this was going on, however, the republic was sinking deeper and deeper into political chaos. The reasons are complex, but the heart of the matter seems to have been the Senate's inability to respond intelligently to the demands of the people and soldiers for recognition of legitimate needs (it was a citizen army, so the army and the people spoke essentially with the same voice). As a result, powerful generals began to realise that they could meet those needs and advance their own power by using their discontented troops as a battering-ram against the state. The result was that the ordered system of government by Senate and elected magistrates (see p. 52) collapsed in the face of onslaughts by men like Marius, Sulla, Pompey and Julius Caesar who, with their own, effectively private, armies at their back were able to enforce their will on Rome and the Senate.

When Julius Caesar defeated Pompey in the civil war between the two surviving power-players in 48 BC and effectively made himself monarch, the end of the republic was in sight. After Caesar's assassination on the Ides of March 44 BC by Brutus and his followers (see p. 85), who thought this single act would restore the republic, there was another period of civil war, ending when Caesar's adopted son Octavian defeated Marc Antony (the two had carved up the Roman world between them) and his Egyptian queen Cleopatra at the battle of Actium in 31 BC.

Octavian was now effective dictator, and was soon to become Rome's first emperor, renaming himself Augustus (for which story, see Chapter 8). I often wonder whether there was any connection between the military revolution of the last hundred years of the republic and the cultural revolution brought about by the Romans' contact with the history of the once dangerously anarchic and freedom-loving democracies of the Greek world (see p. 53). It always strikes me as rather too good to be true that the Roman republic was evidently founded just before Cleisthenes invented democracy in Athens.[9]

The transition to empire was painful but brilliantly engineered by Augustus, and created a yet more stable and coherent Mediterranean. It is impossible to overestimate the importance of this for the survival and impact of Greek and Roman literature. When the army of the emperor Claudius took Britain in AD 43, the Roman empire extended from Britain in the west to Syria and Judaea in the east, from the Rhine-Danube in the north to North Africa and Egypt in the south, and it was now that the taste for what we know as classical literature was formed by educated Greeks and Romans – Homer and fifth/fourth-century Greek, first-century BC and first-century AD Latin. The political, intellectual and moral edification offered by Homer, the philosophers, the tragic poets, by Virgil and Cicero, were felt by the ancients themselves to be unmatched. These were the authors to be offered to the young. These therefore were the texts, endlessly copied and re-copied, that stood the best chance of survival.

For nearly five hundred years under the Roman empire in the West, till its end in the fifth century AD, anyone who wanted an education (restricted largely to the wealthy) spent most of their time studying classical Latin literature, with classical Greek literature on the side (though the Greek was slowly dropped).

Classical Greek literature, meanwhile, was the staple of education in the eastern, Greek, part of the Roman empire. In order to give the eastern élites a Rome of their own, the first Christian emperor Constantine (d. AD 337) had turned ancient Byzantium into a seat of power almost equivalent to Rome, renaming it Constantinople (modern Istanbul). In AD 395 the empire administratively split into two: a western half, nominally centred on Rome, and the eastern half, centred firmly on Constantinople. While the western empire sank under pressure from migrating Germanic tribes, the empire of the Greek east flourished, becoming what we know as the Byzantine empire. Here classical Greek literature was standard, but very little Latin. Latin was simply not needed by the wealthy, Greek being the language of culture and administration. Indeed, in the east, the spirit of classical Greek education effectively survived till the destruction of Constantinople by Ottoman Turks in 1453.

The collapse of the Roman empire in the West in the fifth century was not due to anything like a planned, concerted barbarian assault.[10] Various Germanic tribes, sometimes peacefully, sometimes not, many driven out by nomadic Huns from Mongolia, had taken up residence within the western Roman empire from the late third century AD (e.g. Franks around the Rhineland in Gaul from the 270s).[11] Since the Romans could not keep these tribes out, they often accommodated rather than fought them, giving them lands and federate status within the empire. Enclaves of Goths were to be found in Asia Minor and the Balkans; Goths and Franks settled in Gaul, Goths and Suebi in Spain, and Vandals in north Africa.

Many of these Germans served Rome well. Late emperors, for example, surrounded themselves with them. The last army of the Roman empire stationed in Italy consisted almost entirely of them. And many were happy to serve. They admired the imperial monarchy. In other words, some German tribes had become thoroughly romanised in Roman territory well before the Roman empire broke up. But other tribes kept on coming, and full assimilation proved impossible. Rome never solved the problem of ethnic disunity. When Goths under Alaric sacked Rome in AD 410 (for failing to win land and settlements), it was a sign that the authority of Rome in the West was virtually at an end,[12] and the last emperor was removed in AD 476. The tribes now simply established their new, autonomous, individual kingdoms within what was once the mighty western

Roman empire. In truth, many had already done so, like Euric, king of the Visigoths in Gaul and Spain, and the Vandal Gaiseric in north Africa.[13]

The Roman way of doing things, however, did not disappear with the empire. The Germanic tribes had nothing to match the Roman cultural and educational tradition. Illiterate when they entered the empire, already predisposed to look up to it, many local kings intentionally shaped their kingdoms on the pattern of the Roman, and welcomed Romans into their courts after the fall of the empire. Familiar structures, in other words, remained in place locally, and this gave the Christian Church the chance to continue to work among the pagans in the same way as they had under the empire.[14] As they did so, they established their schools (see p. 24) and maintained major elements of classical culture – especially Latin, the language of legislation, administration, culture and education (in time *clericus* was to become the term for any educated person, as well for a church functionary).

The conversion of Clovis, king of the mighty Franks, in AD 496 and his baptism, with three thousand of his soldiers, at Rheims in 498, were a turning point. The result was that by the end of the seventh century, Roman Christianity was dominant throughout Europe. When the Frankish king Charlemagne was crowned emperor by the pope in Rome on Christmas Day AD 800, he was the first western emperor to be proclaimed since AD 476 – whatever his authority in fact meant (there was certainly no sense of a united Europe). His seal at any rate bore the words *Renovatio Romani imperii* – 'Renewal of the Roman empire' – and his reign was accompanied by a rebirth of interest in classical Latin literature ('the Carolingian Renaissance'). Greek, it must be said, hardly existed in the West at this time, of course, but Roman culture mediated much of it, and from the twelfth century AD Arabic translations of Greek treatises would be translated into Latin well before knowledge of the Greek language returned widely to the West.[15]

Interestingly, Christianity at first made little impact on pagan education. In AD 312 the Roman emperor-to-be Constantine had chosen to fight his civil war for the imperial throne under the banner of the Christian God, and by the end of the fourth century, Christianity had become the religion of the Roman world, with the most profound effect on all subsequent European culture. But Christians immediately found themselves with problems.[16] Pagan literature, full of strange gods, most downright immoral, was at the heart of education. Its values were not Christian values, its philosophies out of keeping with the teachings of Christ. But what alternative could Christianity offer? It had no school text-books and its literature, however celestial, was the thinnest of gruel for those fed on a cholesterol-rich diet of Homer, Plato and Cicero.[17]

To soften the impact, Christians set about re-interpreting pagan literature: new religion, new God, new pagans. So pagan gods were allegorised, pagan philosophies reworked into Christian moulds (see p. 128). Virgil's

Eclogue 4, dated 38 BC, offers the most famous example of the Christianising interpretation. Here Virgil, writing at a time of crisis for the Roman
republic after the death of Julius Caesar, foresees the ancient prophecies
being fulfilled in the return of *Virgo*, goddess of justice, to the earth and
the dawn of a new Golden Age in the birth of a child (probably a hoped-for
son of Marc Antony). Christians viewed the passage somewhat differently.

But it was not easy for these Christians, steeped as they were in the
classical tradition. Take St Jerome. His translation of the Bible into Latin
(the Vulgate, AD 404) was to become the 'authorised' Latin version.[18] But
he loved his pagan authors. He reports in *Letter* 22.30 (dated *c.* AD 374)
that, during an illness, he dreamed of being hauled before a Judge who
asked him what he was. 'A Christian,' he replied. 'No,' said the Judge, 'you
are a Ciceronian, not a Christian, for your heart is where your treasure is.'
Mortified, Jerome cried, 'Lord, if ever again I possess worldly books, if ever
I read them, I shall have denied You.' He claims not to have opened his
classical texts for the next fifteen years. Later, he became more liberal. In
Letter 70, he points out that Moses, the prophets, and St Paul had all used
pagan literature, and argues that pagan literature can be put to Christian
use in the same way that God enjoined the Israelites to take gentile wives
and, by shaving their heads and paring their nails, turn them into Israelites. In the same way, the otherwise unyielding Christian apologist
Tertullian[19] (*c.* AD 160-240) allowed children to go to school as long as they
were aware, in his striking image, that they were being offered poison
(though, bizarrely, he drew the line at Christians teaching in schools).[20]

There was only the occasional reaction to this liberal approach. In the
eleventh century AD, for example, the Byzantine monk John Italos had
anathemas pronounced against him for being over-zealous in his Platonic
studies:[21]

> Anathema on those who go through a course of Hellenic studies and are
> taught not simply for the sake of education but follow these empty notions
> and believe in them as the truth, upholding them as a firm foundation to
> such an extent that they lead others to them, sometimes secretly, sometimes
> openly, and teach them without hesitation.

But he was very much the exception, especially in the tolerant world of
Byzantium.

In other words, Roman education simply continued until a viable Christian alternative emerged. This began in the closed, fourth-century
monastic schools (the Desert Fathers in Egypt providing a typical pattern)
and grew with the far more influential episcopal schools. These were
secular institutions for groups of students hoping for a career via the
Church. They were given both a specialised and general education under
the instructional care of a bishop, though not in a monastery. These
episcopal schools became, in time, the western medieval universities. The

significant point is that, though there were, as we have seen, new German masters of Europe after the fall of Rome, European education continued to be in Latin, the universal language of the educated in the West, and classical authors like Cicero and Virgil still had a serious part to play in it. So it was primarily the Church's influence that maintained Latin as the language of culture and education in the West, for better or worse, up till the seventeenth century. Newton's *Philosophiae Naturalis Principia Mathematica* appeared in Latin in 1687.

I end by pointing out that Classics today no longer respects the ancient boundaries. The school study of Graeco-Roman language, culture and history (the last two in translation) does, it is true, stick mainly with the classical periods. In universities, however, courses in the languages and in translation extend well beyond them. They span over two thousand years, from the prehistoric Greece of the Mycenaeans and Minoans (*c.* 1600-1100 BC) with their early form of Greek known as Linear B, to the end of the Roman empire in the West in the fifth century AD and the beginnings of its continuation in the Greek east (the Byzantine period) in the sixth century AD. Classicists, in other words, define their subject these days far more broadly than it was ever defined by Greeks and Romans. The texts, whether in the original or in translation, are also read with much more emphasis on their cultural context, in tune with the demands of our fast-expanding world. Classicists, as ever, respond to the world about them and cut their cloth appropriately.[22]

3

Excavating the Past: Ephesus and the Temple of Artemis

As one staggers round ancient sites clutching guide-books, brows and overpriced plastic bottles of water while trying to avoid the babble of voluble and ignorant guides,[1] one should rejoice that a million other people seem to be doing exactly the same. To wander round a major city like Ephesus with no other soul in sight gives about as much sense of what it must have been like two thousand years ago as to wander round a deserted London today. But site-seeing raises a thousand questions. How do they know this is Ephesus? What happened to it to reduce it to this state (there were no bombs in the ancient world)? For how long has it looked like this? Ephesus was renowned for its temple of Artemis. Where is that temple? How do they *know* it is the temple of Artemis? How much more is there to discover? Here is the story of the recovery of Ephesus, particularly its great temple.[2]

Ephesus is near the west coast of modern Turkey (Fig. 1). It is a Greek city, founded by one Androclus – remember him – around 1000 BC, and was at that time on the coast. From the fourth century BC, it developed into an important port. Its massive temple to Artemis (Roman Diana), also dating from the fourth century BC, was one of the seven wonders of the world.[3] In 133 BC Romans made that part of Turkey a province, calling it Asia, and Ephesus became its administrative and economic centre, with a population rising to about 250,000 people. St Paul wrote a letter to Christians there and visited it (c. AD 53), being given a rough time by local silver-smiths who saw a threat to their lucrative trade in tasteful miniature replicas of the temple of Artemis.[4] It continued to flourish throughout the Roman and Byzantine period – there was an important shrine to St John there – but, as the harbour silted up, it fell slowly into decline and when it was captured by Turks in 1304, became a forgotten backwater.

Virtually everything of the city that is visible today was built during the Roman imperial period (second-fourth century AD), the time of Ephesus' greatest glory (Plate 1). We know this because of the number of buildings on which inscriptions name Roman emperors in whose rule they were put up. The city is in ruins, but great cities do not just disappear, unless buried under volcanoes or, like Olympia, silt. They are recycled. In other words,

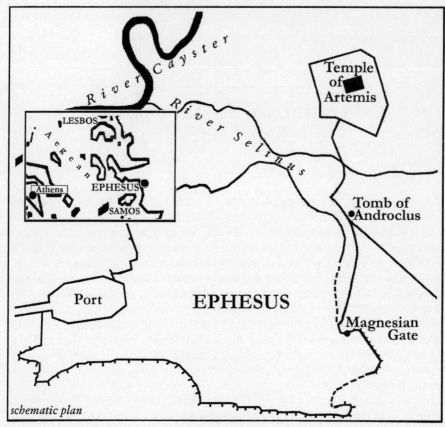

Figure 1

as buildings are neglected, the stone is carted off and used for other purposes, like constructing buildings elsewhere (and squared blocks were more useful in this respect than columns and decorations). When that stone was marble (and much of Ephesus was), there was another yet more destructive use for it: the marble was converted into lime (by heating), and used for mortar. Even more bizarrely, metals were so precious in the middle ages that walls that had been fixed together with metal clamps and dowels were hacked open.

How, then, do we know this place is Ephesus? Coins with 'Ephesus' on them are one answer, inscribed public notices another. One of many such notices found there, for example, begins 'The Council and People of the first and greatest metropolis of Asia, the city of the Ephesians ...'.[5] But early travellers from the West in the seventeenth and eighteenth centuries to this ancient, vast, magnificent city found nothing but a sad collection of scattered, ruined buildings, many half-buried because of the silting up of the plain, and certainly no sign of the fantastic temple of Artemis (Plate 2). This was baffling, given its size: a base measuring 170 by 377 feet (three times larger than the Parthenon), requiring two rows of pillars around the outside to support the roof and three rows at the front, nearly 60 feet tall: 127 columns in all, the elder Pliny tells us. The Greek epigrammatic poet Antipater, writing around 10 BC, describes it as follows in a poem about the seven wonders of the world:

> Rocky Babylon's walls, wide enough for chariots to run along,
> And the statue of Zeus by the river Alpheus I've seen [at Olympia],
> And the Hanging Gardens and the Colossus of the Sun [at Rhodes],
> And the huge labour of the towering pyramids,
> And the mighty tomb of Mausolus; but when I saw
> The temple of Artemis almost touching the clouds
> It put the others in the shade. Except for Olympus,
> The sun never shone on anything its equal.
>
> Antipater, *Palatine Anthology* 9.58

Enter James Turtle Wood, an engineer working for the Ottoman Turks on the single-track Smyrna-Aidin railway (it still functions) and enthusiastic archaeologist.[6] In 1863 he had received permission from the local pasha to do some preliminary investigation at Ephesus, and after following a few hunches which revealed nothing, he asked the British Museum in 1864 for a hundred pounds to excavate the still visible main theatre and the odeion (a smaller theatre, probably in fact the place where the Council met), in the hope that this would lead him to the temple (Fig. 1). He had remembered that large structures like these frequently carried plaques and inscriptions, and he thought he might find one which gave him a clue where the temple was to be found. He also immersed himself in ancient sources that mentioned Ephesus – the elder Pliny, the geographer Strabo, the traveller Pausanias, and many others.

He got his grant for this and the next three years, and in 1867 struck lucky. He excavated a series of slabs inscribed with decrees concerning the gold and silver images given to the temple of Artemis by a wealthy Roman, Gaius Vibius Salutaris, in AD 104. These stated that the effigies should be brought from the temple to the theatre on days when the Assembly met (and on any other days the Council and Assembly decreed) and should be taken back to the temple *via the Magnesian gate*. This was the clue Wood had been looking for.[7] He now put all his efforts into locating that gate. Following the line of the partly visible city walls, he finally found it (it was thus named, and stood near the modern tourist entrance to Ephesus' upper city). His next job, then, was to excavate the road leading out from it. He began in 1868 but found after fifty yards that the road inconsiderately forked in two. Undeterred, he worked on both, and in February 1869 came across a roadside plinth 42 feet square, on which several courses of immense white marble blocks had been constructed. This impressive structure gave no indication of its purpose, but Wood remembered that one of the ancient sources, the traveller Pausanias, had said 'The Ephesians buried Androclus [their founder] in their territory, where the tomb is shown down to my time. It lies on the road which leads from the temple, past the Olympeion, and to the Magnesian gate.' So grand a structure was surely Androclus' tomb, and Wood concentrated excavations on this road.

He dug a further two hundred yards, but it was now April, the plain of Ephesus was sown with barley and it was at its height. He could not dig any further, having no money with which to compensate owners. Meanwhile, the British Museum was getting fractious, warning him that he would get no more money for next season unless he hit the jackpot. It was time for a gamble. Guessing at the probable onward direction of the ancient road, Wood set his men to sink a few trenches in an olive grove some way ahead. Here they hit a thick ancient wall, and noticing that its line followed the line of the modern wall above it, Wood sank another trench beside the modern wall further on. Here, in the angle of the ancient wall, he found the following inscription: 'The emperor Caesar Augustus [a long list of titles follows] caused the temple of Diana to be surrounded by a wall ....'

He had done it. This was surely the boundary wall (*peribolos*) mentioned by the ancient geographer Strabo when he discussed how the temple had been designated as a sanctuary: 'The temple has the right of sanctuary to the present day [first century AD], but its boundaries have varied. Alexander the Great extended them to six hundred feet ... Marc Antony doubled the distance, and thus included a certain portion of the city within the right of sanctuary. But this decree put the city at the mercy of criminals, so Augustus cancelled it.' This wall, then, marked Augustus's new, narrower limits to the area round the temple to be designated as offering sanctuary. Wood excavated this angle of the wall three hundred yards to its north, nearly two hundred to its east, and defined the area within which the temple must have stood. In 1869 he returned with money from the British Museum to buy up the complete site, and on 31 December 1869 struck what he assumed was the temple's marble floor. On New Year's Day 1870, he exposed enough of it to show that it was Greek.

Wood's work continued for the next four years, often in appalling conditions. The temple was some twenty feet below the surface, and if the season was unduly wet, the water could stand seven feet high (the site being some feet below the level of the nearby river Cayster).[8] Nor did the site exactly live up to expectations (Plate 3). The destruction of the temple and recycling of its marble had been very thorough. Individual pieces there were in abundance – slabs, column-drums, mosaics – and sixty tons' worth were shipped back to London in 1873. By the end of four years, when everything was done that could be done, Wood calculated that 132,221 cubic yards of soil had been shifted. But if the temple would never stand again, he had at least identified its site and shape and with the help of coins depicting it (Plate 4(b)) and Pliny the elder's description, was able to offer a reconstruction (Plate 4(a)).

Visitors nowadays will see a large, sunken, in places marshy, area, scattered with meaningless bits and pieces, with a single pillar in the middle, cobbled together out of some remaining column drums, to give some idea of height. A stork nests on top of it – appropriately enough, Artemis being goddess of childbirth (Plate 5).[9]

This compressed account gives a pleasing sense of a ruthlessly logical progress with an air of inevitability about the outcome. After the event, that is always the case. In fact it was at times pretty chaotic. Wood mentions the blind alleys, the problems hiring and retaining even half-decent workmen, the travel (three and half hours each way by train every day), the bandits (Wood had to have a bodyguard, and one of his workers was murdered), and the pestilential tourists (Wood found the Americans by the far the most interested, and 'formed a very high estimate of the American character. I found them generally anxious to make something more than a superficial survey of the ruins, and I do not now remember any party of Americans preferring to sit down to eat and drink, to making a careful examination of all the interesting objects they had come to see').

But nearly all ground-breaking research, whether archaeological or literary, is usually a messy business while it is in progress, and is never one-dimensional. Wood's excavation of the temple of Artemis entailed far more than wielding a spade: knowledge of Latin, Greek, ancient history, scattered historical sources, inscriptions and their conventions, coinage, architectural form, engineering, and so on were all vital to the enterprise, as well as imagination, intelligence, grit, luck and fund-raising skills.

To move to a different area, a scholar dealing with a new papyrus fragment encounters problems no less acute – straightening it out, mending it, ensuring it does not fall apart under examination, dating the papyrus from the style of the handwriting, determining whereabouts in the roll it might have come, decipherment (with all the problems of poor handwriting, odd conventions of spelling, plain bad spelling, holes caused by book-worm, blotches in the papyrus), transliteration, translation (if it is translatable), saying what is going on, determining authorship, emending the text, comparing it with other texts, and so on.

To end with a delicious example of papyrological problems. Ancient texts were written in capital letters with no gaps between the words and no punctuation. The scribe of the fourteenth-century manuscript of Euripides known as L was copying out Euripides' *Hêraklês mainomenos*. Heracles in a fit of madness has slaughtered his children, fallen asleep and now wakes up. His father Amphitryon is in attendance:

Heracles: Father, why are you weeping and veiling your eyes, retreating far from your dear son?
Amphitryon: My son! Still mine, for all the evil you have done!

Heracles: What grievous thing have I done to make you weep?
Euripides, *Madness of Heracles* 1111

The scribe was now faced with a reply by Amphitryon made up of the following run of letters:

AKANTHEÔNTISEIPATHOIKATASTENOI

This stumped him. Like a desperate schoolboy faced with an incomprehensible Greek unseen, he abandoned sense and split the words up in any way he could, in the hope of at least gaining a few marks for effort:

AKANTHEÔN TIS EIPATH' OI KATASTENOI
'A certain one of the spines, say [all of you], whither may it groan.'

Characters on the Greek stage rarely enquire after the emotional well-being of the local flora. The scribe should have divided the words up:

A K'AN THEÔN TIS, EI PATHOI, KATASTENOI
'Such things as a god would groan at, were he to suffer them.'

1. Reconstructions of Ephesus.

2. Site of Ephesus (engraving, c.1860).

3. Engraving of the excavation of the Temple of Artemis (c.1870).

4(a). Reconstruction of the Temple of Artemis (by J. T. Wood).

4(b). Medal, obverse and reverse, illustrating the temple of Artemis.

5. Present site of the temple of Artemis.

4 COMPOSITE

3 CORINTHIAN

2 IONIC

1 DORIC

6. The Colosseum, with drawn orders inset.

enablature

CORNICE
FRIEZE
ARCHITRAVE
CAPITAL

PILASTER

BASE

PEDESTAL

FOOTING

impost

impost

impost

7. The arch of Constantine, illustrating the orders.

8. Long section of the House of the Tragic Poet, Pompeii.

9(a). The *basilica nova*.

9(b). Seventeenth-century painting of the Constantinian *basilica* of St Peter in Rome.

9(c). S. Maria Maggiore, Rome.

11. Il Redentore, Venice (see p. 120).

10. S. Maria Novella, Florence.

12. Il Redentore (interior).

13. The Pantheon, Rome.

4

Greeks and the Near East

Everyone is fascinated by origins, and when we turn to the history of ideas, it seems that the ancient Greeks set a large number up and running for the first time.[1] Any classicist can reel off a check-list: Greeks invented philosophy, history, democracy, tragedy, dialectic, rhetoric, rational medicine, a range of architectural forms, the idea of a library whose purpose is to preserve, edit, explain and transmit a national literature, logic, biology (these last two the work of Aristotle), axiomatic reasoning and so on. One might object that people had been e.g. logical and rhetorical and cured people medically before ancient Greeks ever appeared on the scene. In those cases, then, a more accurate term for the Greek achievement would be 'rationally systematised, turned into a structured discipline for the first time'. In other words, Greeks invented and explained the rules governing logic, rhetoric and the practice of healing.

At the heart of the Greek intellectual achievement lies its rationalism, that is, the Greek insistence that the world be humanly comprehensible, understood without recourse to the supernatural, and their conviction that the human brain, working by observation and logic alone, was capable of explaining virtually everything.[2] This did not mean Greeks refused to acknowledge the supernatural. Far from it: their temples, oracles, rituals and literature bear powerful witness to their sense of the presence of the supernatural in their lives. But they saw, in a way that as far as we know no other civilisation had done, that there was a distinction to be made between (to put it in modern terms) philosophy and theology, science and religion, that different criteria of intelligibility were applicable. This ability to make distinctions has been of the very greatest importance. Consider the shock it would deliver to the system today if a doctor were to say 'We cannot cure cancer because God is ultimately responsible for it and how can we know the mind of God? Besides, it would insult him to peer too closely into his creation.'[3] Thanks to the Greeks, Christian doctors today can insist both that the world is a rationally intelligible place, subject to hard physical laws, and that an only partially knowable God created it.

It is not easy to explain this Greek passion for rationalism. The absence of a priest-caste holding the key to all knowledge has something to do with it; so too does the absence of anything remotely resembling a Bible or creed (Greek religion centred on ritual, not belief or morality). Greeks are also a fiercely independent-minded people, an observation which perhaps merely makes the same point in social rather than religious terms (arguably, only the Greeks could have invented a political system as relentlessly individualistic as radical democracy: see Chapter 5). They are also highly competitive. But whatever the explanation, that characteristically independent-minded, competitive attitude to the gods is there in Greek literature from the very beginning – in Homer.[4] Very well, but the question that observation poses is whether it is as simple as all that. Is Homer a one-off? Is there not an epic tradition on which he drew? And if there is, how far does the human response to gods in Homer conform to the tradition rather than to a particular Greek mind-set? In other words, without some understanding of epic before Homer, we must be wary of making too great claims for him. *Mutatis mutandis*, the same may be said of the Greek achievement generally. First things, however, first.

Homer's *Iliad* begins with the quarrel between Achilles, the Greeks' greatest warrior, and Agamemnon, the Greek leader. It centres on the question of how Agamemnon should be compensated for the loss of the girl Chryseis. Chryseis was daughter of a local Trojan priest of Apollo, and Agamemnon had taken her as part of his war-booty in a raid. The priest had asked for her return in exchange for ransom; Agamemnon had refused; and Apollo, enraged at his priest's treatment, had inflicted a plague on the Greeks. Achilles, realising it must be Apollo (god of plague), now calls a council to discuss how to deal with the matter. It is agreed by everyone that Apollo must be placated with a sacrifice and the girl be returned (and indeed, both are done, and the god is placated and the plague lifted), but Agamemnon demands to receive matching compensation at once. Achilles disagrees, insults are exchanged, and Agamemnon, incensed, threatens to take Achilles' girl, Briseis, in lieu. At this point Achilles wonders whether to draw his sword and disembowel Agamemnon, or hold his peace. The text continues:

> He was drawing his great sword from its sheath, and Athene came
> 195 from heaven. The white-armed goddess Hera had sent her,
> loving and caring for both men equally in her heart.
> Athene stood behind him and seized Achilles by his dark hair,
> appearing to him alone. None of the others saw her.
> Achilles was amazed, and turned round, and immediately recognised
> 200 Pallas Athene. Awesomely did her eyes shine on him.
> And addressing her he spoke winged words:
> 'Why have you come this time, child of aegis-bearing Zeus?
> Is it to witness the son of Atreus Agamemnon's humiliation of me?
> I tell you this straight, and I think it will be done:
> 205 He will very likely lose his life for his insults.'
> The goddess grey-eyed Athene then addressed him:
> 'I have come to restrain your impulse, if you will obey me,
> from heaven. The white-armed goddess Hera sent me,
> loving and caring for you both equally in her heart.

210 But end your quarrel, and do not draw the sword in your hand.
But do insult him in words, how it will be.
I tell you this straight and it will be done:
At some stage three times as many shining gifts will appear
Because of his humiliation of you. You restrain yourself and obey me.'
215 Replying swift-footed Achilles addressed her:
'I must respect the words of you two, goddess,
furious at heart though I am. It is better this way.
The gods pay attention to the man who obeys them.'

Homer, *Iliad* 1.194-218

Two comments are in order. First, observe how rational the sequence of events is. The god Apollo may have sent the plague, but he does so for intelligible reasons – his action is not random – , everyone knows Apollo is responsible, and appropriate action is taken to solve the problem. In other words, the irruption of the divine does not cause chaos: it is almost part of the natural order of things and rational steps can be taken to deal with it. The same can be said of Athene's intervention. She is sent for a reason and she has a perfectly human conversation with Achilles on the matter.

Second, remark Achilles' reaction to a goddess. He may have felt amazed when she pulled his hair from behind (who wouldn't?), and her eyes may have shone awesomely, but as soon as he sees it is Athene he asks why she has come and goes into a very human rant (204-5) about his treatment and what he will do to Agamemnon. These are not the words of a man exactly overwhelmed by the divine presence, let alone keen to hear what a divinity will say. Nor does Athene sound much like a goddess when she replies that she has come to restrain him 'if you will obey me'. Achilles is being addressed by a god, and he has an option?

In other words, for all Athene's divine splendour (those shining eyes), she may as well be human, the way Achilles addresses her and she replies. This style and level of interaction between men and gods are absolutely standard throughout the *Iliad*. Thus, when in *Iliad* 16 the god Apollo attacks Achilles' friend Patroclus from behind, knocks off his helmet, shatters his spear, and breaks his corselet – an intervention of appalling power, pathos and intensity, which leaves Patroclus defenceless, to be finished off eventually by the Trojan hero Hector – no human actor passes any comment on it. It might be harrowing to us, but all Patroclus says before he is dispatched by Hector is that Zeus, fate and Apollo combined to kill him. Patroclus, in other words, accepts divine intervention as par for the course, the sort of thing that could happen to anyone on a bad fate day. As far as the heroes *talk* about divine intervention, then, concepts such as irrationality, mysteriousness, or violation of causality do not feature. They talk to and about gods almost as if they were human. These are powerfully rational and independent heroes, cowed by nothing.[5]

A splendid passage illustrating this feature with particular clarity occurs in *Iliad* 22. Intent on revenge for the death of Patroclus, Achilles has been pursuing Hector round the walls of Troy but failing to catch him: for once his swift feet (the mark of an expert in the rout) are not up to the task. Athene now intervenes, telling Achilles to take a breather while she persuades Hector into standing and fighting. Achilles is delighted and obeys.[6] She disguises herself as Hector's brother Deiphobus, approaches Hector and suggests they both take on Achilles. Hector agrees, and turns to face his rival. Words and spears are exchanged, neither conclusive; Athene returns Achilles' spear but not Hector's. Hector at once calls on Deiphobus to give him his spear – and finds he has disappeared. He reflects on his situation in the following words:

> 'All over: the gods have surely called me to my death.
> I thought the hero Deiphobus was here.
> But he is on Troy's wall, and Athene deceived me.
> Now evil death is upon me, not far off,
> and there is no escape. Long ago this must have been the preference
> of Zeus and the far-shooting son of Zeus [Apollo], who before this
> carefully protected me. But now my fate comes to meet me.
> Let me not die an unimpassioned, inglorious death,
> but with some great deed to my name, for future generations to hear.'
> Homer, *Iliad* 22.297-305

Here is a man who has been utterly betrayed by the powers above. Zeus and Apollo have tossed him aside; Athene has most foully tricked him into facing his killer. His analysis of the situation is almost inhumanly icy in its rationality. He understands precisely how the gods have treated him. He acknowledges, but does not examine, its implications. No protest escapes his lips at that divine treatment. No ounce of fear betrays him. His sole concern now is to die a death that men will remember. Hector's independence of mind, his rationalising of everything that has happened, his lack of interest in probing the deeper theological implications – all are typical of the Homeric hero.[7]

So much, in brief, for the gods in the *Iliad* – or at least, for the human response to them. We now turn to the problem this raises: is this feature of heroic behaviour in the *Iliad* an index of a uniquely independent mentality, somehow looking forward to and anticipating the Greek sixth-century intellectual revolution that was to witness the invention of philosophy and the first efforts to describe the world as the product of other than supernatural forces? Or is it a feature of the oral epic tradition generally, which Homer has simply hellenised for the sake of his story?[8] To answer the question, we must turn to the Near East, and I take one telling example.

The Babylonian *Epic of Gilgamesh* in its original form antedates the *Iliad* by nearly two thousand years (in Sumerian, its original language, the hero is called Bilgamesh). There is a moment in both epics when the respective heroes, Achilles and Gilgamesh, with his companion Enkidu, encounter a god. In *Iliad* 22, Achilles has been led a merry dance by Apollo. Disguising himself as the Trojan Agenor, Apollo has drawn Achilles away from the fleeing Trojans in order to give them the chance to retreat back inside Troy in the face of the Greek hero's irresistible onslaught. Mission accomplished, Apollo mockingly reveals himself and the furious Achilles screams 'You have deprived me of great glory, and saved these Trojans easily! Why? Because you were not afraid of any reprisal! You would have got it from me, if I had the power!' Similarly, in the *Epic of Gilgamesh*, Gilgamesh and Enkidu have killed the Bull of Heaven which the goddess Ishtar sent against them. Enkidu rips off its shoulder, and slaps Ishtar in the face with it, crying 'I wish I could get you too! I wish I could make you like that! I wish I could hang up its guts and yours side by side!'[9]

Only one example, as I say, but of the highest importance. For it demonstrates that one of the points of being a hero in the near eastern tradition too is to take on gods. In other words, the Homeric example tells us little specific about the independence of the Greek mentality: it was a mentality shared equally by Babylonian heroes. That might, of course, be merely coincidence, but it does raise the possibility that Greek culture, far from being a unique, highly original, one-off, in fact has it roots in the Near East. Is it, then, to the Near East that we should look for an explanation of the Greek miracle, abandoning all these claims for 'firsts'?

This in principle is perfectly plausible. Since neolithic times, the Greek world had been receptive to near eastern influences – religious, musical, technological, agricultural, cosmological and so on. The cultivation of cereals, flax, olive, and vine; pottery; the working of copper, bronze and iron; writing; walled towns; harp, lyre and double oboe; the Mycenaean/Homeric concept of kingship; conventions relating to treaties, sacrifices, holy places, prayer – the Greek versions of these are all of near eastern origin. The Greeks were fully aware of much of this debt. It is telling that Homer, author of the first Greek literature, makes no effort to distinguish Greeks from eastern Trojans, linguistically or culturally. Certainly the fifth-century BC Greek historian Herodotus had the greatest admiration for eastern peoples, especially the Egyptians.[10]

But the game has taken on a fresh impetus with the recent publication of M.L. West's monumental *The East Face of Helicon: West Asiatic Elements in Greek Poetry and Myth* (Oxford, 1997), a massive and authoritative assessment of Greece's literary debt to the east.[11] In examining the total literary output of Mesopotamian, Anatolian, Syrian and biblical sources over two thousand years, West (Senior Research Fellow at All Souls College, Oxford) has found a mountain of compelling evidence for literary receptiveness as well, in particular, for features shared between near eastern literature and early Greek poetry and myth (Homer, *c.* 720 BC, via Hesiod and lyric poets like Sappho, to Aeschylus, d. 455 BC) in everything from vocabulary, phrases, idioms, and figures of speech to myths and the sort of detailed links between Homer and *Gilgamesh* mentioned above. Something, in other words, is going on here in the literary world that cannot be ignored. The Greek literary debt, conscious or not, to its eastern neighbours is massive.[12]

I select here, with minimal comment, a number of examples from West's work, to indicate the range of shared features which he has found. Some, as he admits, are slight; others very thought-provoking; all are open to further debate. The translations are West's.

1. Gilgamesh and the *Iliad*

'Gilgamesh is based in his own city of Uruk, from where he makes a couple of excursions to remote lands, whereas Achilles is taking part in a war on foreign soil. But upon these different backdrops is projected a remarkable similar personal drama: a man of abnormally emotional temperament, with a solicitous goddess for a mother and a comrade to whom he is devoted, is devastated by the latter's death and plunges into a new course of action in an unbalanced state of mind, eventually to recover his equilibrium. Similar too is the overall ethos, the sense of heroic man brought face to face with issues of life and death, railing against mortality, but coming to understand and accept it. It is this ethos, more than the exotic mythology, that gives the Gilgamesh epic its singular appeal to the modern reader, an appeal unmatched by the other Akkadian narrative poems. It has been called the first great embodiment of humanism – a title others would willingly bestow on the *Iliad*' (*EFH* 338).

West goes on to demonstrate a very large number of more intimate connections between the *Iliad* and other near eastern epics (*EFH* 347-401), leading him to conclude (among other things) that the divine comedy of the gods is also a near eastern epic reflex ('It is not that the Greek poet is drawing capriciously from models in different countries; it is rather that there is a broad stream of international tradition, the present evidence for which is somewhat fragmented', 401). One of the most interesting connections is the description of Achilles lamenting the dead Patroclus and Gilgamesh the dead Enkidu:

> And Achilles led [the Greeks] in their heavy wailing,
> laying his man-slaying hands on his comrade's chest,
> groaning again and again, like a full-bearded lion
> whose cubs a huntsman snatches away
> from the dense woodland, and it comes later, and is chagrined,
> and it roams many a glen, seeking after the man's tracks,
> hoping to find him, for it is in the grip of bitter anger –
> so he groaned deep, and spoke among [the Greeks].
>
> Homer, *Iliad* 18.316-23

Here Gilgamesh addresses the people of Uruk, before turning to the dead Enkidu:

'Hearken to me, young men, hearken to me;
hearken to me, you elders of [Uruk].
I weep for my friend Enkidu;
like a woman mourner I lament (him) bitterly ...
You there, turn to me! Don't you hear [me]?'
But he did not raise his head.
He touched his heart, but it was not beating at all.
He veiled <his> friend's face like a bride's.
Like an eagle he circled over him;
like a lioness whose cub[s are caught] in a pitfall
he kept turning to and fro.

Gilgamesh VIII.ii.1-4, 15-21

West points out that Gilgamesh feels Enkidu's heart in case it is still beating, but there is no reason for Achilles to lay his hands on Patroclus' chest, since he is clearly dead, and wonders whether this feature was 'taken over from the source version and has lost its rationale'.

2. Gilgamesh and Odysseus

The *Odyssey* opens:

Tell me, Muse, of the man so versatile, who wandered
far and wide after he had sacked Troy's citadel.
Many were the peoples whose cities he saw and whose mind he came
   to know,
and many the woes he suffered in his heart at sea
as he ventured his life and his comrades' safe return.

Homer, *Odyssey* 1.1-5

In the Standard Babylonian version, *Gilgamesh* begins:

[Of him who] saw everything let [me te]ll the land,
[of him who] knew [the entiret]y [let me tea]ch his whole story.
[the] la[nds] altogether.
[He was compl]eted in wisdom, he who kn[ew] the entirety;
he saw the [se]cret, and opened up what was concealed;
he brought back intelligence from before the Flood;
he travelled a distant path, weary and resigned.

Gilgamesh I.i.1-7

West adds that there are other near eastern travellers, but continues 'The figure of the world traveller, then, was established at an early date in Babylonian tradition. But it is Gilgamesh, the wanderer in remote, mysterious lands where strange beings are to be encountered, who provides much the closer model for Odysseus' (*EFH* 404).

3. Sappho

One of Sappho's most famous poems is the one in which she lists the physical symptoms she experiences when she looks at a certain woman:

> Speech fails me,
>
> my tongue is crippled, a subtle fire
> is straightway running beneath my skin,
>   with my eyes I see nothing, and my ears buzz,
>
> the sweat pours down me, a trembling
> seizes my whole body, I am greener
>   than grass; I seem to myself little short of dead.
>
> Sappho, 31.7-16

Here is a Babylonian poem in which the speaker prays for deliverance from an evil demon:

> My eyes bulge but see not, my ears are open but hear not;
> my whole body has been gripped by weakness,
>   a stroke has fallen upon my flesh;
> stiffness has seized my arms, debility has fallen upon my knees;
> my feet have forgotten how to move;
> [a seiz]ure has overtaken me, I suffocate in a collapsed state:
> signs of death have clouded my face.
>
> *Ludl* II 73-81

West comments 'Half a dozen similar passages could be quoted' (*EFH* 527).

West's book runs to 662 pages. Thousands of comparisons are drawn, and compelling reading they make. By itself, of course, a comparison, tells one nothing. One still has to ask the question – so what? The big question for the historian is how far the similarities between early Greek and near eastern literature are conscious, or if not conscious, then at least indicative of some sort of inter-cultural influence (however that may have come about). Then again, however great the similarities, it is arguable that only differences count. Here is a mammal with a mouth, teeth, two ears and eyes, a heart, lungs, reproductive organs, and digestive organs – is it a field-mouse or a dead professor of business studies?

West is well aware of the problems inherent in his exercise, but it seems to me that his case for a high level of literary interaction between the Near East and the Greek world is unanswerable. Cultural interaction of other types is, as we have seen, undisputed. Why not literary too? Was there even, as West speculates, a sort of epic 'hot-line' to the *Gilgamesh*-singers of the Assyrian court of the seventh century BC? Such activity could also explain the large number of Semitic loan-words in the Greek language.

At one level, none of this makes the slightest difference to the Greek achievement, which is a matter of historical record. The Greeks, for example, learned about monumental statuary and probably temple building from the Egyptians. But no Egyptian ever produced anything even remotely resembling the Parthenon. Some near easterners lived in something resembling city-states, but none of them invented democracy. Greek literature is a brilliant achievement, whatever its sources (no one demeans the Roman literary achievement because we know its origins to be Greek). Most important of all, however, is that West's intensive scrutiny of the full range of near eastern literature reveals nothing comparable with the Greek intellectual, rationalising revolution. This is what marks Greek culture out as so different and so important. Indeed, given the sheer weight of near eastern influence but its profound silence in this area, the uniqueness of the Greek intellectual achievement is thrown into even sharper relief.

In making this claim, no one is playing off culture against culture. Babylonian technical achievement, for example, which cannot have been realised without the highest levels of thought, observation and testing is not diminished because Babylonians did not speculate rationally about the nature of the universe, any more than the Greek achievement is diminished because Greeks did not invent metal inlay. To acknowledge one culture's strengths and weaknesses is not to demean another's. So it is an exciting new development that our understanding of the Greek literary achievement literature can now be sharpened as a result of our greater understanding of the near eastern influence on Greek. Yet even if it does emerge that every one of the Greek 'firsts' mentioned at the start of this chapter is mistaken, it will not alter the fundamental fact that the Greek way of looking at the world, whether unique to Greeks or not, is the *source* from which the West's way of looking at the world has largely flowed.

This is well illustrated by Greek myth. There is no doubt that much Greek myth is taken directly from the Near East. The case is massively documented. I take a few Greek gods and myths by way of example. Zeus shares the same name as the Indic sky-god *Dyaus pita*, father of the day (cf. the Latin *Diespiter/ Juppiter*). *Dyaus* in Indic religion is not the king of the gods. In the Greek pantheon, Zeus is, as sky-god, god of storms and thunder and lightning. Aphrodite is closely associated with the Phoenician goddess of sex, Ishtar-Astarte (a connection also made by Herodotus): Astarte is called 'queen of heaven', as is Aphrodite (*Ourania*); Astarte is worshipped with incense and doves, like Aphrodite. The man-god Heracles has parallels in Babylonian myth, where a hunter wearing lion-skin, bow and club is depicted and associated with Ninurta, son of the storm-god Enlil, who undergoes many exciting adventures; and so on.[13] Whatever the origins of these gods, Greeks naturally hellenise them and give them their own genealogy, role, function and imagery. Homer obviously played an important part in turning them into a large, squabbling family and giving them human characteristics. Hesiod's *Theogony*, 'Birth of the Gods', invents a full family tree for them from the beginning, groaning with near eastern connections.

The Hurrian *Song of Kumarbi*, for example, closely parallels Hesiod's story of the early succession of the gods. Hesiod's story tells of Ouranos (Sky), who has his genitals lopped off by sickle-waving Kronos (a harvest-god). Kronos swallows his children so that no one will succeed him, but his wife tricks him into swallowing a stone instead of baby Zeus (the sky-god), and Zeus grows up to overthrow his father and become king of the gods. The *Song of Kumarbi* (c. 1200 BC) tells how Anu ('Sky') has his genitals lopped off and disappears from heaven after a battle with Kumarbi, a harvest-god; how Kumarbi holds some gods in his belly, is given a stone to eat but spits it out; and how Tessub (storm-god) then emerges from his body and ... presumably comes to power, but the tablet is damaged and ends here (only the first tablet is preserved). There are comparable Babylonian, Phoenician and Hittite versions. The detailed connections with Hesiod are too complex for this sequence to be the result of anything other than direct transmission.

Myths for Greeks served a wide range of functions. Whatever modern scholars make of them,[14] Greeks saw them as preserving for posterity the great stories of a heroic past; offering salutary lessons in the shape of moral paradigms (often through allegorisation); explaining the origins of things, especially ritual; and all the time arousing intense pleasure in the hearing. We too can see groups of myths that are historical or foundational (e.g. the myths surrounding the Trojan war and the myths of Theseus as founder of Athens);[15] myths that explain the origins of rituals (e.g. why men get the good meat at sacrifice and offer up the bones and rubbish to the gods – because Prometheus tricked Zeus into accepting the worse side of the bargain); myths that offer allegories of human situations (when the gods fight each other, it is 'really' a battle of the natural elements, hot *vs.* cold, moist *vs.* dry, etc.); and myths that explain man's position in the world (particularly their difference from the gods) and offer salutary lessons e.g. Oedipus. Greeks adored their myths – taught them from the cradle, they met them in the most prestigious public places (e.g. illustrated on the friezes of their temples) and at their great, annual religious events, like the dramatic and choral festivals. Romans ran with them too, signalling their cultural aspirations by being able to recount the most trivial details.

However one defines myth – Walter Burkert defines it as 'a traditional tale with secondary, partial reference to something of collective importance' – Greek myths can generally be seen to relate to some contemporary Greek concern, among which gods and ritual, the city and its origins, the family, the past and the natural world bulk especially large. But even so, myths are not sacred or canonical – a sort of Bible – but open to reinterpretation and reuse, as we saw from the tragedians' re-workings of the Philoctetes' myth (p. 10). What is most striking about them, however, and what differentiates them most forcefully from near eastern and other

myths, is their comparative rationality. Amazing things certainly happen
in them, but the bizarre, the fantastic, the magical and the grotesque are
for the most part firmly excluded. When the absurdly supernatural is
(rarely) admitted, every effort is made either to play down or to rationalise
it. To quote, by way of contrast, an extreme, and to classicists well-known,
example from the myths of the Bororo of Brazil:[16]

Long ago a young man called Geriguiaguiatugo followed his mother into
the forest, where she was going to collect special leaves for the initiation
of young men after puberty. He raped her, and his father, discovering by a
trick that his son was the culprit, sent him on a deadly mission to fetch
various kinds of ceremonial rattle from the lake of souls. The young man's
grandmother advises him to enlist the help of a humming-bird, which
obtains for him the object of his quest. Other missions aided by other kinds
of bird are also successful, so that eventually his father takes him on a
parrot-hunting expedition and strands him half-way up a cliff, hanging on
only by a magic stick given him by his grandmother. Father goes away, but
son manages to climb the cliff. On the isolated plateau above, he kills
lizards and hangs them round his belt as a store of food but they go rotten,
and their smell makes the young man faint, then attracts vultures who
devour his posterior as well as the maggoty lizards. The sated vultures
turn friendly and convey him to the foot of the cliff. The young man is now
hungry again, but the wild fruits he eats go straight through him, devoid
as he now is of a fundament. Remembering a tale of his grandmother's, he
fashions a new posterior out of a kind of mashed potato. He returns to his
village, which he finds abandoned; but eventually discovers his family,
after taking the form (according to the main version) of a lizard. He
appears to his grandmother in his own shape; during the night a terrible
storm extinguishes all the fires except hers; the other women, including
the father's new wife, come from embers the next day. Father pretends
that nothing has happened between him and his son, but the son turns
into a stag and casts him with his antlers into a lake, where the father is
devoured by cannibal piranha fish. His lungs rise to the surface and
become the origin of a special kind of floating leaf. The young man then
kills his mother and his father's second wife.

The fact is that one will search the corpus of Greek myth in vain for
anything remotely resembling the Bororo story. Certainly the Odysseuses,
Jasons, Orpheuses, Medeas, Heracleses, Theseuses and Minoses of the
Greek world get up to some pretty rum tricks from time to time, but when,
for example, Minos' wife Pasiphae wants to be impregnated by a bull she
persuades Daedalus to make a comfy cowhide frame into which she can
insert herself in preparation for the delightful consummation, and what
could be more practical than that? As I say, I do not deny the element of
the supernatural in Greek myth, but Greek myths sound like the minutes
of the Rationalist Society compared with the Bororo example.

There is, however, a reason for this. Most of the Greek myths we know best come to us not raw, but mediated through a sophisticated literary tradition, beginning with Homer and continuing through Greek tragedy and (in Roman times) Ovid's *Metamorphoses*. While the Bororo myths are collected 'in the field', Greek myths are collected off the pages of artists like Sophocles. No wonder the differences are so radical (one wonders what the adventures of Geriguiaguiatugo would look like in Sophoclean hands). Selected, then, and superbly articulated to focus on the great issues, it is no wonder that so much Greek myth has had such a rich afterlife in the western tradition. It grapples in human terms with the very basic, universal conditions of existence – life, death, survival, identity, marriage, the family, transition, justice, conflict, suffering, especially the points at which the human and the divine cross – and yields interpretation at many levels.[17] Greek tragedy, in particular, uses myth to focus on some of Athens' most important concerns, both particular and general. The *Oresteia* examines the idea of justice, *Philoctetes* explores the tension between success and goodness, *Oedipus* of (self-) knowledge and ignorance. George Steiner points out that the story of Antigone alone embraces all the major conflicts of western literature: male-female, young-old, society-individual, man-god, living-dead.[18]

This morning I read a twelfth-century life of Judas Iscariot, which told how Iscariot was cast out by his father because he had received a vision that his son would kill him; how the baby Iscariot had been rescued by shepherds, was reared and found employment in Herod's palace; how Iscariot one day broke into his father's orchard to pick fruit for the king, was discovered by his father, and killed him in a fight; and how, to help compensate for the crime, Herod persuaded Iscariot to marry the murdered man's mother ...[19]

5

Democracy's Brief Day

Aristocratic families ruled early Athens. According to the historian Plutarch (*c.* AD 100), the mythical founder of Athens, Theseus, made it their function to 'carry out rituals, provide archons (state executives), teach the laws and rule on sacred matters'. All secular and religious power was thus in their hands. The reformer Solon in 594 BC deprived the aristocrats of their monopoly of power and replaced them with the non-aristocratic rich, but it was still the rule of the few. It even became the rule of the one in Athens when about 560 BC the aristocrat Pisistratus briefly seized power as one-man *turannos* (origin of our 'tyrant'). That 'tyranny' was broken with the help of Spartan intervention in 510 BC, and aristocratic rule returned.

But not for long. In 507 BC, the Athenian Cleisthenes took the first steps to blowing that whole world apart when he instituted the world's first and last democracy. The word derives from a combination of *dêmos*, 'people, citizen-body, parish/ward, masses' and *kratos*, 'power, grasp, authority, rule'. But the new order was not so named immediately. Since *dêmos* was frequently deployed as a term of abuse by those who saw themselves as superior to it, it was inviting trouble to replace the previous oligarchic rule of the rich and aristocrats with something that could be taken to mean 'mob-rule'. So *isonomia*, 'equality under the law' (*isos* 'equal' + *nomos* 'law') was the early, perhaps more tactful, formulation.

Cleisthenes, then, broke the oligarchic system. Still, even under the later fully-fledged democracy, the people never shook off a sense that aristocrats had an inborn right to rule, and members of aristocratic families like Pericles regularly found themselves in positions of power. Pindar, the fifth-century poet who celebrated winners at various athletic competitions (e.g. Olympia), sums up the idea that rule is in the blood when he says:

> Through inborn splendour a man carries great weight.
> He who has only taught skills is a lightweight,
> blowing this way and that, never standing
> secure, merely sampling countless exploits, getting nowhere.
>
> Pindar, *Nemeans* 3.40-3

This is the aristocratic ethos writ large.

That said, it must be emphasised that under the democracy aristocrats came to positions of power only because the people voted them there, and that they wielded power only in as far as the people allowed them to. There was never any doubt about who the bosses were – the people. It is the extraordinary achievement of Greek democracy that, for the first and last time, a political order was instituted that did not reflect the social hierarchy, but put the power of self-government into the hands of all citizens, united by horizontal bonds of solidarity based on the link between equality and the law. No French revolution was required to effect this remarkable and unique development.

Democracy did not spring fully-formed from Cleisthenes' head. During its 180 years of existence – it was extinguished by the Macedonian general Antipater in 322 BC (see p. 16) – it underwent increasing radicalisation. The synoptic description given here draws together its most important features.

The four elements of Athenian democracy were:

(i) The *ekklêsia*, the Assembly, consisting of all citizens (Athenian males aged over eighteen). This was the state's sovereign body, taking all decisions by a show of hands.

(ii) The *boulê*, the Council, consisting of 500 citizens aged over thirty, who served for a year as a sort of Assembly steering committee, preparing all the Assembly's business and ensuring its decisions were put into effect. No one could serve on the Council more than twice.

(iii) The *dêmos*, 'deme', here meaning the 'parishes' or 'wards' of Attica (the city-state of Athens, consisting of the city and its surrounding countryside and coast). Cleisthenes created 139 demes in Attica. Members of the Council were appointed at deme level.

(iv) The *phulai*, or 'tribes'. There were ten of these. Cleisthenes created each tribe by combining a block of demes from the city with a block from the coastal areas and a block from the country areas. These tribes elected the top executive officials and formed the basis of military organisation.

The results of this new system were (i) to hand power over to the people, (ii) to create strong commitment to democracy at deme level, and (iii) to make it very difficult for any individual or family to fix appointment to offices, let alone to the top offices that the tribes controlled. The mixture of far-flung demes out of which each tribe was constructed ensured that.

Now for a little more detail.

(i) The sovereign body, the **Assembly**, met once about every nine days, and could be specially summoned at any time. Convened as the Assembly, it was the state's legislature. The following, very approximate, figures give some idea of what the balance of political power was in the city-state of Athens:

	431 BC	**317** BC
Male citizens	50,000	21,000
Athenian women and children	200,000	84,000
Male resident aliens	25,000	10,000
Resident alien women and children	50,000	20,000
Slaves	100,000	50,000
Totals	325,000	185,000

The fate of Athens, then, at the start of the Peloponnesian war in 431 BC was in the hands of about 50,000 citizens. This assumes, of course, that they all attended the Assembly. But they did not. The Assembly's meeting place, the Pnyx, could hold only about 6,000 people at the time. Besides, Attica was the size of present Oxfordshire (about 100 square miles). The furthest deme from Athens was Thoricus 25 miles away, a good day's journey. Anyone attending an Assembly from there would have to spend three days to do it, two travelling. We can assume that politics was dominated by the citizens who lived in Athens. Some politics too – war, peace, treaties, alliances, expeditions, building projects, taxes, expenditure, regulation of officials and so on. In short, everything that government does today was done in Athens by the people meeting in Assembly.

(ii) The **Council** acted as the Assembly's steering committee. It consisted of 500 citizens over age thirty, fifty from each of the ten tribes. There was a formula for determining which demes from each of the tribes should provide the Council members in any year. Councillors were appointed at deme level by lot, not vote. The Council had no power to initiate policy or legislate. Its function was executive, to prepare the agenda for the Assembly (the Assembly could throw the agenda back if it did not like it) and ensure its decisions were carried out.

(iii) To help the Council carry out its responsibilities, the civil calendar was divided into ten 'months', each of about 35 days. Each month one of the ten tribes was obliged to put its fifty Council members on 24-hour stand-by. This stand-by committee, called the ***prutaneis***, lived at state expense in a hostel adjoining the Council Chamber, and received all business, embassies, etc. and transmitted details to Council. There was a different chairman of the *prutaneis* every day, who also acted as chairman of the Assembly on that day, if needed. On one day, we hear, Socrates was chairman. On that one day, Athens' fate was to some extent in his hands. It was a privilege and responsibility that, over the years, fell to a very large number of ordinary citizens.

Here are two snapshots of the Assembly, Council and *prutaneis* at work.

Aristophanes' comedy *Acharnians* was staged in 425 BC. Athens was then at war with Sparta and the comedy opens with the farmer Dikaiopolis moaning about the fact that the Assembly has not started yet. He wants peace, but no one seems interested:

> There's an Assembly called for sunrise and who's here? No one. Not even the *prutaneis*. They'll come late and then they'll all pile in together, shoving each other to get the front seats like there's no tomorrow. As for how we'll get peace, they don't give a toss. O my city, my city! I'm always first to take my seat here in the Assembly. All on my own, I sigh and yawn, stretch and fart, don't know what to do. I doodle on the ground, pull a few hairs out, do some sums in my head, all the time gazing out over the countryside, yearning for peace, hating the city, longing for my deme ... Now I'm here all ready to shout, interrupt and slag off any speaker who doesn't talk about peace. Hullo, here come the *prutaneis*, right on the dot of midday. Didn't I tell you? Just like I said, all pushing to get the front seats.
>
> Aristophanes, *Acharnians* 19-42

Here in November 339 BC the orator-politician Demosthenes describes what happened when news reached Athens that Philip of Macedon had taken Elateia and was now threatening Athens itself:

> It was evening when the messenger arrived to tell the *prutaneis* that Elateia had fallen. They were in the middle of supper, but rose at once ...
>
> At dawn next day the *prutaneis* summoned the Council to the Council Chamber while you all made your way to the Assembly. The whole citizen body had taken their places before the Council proceeded to business or proposed a motion. When the Council arrived and the *prutaneis* reported the news they had received, the messenger was introduced and told his tale. The herald then asked 'Who wishes to speak?' Not a soul stirred. He put the question again, and again. Still there was no response, though all the commanders were there and all the politicians, and though our fatherland was crying out for someone to speak and save her. It was I who answered her call that day, and came forward to address you.
>
> Demosthenes, *de corona* 169-70

(iv) Now to those who did the business: the **executive officials**, or **archons**, appointed to carry out the wishes of the Assembly. These ranged from military commanders, treasurers and tax-collectors to those concerned with weights and measures, regulation of markets and street-cleaning (Aristotle says they numbered seven hundred). They had to be citizens in good standing, over thirty. Most were appointed by lot and served one year only in that office. Only the very poorest citizens were debarred from standing.

The only exceptions to the appointment of archons by lot were the treasury officials and the ten *stratêgoi*, 'military commanders' (with some other military posts). These were not only appointed by vote of the Assembly, but could also hold office year on year. The *stratêgoi* in particular were held in great esteem, and this was where the possibility of continuity in high command and so in state policy existed. Pericles, for example, was elected *stratêgos* fifteen times on the trot from 443 till his death in 429 BC.

All officials were responsible ultimately to the Assembly. At the end of their term of office – and during it if necessary – their performance was subjected to review by the Assembly. If the Assembly did not like what it saw, punishments could be imposed, ranging from fines to loss of rights, exile and death. It was no good pleading that one had only followed Assembly instructions. The Assembly could do no wrong.[1]

(v) Finally, the **judicial system**. Law in ancient Athens was in the hands of the individual. There was no such thing as a state-controlled Director of Public Prosecutions or what we would know as a police force: all cases were brought personally. But there was a distinction between private prosecutions, which had to be brought by the person injured, and public ones, where 'anyone who wished', as the terminology had it, could bring them. To encourage citizens to bring cases that were (by definition) in the state's rather than the individual's interests (e.g. against someone defying citizenship laws), there were automatic rewards for successful prosecution (e.g. a percentage of the fine levied). To discourage irresponsible prosecutions, a fine was levied on the prosecutor if e.g. he received fewer than one fifth of the jury's votes.

For example, a writ could be issued by 'anyone who wanted' against someone who had proposed an illegal decree in the Assembly. The original purpose of this law was to prevent attacks on the democratic constitution, but it could also be used as a weapon against political enemies. It was tried not in the Assembly but by a jury. So anyone who e.g. had persuaded the Assembly into a course of action which turned out to be a disaster could be prosecuted under this head. Since the Assembly could do no wrong, it was always the individual who suffered, if found guilty.

In the UK, the judicial and parliamentary systems function separately (except in the position of the Lord Chancellor, who straddles both). The law lords can overrule parliament. In Athens, there were no law lords, or even judges. Citizens over age thirty – the same citizens who attended the Assembly – sat in the law courts, in juries usually about 500 strong, hearing both political and civil cases. The format was fixed: one (timed) speech from both sides; evidence read out, but no witnesses cross-examined; then without further discussion or guidance, a vote on innocence or guilt. If guilt was established, but the penalty not fixed, there could then be a further speech from both sides on the appropriate punishment, and a vote taken on that. Both in the Assembly, then, and the courts, the *dêmos* ruled supreme. It was legislature and judiciary rolled into one.

An example of the democracy in action. In 427 BC, Athens put down a revolt stirred up throughout most of the island of Lesbos by the leaders of its main town, Mytilene. The revolt was put down, and Thucydides says that the Athenians, in Assembly, passed a decree ordering the execution not only of the leaders of the revolt but also the entire male population of Mytilene, and the sale of the women and children into slavery. The Assembly then instructed a trireme to be sent to Mytilene, with instructions to Paches, the Athenian commander there, to carry out their decision. Thucydides continues:

> Next day, there was a sudden change of feeling among them and a reckoning that a savage and excessive resolution had been proposed, to destroy a whole city rather than the guilty. When the ambassadors of Mytilene who were in Athens and those Athenians who supported them realised this, they arranged with the authorities [i.e. the *prutaneis*] to reopen the debate. They won them round quite easily because it was clear to the *prutaneis* as well that the majority of the people wanted someone to give them a chance to reconsider the matter. So an Assembly was summoned.
>
> Thucydides, *History* 3.36

Cleon spoke on behalf of the original resolution and was opposed by Diodotus. After a fascinating debate on the purpose and efficacy of capital punishment,

> the Athenians engaged in a struggle between the two opinions [i.e. *intense debate followed the two main speeches*], and the show of hands was very close, but Diodotus' motion won. Another trireme was sent out at with all speed so that they should not find Mytilene destroyed, the earlier trireme having got there first. The ambassadors from Mytilene provided wine and barley meal for the crew, and promised great rewards if they overtook the first trireme. So the men made great speed, eating barley-meal mixed with wine and oil as they rowed, and they slept and rowed by shifts [triremes usually beached to eat and sleep]. Luckily there was no headwind, and since the earlier boat had not hurried on its distasteful business, while the second boat pressed on in the manner described, it arrived just as Paches had read the decree and was on the point of carrying out its orders, and prevented the slaughter. So close was Mytilene's escape.
>
> Thucydides, *History* 3.49

The Athenian people were not always so merciful,[2] but the passage well illustrates the extent of the people's control over affairs, not to mention their willingness to change their minds.

It is self-evident that our democracy bears no relation to Athenian democracy. We, the people, do not govern the state, let alone rule supreme. Parliament does. But it is still democracy, we are told – 'representative' in style, a 'parliamentary democracy', under which MPs 'represent' us in parliament. That this is nonsense is quickly demonstrated with a few questions. Who decides who shall stand as a candidate at an election – the people or the parties? The parties. Who decides what policies the candidates will pursue – the people or the parties? The parties. Who decides how an MP votes in parliament – the people or the parties? The parties. In other words, 'parliamentary' or 'representative' democracy does not represent the people – it represents the parties. And if we reply that at least we elect our MPs, that does not mean our system is democratic. Elections are a necessary, but not a sufficient, condition of democracy. Stalin was elected time and again with huge majorities.

The simple fact of the matter is that we do not live in a democracy. We live in an oligarchy – the rule of the few. Since we elect these oligarchs every five years, we live, to be strict, in an elective oligarchy. There is nothing wrong with oligarchy. In a debate about the best form of constitution, the ancient Greek historian Herodotus defines oligarchy as 'choosing the best men in the country and giving them power ... it is only natural to suppose that the best men will produce the best policy'. Is not this precisely what we attempt to do at elections? The history of the West is the story of the triumph of oligarchy, not democracy. Our system, in fact, is the means by which an élite, defined by membership of a party, can legitimately (by election) assert its power over a whole country, allowing individuals like the Prime Minister to rise to almost monarchic status. Athenians would have been amazed that we think this has anything to do with democracy.[3]

At this point it is traditional to round on the Greeks and accuse them of not giving the vote to slaves or women. It is again worth posing a few questions in return. When did all citizen males in England get the vote? 1918. When did all females get the vote on the same terms as men? 1928. So, with the Greek example before us for 2,500 years, it is only within the last hundred years that we have finally adopted their voting practices for male citizens, and amazingly gone one better with females. Even so, we have not yet managed to turn ourselves into a democracy. As for slavery, it was the norm in England and everywhere else in the world till the nineteenth century. Early Christianity, for example, had nothing of interest to say about it (let alone about 'votes for men and women'). So one can hardly point the finger at ancient Greeks. The argument that Greek democracy is shameful because it depended on slavery is similarly vapid. Shakespeare and Newton depended on slavery in exactly the same way. So did every free person in the British empire up till 1838. It is also difficult exactly to remember when we gave the vote to slaves in that enlightened way so characteristic of us (and so different from those hopeless Greeks). I do not, then, think we are in any position to judge ancient Greeks on any of these issues.

To summarise: Athenian male citizens, irrespective of anything other than their citizenship (defined by birth) ran their city-state by listening to arguments and voting for or against them in the Assembly. Any of them, bar the poorest, could stand for an executive position and win the position by lot (true democracy: voting, as Aristotle pointed out, is aristocratic, because it chooses the best). This is genuine people-*power*, the meaning of democracy. At the same time, there was a constraint: all executive officials were responsible to the Assembly and their performance was monitored and reviewed. This is why the system worked: no one was going to put himself up for appointment for the fun of it, if he knew he stood a high chance of being executed for incompetence when his year was up. The contrast with our MPs who, after a lifetime of non-achievement and sometimes rank incompetence, find themselves in the Lords for *our* pains, is striking.

Then again, *stratêgoi* like Pericles did not wield power because it was vested in them (as it is with parliament). In Assembly, Pericles was up against any other citizen who wished to put a point of view. He wielded power merely through his ability to persuade the Assembly of the advantages of his policies. It was the sweetness of Pericles' tongue and the Assembly's favourable perception of his policies that made him a powerful figure – nothing more, and certainly not his aristocratic background.

For all our boasting about democracy, our system owes much more to the Roman republic, a true elective oligarchy yet still more democratic than anything we have to offer. To simplify, its executive officials, (magistrates, *magistratus*), like *quaestor*, *praetor* and *consul*, were all appointed by Roman citizens voting in electoral colleges. Once appointed, a magistrate became a life member of the Senate, the body which, in concert with the serving magistrates, effectively did the legislating. The two democratic elements were that the Senate contained officials known as tribunes of the plebs (i.e. of the people) who had the power to veto any legislation which did not meet with their approval; and when the Senate had made a decision, it could not be put into effect until the people, voting again in colleges, approved of it.

There is no denying that as much wheeler-dealing went on in the oligarchic high places of power in Rome as it does in our parliament. There is no doubt that the powerful oligarchic families ran the show under the republic, and that Rome did not remotely resemble a democracy in the Greek sense. It is also the case that the Roman people could for the most part only react to the Senate's decisions, not control them, and that plenty of electoral fixing went on (some of the electoral colleges were intentionally skewed).[4] Much the same is true of our system. But imagine the uproar in our 'democratic' parliament if someone were to propose people's representatives in parliament vetoing any legislation they disliked; or if all legislation that parliament agreed had to go back to the people for approval before it became law. Far too democratic, what? Indeed, our system often smacks more of the post-Republican world of the Roman empire, where the trappings of magistrates and Senate survived, but all power was in fact gathered into the hands of one man, the emperor (see Chapter 8).

The history of the debates about Athenian democracy down the years make fascinating reading. Until the nineteenth century, 'democracy' was a dirty word. It was regarded with the deepest suspicion by intellectuals and the powerful ever since it was invented, and has never been tried since.

The stability represented by Rome and Sparta was the model generally preferred by the power-hungry, who saw nothing but a threat to their own position in a state where people, not politicians, made the decisions.

But in the nineteenth century there was a U-turn so sudden and total that by the twentieth 'democracy' had become a shrine before which the whole world grovelled in untimely worship, the West, Russia, even China.[5] This alone tells one all one needs to know about the meaninglessness of the word in current usage. But for all its meaninglessness, democracy is now inviolable, a sacred cow, not to be attacked or questioned.[6] The story of this U-turn is worth telling.

In the Greek world, many Greeks were themselves critical of democracy (Greek criticism of some of their most sacred institutions is an object-lesson to us all – see Chapter 8, note 1). Plato, for example, pointed out that, in the Assembly, if the topic under debate was shipbuilding, and some who knew nothing about shipbuilding piped up, he would be shouted down: but when policy was at issue, any blacksmith or cobbler could pipe up and was heard with equal respect, as if 'policy' required no expertise.[7] The Greek historian Thucydides admired Pericles, but was frequently scathing about the Assembly. Polybius, writing his admiring history of the rise of Rome (p. 19) in the second century BC, dismissed the Athenian constitution as worthless.[8] Roman writers, with their disparaging view of the plebs, were never very sympathetic. Pliny the Elder (who died inspecting Vesuvius while it was erupting in AD 79) offers a more balanced view. He describes a picture of the Athenian people painted by the fifth-century BC Greek artist Parrhasius which displays them as 'moody, angry, unjust, fickle, but also biddable, merciful, compassionate, boastful ..., proud, humble, bold, timid – all at the same time'.[9]

This volatility was to become their enduring characteristic in the eyes of future generations. The essayist Plutarch (*c.* AD 100), a Greek who saw everything through autocratic, imperial Roman spectacles, took Athenian history to be the story of unscrupulous demagogues and a few worthy but persecuted statesmen trying to manipulate a volatile mob. His *Parallel Lives of Greek and Roman Statesmen* became the intellectuals' standard text from the Renaissance onwards (in eighteenth-century America, it was outsold only by the Bible) and heavily biased the debate against the Athenians, even though the idea of the self-governing city state did trigger some interest in places like Renaissance Florence. Venice, deliciously, saw itself as resolutely Spartan.

In 1576 Jean Bodin's popular *Six Books of Commonwealth*, translated into English in 1606, lambasted Athenian democratic principles: 'to aske councel of a Multitude ... is to seek for wisdome of a mad man.' But monarchist Europe was never going to see much virtue in Athens. The anti-monarchist cause espoused by Thomas Hobbes presented Athens in a better light, but the ancient republics like Rome, not the direct democracy of Athens, were the real subjects of that campaign. At the start of the eighteenth century, attempts by British Tories to impeach Whigs led to a wide-ranging discussion of accountability in government, and the fact that even Pericles was once impeached for mismanagement of funds was held up as a magnificent example. But this did not shake off those like Hume who continued to see the Athenians as an uncontrollable mob.

The fathers of the American revolution have it to their credit that they argued long and hard about different types of constitution, and the Athenian model occurs again and again in their analyses. Tom Paine claimed that 'what Athens was in miniature, America will be in magnitude' (1792), but in the constitution of 1787, not one Athenian institution was to be found. The Athenians' reputation for instability and disorder told against them, and the republican model was adopted. Even the French revolution made little use of the Athenian precedent. The revolutionaries looked primarily to those stable models of Rome and Sparta rather than fickle Athens. Britons over the water, however, characterised events in France as typical of what happened when a people was 'deluded by democratic theories'.

In eighteenth-century Germany, however, a different perspective was developing. In 1755 the art historian Winckelmann argued that democracy made Athens' brilliant cultural achievements possible – no democracy, no Parthenon, no tragedy, nothing. This proved a dynamic notion, and Germans like Herder and Schiller took up the theme enthusiastically. In Victorian England, meanwhile, an interest developed in Greek myth and religion, which seemed more intense and deeply felt than Roman and was represented as a pre-Christian means of perceiving the divine. Plato and Aristotle too were appropriated by Victorians in the Christian cause: their teachings, it was claimed, foreshadowed those of the liberal Anglican Church (cf. p. 23). These precedents, set by such highly respectable ancient figures, proved a useful antidote to the attacks on Christianity launched by science and Darwinism.[10] The struggle for Greek independence from the Ottoman empire in the 1820s generated further sympathy, and suddenly democracy did not look quite such a bad bet after all. But not direct, Athenian democracy. This was 'new' democracy: the previously forbidden term was adopted, buffed up and made safe for consumption by being applied to any constitution with an elective element in it. In other words, it was just an alternative, sexier term for elective oligarchy, or plain old republicanism (give or take a monarch or two). And so it remains today, a magnificent word, evoking magnificent ideals, utterly betrayed. So when Professor Anthony Giddens, in his 1999 Reith Lectures, claimed that democracy was one of twentieth century's great 'energising forces', all he was saying was that the idea of an elected oligarchic élite caught on among the competing oligarchic élites. Very energising.

6

Rhetoric: Persuasion for All

Persuasion, whether by words, gesture, look or touch, is one of the main purposes of communication. But while to some it comes naturally, to others it comes most unnaturally, and that is perhaps why rhetoric, the rules governing persuasive speech, began to be formalised by Greeks around 480 BC, shortly after the Athenian Cleisthenes invented democracy (see Chapter 5). The very essence of direct democracy is that in the people's Assembly everyone should have a voice. But if that voice is clumsy and hesitant, how persuasive will it be? How willing will that person be to voice an opinion in the first place, surrounded, as he will feel himself to be, by all too fluent speakers? Yet persuasion itself is a two-edged sword. There are, after all, right and wrong arguments, and the unscrupulous speaker will use his rhetorical skills to promote the worse cause. This is the subject of Aristophanes' comedy *Clouds* produced in 423 BC, in which Socrates, quite unfairly, is characterised as the master of wrong arguments – not that comedy ever had anything to do with fairness.

It is important to stress that we are talking here about the formalisation of rules. Greeks did not need rules to be rhetorical, of course. Nearly half of Homer's epics the *Iliad* and *Odyssey* (*c*. 720-680 BC) consists of gods and heroes talking to each other, and they were taken as models of persuasive speech by later teachers of rhetoric. Indeed, as Achilles' old tutor Phoenix said, a hero was brought up to be a speaker of words as well as a doer of deeds:[1] it was just as important for a hero to win his case in public debate (where the decisions were made) as on the battlefield. But Greeks of the early fifth century BC were the first people we know of actually to describe how to do it, turn an art into a craft, produce handbooks on that craft and make it available to anyone who wanted to learn it. Rhetoric and democracy go hand in hand.

There were, however, serious implications lurking behind this apparently innocent activity. One early example of a rhetorical handbook points out how to argue the good and bad side of everyday occurrences:

> Sickness is bad for the sick, good for doctors; death is bad for the dead, good for undertakers and monumental masons; a good harvest is good for farmers, bad for grain-traders; shipwrecks are bad for the owners, good for shipbuilders ... (and so on).[2]

Clearly, a successful speaker has to know how to put a gloss on anything. But if there are two sides to every question, is everything relative? Are there no absolute values? The fifth-century BC thinker Protagoras' dictum 'man is the measure of all things, of things that are, that they are, and of things that are not, that they are not' did indeed strike at the heart of absolutist thinking. One of the most common of ancient polarities typifies this clash: the debate between *nomos* 'law, custom, convention' and *phusis* 'nature, reality'. Do gods really exist? Or are they merely conventions? Is there such a thing as real goodness, or is it all a matter of interpretation? Is it natural that human races are different, or just a matter of custom? And so on.[3] Plato set his face firmly against such relativist stances. Arguments like this seemed to be the very essence of rhetoric, whose purpose (for him) was to juggle with such positions, not in order to establish the truth but to come out on top, by fair means or foul. Rhetoric and pulling the wool over people's eyes became inseparably linked.

This is fair criticism, but can itself be turned into a defence of the teaching of rhetoric: it takes one to know one. Then again, even Plato, after the most violent attacks on it,[4] came to see that rhetoric was only a means to an end, and the real question was whether the rhetorician's ends were noble (so, in his view, rhetoric was fine if you were a philosopher. Advertising agencies who hired Platonists would therefore escape his wrath). But whatever the ethical problems associated with rhetoric, the ability to speak persuasively in public was the central skill that ancient education tried to develop (see p. 100) because, as the Homeric hero knew, that was the way to fame and fortune in the political arena. Greeks distinguished three methods of getting your way – force, trickery and persuasion. Only the last guaranteed a victory without physical conflict. In the hotly competitive world of the ancients, such a consummation was devoutly to be wished.[5]

Whatever the state of the teaching of rhetoric in fifth-century Athens, Aristotle's *Art of Rhetoric* became a definitive statement of the theory and practice. Aristotle argued that rhetoric dealt with the presentation of a case under three broad heads: logical, stylistic and emotional. To put it another way, the successful orator will be a master of argument, have a good ear for aesthetically pleasing utterance, and a rich understanding of human character (you can persuade people only if you know what makes them tick). Discovering the best means of persuasion under each of these headings forms the substance of his *Art*.

It was not, however, to have an immediate effect. Rhetoric flourished under democracy. When that democracy was killed by the Macedonians in 322 BC, the political and legal forums where its impact was most felt disappeared. Rhetoric's revival, then, awaited the Romans. For Romans, as for Greeks, the capacity to win your argument in public, before Senate, jury and people, was the key to success. In the second century BC Rome was a growing Mediterranean power (p. 18): never were the stakes of that power so high for individual generals and politicians. So they fell upon the Greek rhetorical example as hungrily as they had upon Greek literature and theories of language (p. 94), and made it Roman. Cato the Elder protested, as usual (p. 20): *rem tene, verba sequentur*, he cried 'Keep to the subject and the words will come', i.e. forget all this fancy Greek theory. It was not a plea Romans heard. To take a single author, six of Cicero's treatises on the subject survive, and there are two more attributed to him. Quintilian's vast *Institutio Oratoria* and Tacitus' *Dialogus* give some idea of the development of rhetoric under the empire. It is not surprising that, since it was at the heart of Roman education, rhetorical technique was to have such a profound effect upon Latin literature.

There were many rhetorical schools of thought in Rome, all of them offering different emphases and preaching different skills. I do not intend to describe them. But it is of interest to summarise the basic rules of ancient rhetoric common to most theorists because they are as relevant today as they were then. Modern 'communication skills' is just another term for rhetoric, and the craft has not changed. The following pages will therefore save lawyers, spin-doctors, advertisers and salesmen in particular large sums of money in expensive training courses, which merely regurgitate, with the help of a particularly rebarbative terminology, principles at least two thousand years old. Not that that will help with the one problem rhetoric cannot solve: wielding all these wonderful communication skills, what is it you want to be communicative *about*? Do you have anything worth communicating? The medium, *pace* Marshall McLuhan, does actually require a message.[6]

I must warn here that the subject is vast, and presented in many different ways by ancient rhetorical theorists. I have tried to identify the major headings under which they worked. The rest of this chapter is divided, then, into a variety of sub-headings under, first, subject, argument and refutation; second, the speaker's resources; and finally, the structure of the speech. Ancient rhetoric tends to concentrate on legal and political affairs, but what is said here can be fruitfully applied to many situations – intellectual, business, social and so on – where exposition is required.

A. Subject, argument and refutation

Subject

First one must decide what sort of case one is arguing, and two types were identified: the *thesis*, a general argument about human behaviour, and the *causa*, a specific case about a specific issue.

Thesis

The *thesis*, a debate about universal patterns of human behaviour, e.g. 'Should a man marry?', was the staple of ancient school education for over a thousand years. Cicero originally thought it was not the true business of the orator, but more of the philosopher. In time, however, he came to change his mind, on the grounds that a specific case is always best argued in terms of the universal: only when one has established whether X is a good or bad course of action in principle can one then decide whether Y, in this specific instance, should do/have done it.

Cicero identifies three types of debate:

(a) Seeking to know/learn/understand, e.g. 'what is justice?'

(b) Seeking to define questions of duty, e.g. 'How should a state be administered?'

(c) Seeking to discover how to get or avoid something, e.g. 'How can I be happy?', 'How can I avoid poverty?'

Causa

The *causa*, a specific case, was defined under three headings: legal (judicial), political (deliberative) and epideictic (occasional, celebratory).

Legal (judicial)

The justice of past actions is the subject of these cases. For Aristotle, a crime is 'an injury voluntarily inflicted, contrary to the law'. He discusses laws, contracts and so on intensively, because most cases consist of conflicts between the letter of the law and equity (or fairness), or between the wording of a contract and its intentions, or between laws on the same subject. Three things need ascertaining, says Aristotle:

(a) Why someone does wrong.

Under this head he lists seven causes of criminality: chance, character, need, habit, reasoning, anger, desire. These help the advocates on both sides find arguments for or against a person convicted of crime.

(b) The state of mind of criminals.

Criminals must suppose first, that the crime can be committed; second that they can commit it; third, that they will not be found out or, fourth, if they are found out, that they can escape punishment. Arguments about motivation spring from these.

(c) The kind of people who are wronged.

These people have something the criminal wants, either necessities or luxuries. Such people are any or all of trustful, easygoing, sensitive or frightened. These can be the subject of arguments about third parties.

Political (deliberative)

In this kind of speech one persuades or dissuades someone from a course of action, by categorising it under four extremely important, widely used headings, which Cicero suggests should be dealt with in the following order: is the action possible? Is it necessary? Is it advantageous (e.g. easy, important, pleasant, free from danger)? Finally, is it honourable (e.g. just, pious, merciful, moral)? The purpose is to identify for listeners the ends of the course of action in view and the means to those ends. The point about these categories is that they are quite distinct from each other; the result is that conflicts will occur between them, e.g. honour against advantage, possibility against necessity, and so on. Subjects will include the political – war and peace, finance, legislation – and the personal – how to become happy (here sub-headings will include friends, wealth, children, old age, health, beauty, strength, fame, goodness). Since maintenance of the established order is advantageous to everyone, Aristotle insists, one must take into account people's political circumstances, customs, habits and interests.

Epideictic (occasional, celebratory)
These include e.g. speech days, commemorative addresses, ceremonial occasions. They have nothing to do with deciding the justice of a past action or considering what course of action is now expedient. Their subject is the present, usually to praise or blame. Is a man extravagant? Call him generous. Rash? Call him courageous. Stupid, call him honest; thick-skinned, call him good-tempered; treacherous, call him cautious. The headings under which Aristotle thought a man should be praised were for his sense of justice, courage, self-control, wealth, generosity, kindness, foresight and wisdom.

Argument

There are broadly two types of argument. One is non-artistic, i.e. based on tangible evidence (documents, wills, contracts, etc.). This I say no more about. The other is more important – what the ancients called 'artistic', i.e. invented, arguments.

Events
When one is talking about events, one should ask why did something happen (cause)? Where did it happen (place)? When did it happen (time)? How did it happen (manner)? By what means did it happen (means)? Further questions could be added – what of the effects as well as causes of the action? Is it similar or dissimilar to anything else? What is the sequence of events?

Persons
In relation to persons rather than events, one is advised to investigate parents, race, nation, age, sex, education, experience and reputation.

Focus
At law in particular, it is essential to identify the focus of the problem, the precise issue on which the argument hinges. Ancients saw three major points at issue:
(a) Is it a matter of fact? i.e. did it actually happen?
(b) Or of definition? Is it a matter of categorising what happened?
(c) Or of quality? Is it a matter of evaluating it?
For example, A kills B – or did he? (Fact). If he did, was it murder? Manslaughter? Accident? (Definition). Whatever it was, was it a good or bad thing? (Quality). The skilful speaker can try to conclude the case at any of these three points e.g. his client A did not kill B; but if he did, it was

an accident; but if it was murder, it was an excellent thing to have done it, or it was someone else's fault, or the circumstances told against my client, and so on.

Hermogenes, for example, shows how to shift the blame on to a third party: first, agree a wrong looks as if it has been done but show your intentions are innocent; then blame someone/thing else; then minimise the wrong done; then argue no real wrong was done at all.[7] *Mutatis mutandis*, these headings work for the prosecution.

Emotional appeals

It is just as important to determine how to organise the emotional impact of a speech. Aristotle identifies two areas to work on:

(a) *ethos*: i.e. the personal character of the speaker – Aristotle emphasises that the speaker must show himself to be a person of good sense, good moral character, and good will.

(b) *pathos*: appealing to the emotions of the listeners and putting them in the right frame of mind. Aristotle points out that emotions like anger, pity, fear, etc. change men's judgement. We should find out what makes people angry/ pitiful/ afraid (etc.), at whom this feeling is directed, what their consequent state of mind is, and how this can be turned to the speaker's advantage. Another writer puts it more simply: 'our aim is to win over, instruct and move our audience.'

Refutation

I list here the five most important devices:

Deduction (especially the syllogism, or enthymeme)

A simple example: All men are mortal. Socrates is a man. Therefore Socrates is mortal. This is a form of deduction – i.e. taking the general case and deducing the specific example from it. 'People who do X are the sort of people who will do Y' is a typical deductive argument. Many of these types of argument are fallacious, e.g. fire produces smoke. I see smoke. Therefore there is a fire. But the syllogism does not say that *only* fire produces smoke.

Induction

These arguments are the opposite of deduction, taking a specific and reaching a general conclusion e.g. the sun rises every day. Therefore it always rises. 'X once did Y. Therefore he did Y this time' is a typical inductive argument. Inductive arguments are famously uncertain. Because X has happened in the past does not *prove* it will happen in the future.

Arguments from probability

These relate to deduction and induction, and take the form 'Given X, it is probable/likely that Y happened'. Quintilian identifies three degrees of probability: very strong (like a sound deductive argument), less certain (like an inductive argument), and straining credibility ('a theft committed in a household was committed by a member of the household').

Maxims

These again relate to syllogisms, because they take a universal truth and apply it to a specific case. 'Too many cooks spoil the broth. So we do not need a committee, but a single person to ....'

Examples

This involves the use of a case parallel to the one at hand, most commonly some past event that throws light on the present. Thus 'X made himself a tyrant by taking a personal bodyguard. Therefore do not allow Y to take a personal bodyguard.' Aristotle recommends that the example should always follow the proof. Thus, having made your point by argument, then clinch it with a telling example.

B. The speaker's resources

Five headings helped a speaker think about how to ensure a successful speech.

Inventio: discovering what to say

This is covered by **A.** above.

Dispositio: arranging the speech

This is dealt with structurally under **C.** below. Rhetoric has least to say about this in detail, because every case is different. Some hints do emerge. It was not thought wise to leave the strongest argument till last: the audience's expectations must be met early or you will lose them. Others point out that where a client has the law against him, but equity, or fairness, on his side, the best thing to do is attack the law first and then appeal to fairness.

Elocutio: language

This subject is probably the least relevant to us, given that we are less concerned about correctness than the ancients. Five topics were very important to them (see p. 96):

Correctness

Grammar was taken for granted; use of language was the main issue. Is this the best Greek and Latin, from the best authors?

Clearness

Be specific, says Aristotle, use simple words and simple everyday images, keep sentences sort, avoid vagueness.

Embellishment

Many possibilities, especially figures of speech designed to imply or suggest what is *not* the case, like rhetorical questions; anticipation ('my opponent will say that ...'); hesitation ('What can I say ...?'); consultation ('I must now ask the judge/my opponent what to do in this matter ...'); feigning emotion; impersonating characters so as to produce an imaginary conversation; giving a vivid word-picture of what took place ('Picture the scene …'); irony; pretended repentance for something said; mimicry.

Verbal repetition

Tricolon (groups of three), anaphora (repetitions), no 'and' (asyndeton), balance, alliteration and antithesis (contrast) are advocated. *Veni vidi vici*, and its translation 'I came, I saw, I conquered', illustrate the first five: (Latin) group of three, (English) repeated 'I', no 'and', (Latin) balance in single words each of two syllables, (Latin) alliteration in repeated *v* and *-i*. There is also a strong sense of climax, very often helped on by 'ascending' tricolon, i.e. each 'leg' of the tricolon lengthens. E.g. 'Friends (one syllable), Romans (two syllables), countrymen (three syllables)'.

Appropriateness

Known today as 'register'. Grand subjects require the grand style (lots of flourishes, long, weighty sentences), but should not fall into bombast; intermediate and low subjects should be similarly styled (by low, one author compares writing a letter, 'a simple subject in simple terms', whose aim is 'to be the heart's good wishes in brief'). Cicero says that the grand style is for moving, the plain for proving, the intermediate for pleasing.

Memoria: memorising

The Greek poet Simonides is said to have invented the first aid to memory. He had just left a party when the roof fell in, killing everyone. But he knew who was who because he remembered where they were sitting. So the speaker should associate each point in his speech with (say) rooms in a well-known house. As he moves from room to room, the next point in his speech will spring to mind.

Pronuntiatio or *actio*: delivery

When the Greek orator Demosthenes was asked what was the most important thing for an orator to get right, he answered 'Delivery'. And the second? 'Delivery'. And the third? 'Delivery'. Great emphasis was placed on correct pronunciation and distinct utterance; the speaker should avoid annoying mannerisms, excessive speed or slowness, panting, spraying saliva, walking about, and excessive gesturing.

C. The structure of the speech

Speech structure is infinitely flexible. The following was recommended as a good pattern for legal cases in particular, but has general application too.

Exordium: the opening statement

It has three aims: to make the audience well-disposed, attentive and receptive. The vital thing is to identify unambiguously the point or points at issue as far as you are concerned. One must also try to arouse expectations by e.g. foreshadowing briefly what will come or suggesting how surprising it will be.

Narratio: the facts of the case

This section is usually confined to the courtroom. It should be 'brief, clear and plausible' – though not so brief as to be unclear. This section should generally stick strictly to the narration of events, avoid argumentation and not play on the emotions of the audience: but as Cicero points out, all these rules can be broken if it will add to the effectiveness of the case (e.g. an element of wonder, suspense, the unexpected, dialogue between participants in the action, and so on).

Divisio: a preview of the main points of the case
This will briefly summarise the next heading.

Confirmatio and *con/re-futatio*: positive and negative proofs
See above under **Refutation**.

Conclusio or *peroratio*: closing statement
There are three requirements of a good conclusion:

Summary
Aristotle: 'In your introduction you should state your subject, in order that the point to be judged may be quite plain. In the conclusion, you should summarise the arguments by which your case has been proved. The first step in this reviewing process is to observe that you have done what you said you would do. The second is to state what you have said and why you have said it' (Cicero points out that recapitulation all through the speech may be helpful if the case is complex).

Sympathy
Make your listeners' hearts go out to you: this is a place for gently twanging the heartstrings.

Eloquence
Rise to the heights of eloquence to reach a memorable conclusion in a grand thunderclap of a finale (though avoid rant, bombast and hysteria, warns Quintilian).

It cannot be emphasised enough what a deep and lasting effect rhetorical principles had on classical literature. Both Greek and Roman literature consciously shapes and argues: it does not emote. This does not mean it is not emotional: it certainly is. But the emotion is contained within clearly structured and organised argument. This can be off-putting to readers happier wading about in umbrella and galoshes under emotional waterfalls spraying feelings all over them. It is probably the reason why classical literature is often described as 'restrained' or 'objective' or 'frigid'. It was certainly easy to write by numbers in the ancient world, turning the same tired arguments and ideas round and round in the same tired way, as the survival of a certain amount of duff stuff demonstrates.

The Romantic movement that swept Europe in the early nineteenth century is largely responsible for our problems with even the best of classical literature. Romanticism deliberately opposed classical 'rationalism' in favour of creative freedom, spontaneity, sincerity, emotionalism, yearning, dreaming, and generally poking about in the soul with a pole to find 'the truth', for the romantic a hopeless search for something that one felt was there but could never be found.[8] Sentimentality and fantasy soon followed: whatever you think or believe is right. The distinction between humans and animals became less clear.

This is very democratic and inclusive – as if anyone could be a writer or painter or thinker merely by wishing to be so – but it does not work. Artistic excellence is usually tied up with the capacity to make distinctions and exert control (if the artist himself is not able to give an account of his work in these terms, that does not mean an account cannot be given; the critic can do it). The rallying call of 'freedom' in cultural matters sounds an uncertain note at the best of times. For example, the present leader of the Conservative party William Hague said recently that popular culture was good because it was the expression of freedom. There is nothing wrong with popular culture, but its excellence or otherwise is a matter of judgement and nothing to do with expressions of freedom.

7

Men on Women

A standard book on the Greek law of family and property has one entry in the index under WOMEN: it reads 'disabilities'.[1] But life is not law.

The ancient world was a male world and virtually without exception all our documentation was written by males. It is impossible to recreate women's experience.[2] We can judge only how they were perceived by men, and in most cases the men who composed the texts were wealthy aristocrats for whom honour, respect and high status among their fellow men were life's absolute priorities. It is not likely that powerful and (self)-important males would present themselves in public in anything less than a most masterful and sympathetic light. Further, Greek thinking in particular had a tendency to polarise the world, each entity defining its opposite – male-female, Greek-barbarian and so on – and never the twain shall meet.[3] Aristotle reports a fascinating list of opposite principles recognised by followers of Pythagoras: limited-unlimited; equal-unequal; unity-plurality; right-left; male-female; still-moved; straight line-curve; light-dark; good-bad; square-oblong. It was no accident that women were linked with the unequal, dark, left and bad.[4] Nevertheless, life is not philosophy either.

Before I offer some texts for consideration, six generalisations applicable to both Greek and Roman women are in order:

(i) There was a broad link between status and dependency in the ancient world. On those terms women, being dependent on their men, could never aspire to men's status. The Roman satirist Juvenal's crushingly obscene onslaught on women in *Satire* 6 (sex-mad, spendthrift, faithless, loud-mouthed blue-stockings, uninterested in babies and keen to assume the roles of men) reads like the work of man terrified of a new order where women could no longer be assumed to be dependants. In general, male authors cast aspersions on women who tried to act like men and men who knuckled under to them.

(ii) Men rationalised this position intellectually by judging that women were inferior in intelligence and self-control, though dangerous for the sexual charms that could addle the brain of even the strongest-willed males (women are commonly stereotyped as drink- and sex-mad). Both cultures institutionalised the guardianship of women: if women had no father or husband, they were assigned a male to oversee their affairs. How tightly this institution functioned is hard to say. Certainly it had become something of a formality by the time of the empire in Rome, when (for example) one Eumachia is celebrated in Pompeii as a woman of considerable wealth and business interests, with a statue erected to her for her donations to building projects.

(iii) Women had no political rights and were debarred from speaking at or voting in political assemblies. This did not prevent some women exercising power through men. Pericles' mistress Aspasia was said to have written his speeches[5] and the comic poet Aristophanes, absurdly, claimed she trained prostitutes, of whom the Megarians stole two, thus starting the Peloponnesian War (*Acharnians* 526-9). Aristophanes could not have thought this would raise a laugh had Aspasia not had a public reputation worth exploiting. Then again, the prosecutor in a case against the woman Neaera, who (he argues) is falsely claiming all the advantages of legitimate marriage and legitimate children, speculates what the jury's womenfolk will say if the jurors return home and say they acquitted her:

> And if you acquit her, what will you say to you wife or daughter or mother when you return home and they ask 'Where have you been?' and you reply 'At the courts' and they ask 'Who was on trial?' and you say (of course) 'Neaera because, as an alien she lived with an Athenian citizen against the law, and married off her daughter, who had been a prostitute, to the king *arkhôn*, and this daughter performed the most secret rites on Athens' behalf, and was given in [ceremonial] marriage to the god Dionysus, and all the rest of it.' When they hear this, the women will say 'And what did you do?' and you will say 'We acquitted her!' Will not these women in all their virtue rise and denounce you in fury that you considered that woman to be no different from them in matters of public ceremony and religious ritual?
>
> [Demosthenes],[6] *Against Neaera* 110-11

Whatever the speaker's agenda, there would be no point in him talking like this if his description of the scene at a juror's home bore no relationship to a possible reality.

On the Roman side, females in the imperial family, as members of the emperor's inner ring, wheeled and dealt with the best of them. Agrippina, for example, ensured that her son Nero would succeed the emperor Claudius, rather than his son Britannicus. The historian Cassius Dio records the following recipe for success of the most famous of them all, Augustus' wife Livia:

> When someone asked her what she did to maintain her grip over Augustus, she replied that she remained scrupulously chaste, gladly did everything he wanted, did not meddle in any of his business, and pretended not to hear about or be aware of any of his love-affairs.
>
> Cassius Dio, *Roman History* 58.2.5ff

Up to a point: an inscription (admittedly from early in their marriage) records the young Augustus' displeasure at Livia's attempts to win favours from him for the Greek island of Samos.

(iv) Women's primary function was to marry and produce legitimate children ('women are married for the sake of bearing children and heirs, and not for pleasure and enjoyment', says the doctor Soranus, sternly). Medical texts concentrate almost exclusively on this aspect of her function: unsurprisingly, since the production of children was so important in the ancient world and childbirth the moment of highest hopes and highest danger for the family.

(v) Religion. In the ancient world, there were male and female divinities overseeing a vast range of human concerns, designed to cover for any surprise that life might spring, and men and women had their full parts to play in the great public rituals played out on behalf of the city in which these divinities were acknowledged. In the Greek world, goddesses were mostly served by priestesses, but in any event priest and priestess had precisely the same ritual functions. Festivals dedicated to women alone, and cults open to both sexes, were widespread.

In the Roman world most priestly functions were performed by men, though in some offices their wives had an official status. The six Vestal Virgins, who served for thirty years from before puberty preparing grain for public sacrifice and guarding the sacred flame (whose extinction proved that a Virgin was impure and Rome in danger), were a major exception. Female cults existed (e.g. the *Bona Dea*, 'Good Goddess', the equivalent of the Greek *Thesmophoria*, a fertility cult), and foreign cults (including Judaism and Christianity) seem to have been of particular interest to women. The Christian belief that God's service should come before everything else, combined with 'official' Graeco-Roman disapproval of sexual pleasure in women, had many interesting consequences, e.g. the honour accorded to chastity, celibacy and the nun (Latin *nonna*, 'grandmother').

(vi) Greek myth, on which the Romans drew very heavily, frequently assigned nightmare roles to female figures (e.g. the Furies, the Harpies, the Sirens, Scylla and Charybdis, Medusa, the Sphinx) and often portray them as destroyers of men (e.g. Medea, Clytaemnestra, Phaedra, Agave). At the same time, figures like Antigone, Alcmena, Penelope and Andromache exhibit a moral and intellectual gravity quite the equal of any male's. Destructive or saint-like, women were nevertheless felt worthy of intensive examination by (male) poets like Homer and especially the Greek tragedians, for whom the family and its capacity to destroy itself were the themes to which they constantly returned. It is (in my view) hard to draw any particular lessons from those examples where male and female figures were pushed to the limits for literary purposes.

By way of a coda, it is worth adding that Romans tended to be more liberal than Greeks in these and related areas. As we have seen, by the time of the empire, Roman guardianship of women was a formality. Likewise, Romans freed slaves as a matter of policy and used their skills, freed or not, in positions close to the centre of power under the empire (see pp. 80-1). Roman marriage laws were notoriously relaxed: living together confirmed marriage, separation confirmed divorce. The poet Catullus had an open affair with Clodia (pet name, Lesbia), wife of Metellus (consul 60 BC); the first emperor Augustus became so concerned about the state of marriage among the upper classes that he even legislated on the matter, to no effect. Finally, Romans welcomed fellow-Italians and foreigners into Roman citizenship (p. 78). None of this was quite the Greek way.

I here offer a selection of texts, with brief commentary.

Greece

1. Homer: Hector and Andromache

Hector has left the fighting and returned into Ilium to make a sacrifice. There he meets his wife Andromache, with their baby Astyanax. Andromache has begged him not to risk his life – he is all she has left:

	'Hector, you are father and lady mother to me
430	and brother, and you are my fertile husband.
	Please, take pity on me and stay here inside the rampart,
	And do not make your son an orphan and your wife a widow.
	Rally the troops by the fig-tree, where in particular
	The city is vulnerable and the wall can be scaled.
435	Three times the best of the Greeks have made an attack on it
	Under the leadership of the two Ajaxes and renowned Idomeneus
	And the sons of Atreus and Diomedes, brave son of Tydeus.
	Someone skilled in prophecy has been talking to them,
	Or their own heart has urged them forward and commanded them.'
440	Then great Hector of the shining helmet answered her:
	'All this is in my mind too, lady; but greatly
	Do I feel shame before the Trojans and their long-robed women
	If like a coward I withdraw from the battle.
	Nor does my heart urge me, since I have learned to be noble
445	And always to fight in the front rank of the Trojans
	Winning for my father and for myself great glory.
	I know this well in my heart and mind:
	The day will come when holy Ilium is destroyed
	And Priam [father] and the people of Priam of the good ash spear.
450	But at that time I shall not rate the suffering of the Trojans,
	Or of Hekabe [mother] herself or of king Priam
	Or of my brothers who in their noble multitudes
	Will fall in the dust at the hands of their enemies,
	As much as yours, when one of the bronze-armoured Greeks
455	leads you away in tears, removing your day of freedom.
	... But may the earth cover me in death first
465	Before I hear your cry and know you are being dragged away.'

So speaking bright Hector reached out for his child.
His child at once into the bosom of his fair-girdled nurse
Shrank back, crying, terrified at the sight of his dear father,
Frightened by the bronze and horse-hair crest
470 that he saw nodding so fearfully from the top of his helmet.
At once bright Hector removed the helmet from his head
And placed it all-glittering on the ground.
Then he kissed his son and dandled him in his arms …
[*and prayed: 'May he be a better warrior than his father'*].
482 So he spoke and in his dear wife's arms placed
His son. She took him to her fragrant bosom,
Laughing in her tears. And her husband took pity on her
[*and attempts to console here: 'No man dies before his time is up'*].
490 '… But return to the house and see to your work,
The loom and the distaff, and tell your slaves
To get to work too. War will be the work of men,
All of them, and especially me, of those born and bred in Troy.'
So he spoke and bright Hector retrieved his helmet
495 With its crest. His dear wife went home,
Turning to look back time and again, the tears falling.

Homer, Iliad 6.429-55; 464-73; 482-4; 490-6

This uniquely touching and affectionate scene between husband, wife and baby – a private encounter, even though they meet outside the home – exemplifies the different roles of parents. For Andromache, the running of home and family is the centre of her life (490-2), for Hector, the battlefield (444-6, 492-3). Andromache attempts to cross the boundaries (429-30, 431-9), to no avail. It is often remarked how deep is the sympathy between man and wife in Homer. While individual roles are clearly demarcated, one does not get a sense that Hector is a tyrant.

2. Aristotle's will

Aristotle had a daughter Pythias by an earlier marriage; he had a son Nichomachus by his later partner Herpyllis; and an adopted son Nicanor.

- It will be well. But if anything happens, Aristotle has laid down the following:
- Antipater is overall executor.
- Until Nicanor arrives, Aristomenes, Timarchus, Hipparchus, Dioteles and Theophrastus (if he agrees and circumstances permit) shall look after the children and Herpyllis and the estate.
- When the girl [Pythias, his daughter by marriage] comes of age, she shall marry Nicanor.
- If anything happens to her – may it not and it will not – before she marries, or when she marries but in the absence of children, let Nicanor be her guardian to take decisions, worthily of himself and us, about the child and everything else.
- Let Nicanor take charge of the girl and the boy Nicomachus [Herpyllis' son by Aristotle] as he thinks fit, as a father and brother.

- If anything happens to Nicanor – may it not – either before he takes the girl or when he has taken her but in the absence of children, let those arrangements stand that he has made.
- If Theophrastus wishes to live with the girl, let him have the same rights as Nicanor.
- If not, the executors, in consultation with Antipater, shall take decisions concerning the girl and boy as seems best.
- The executors and Nicanor, in memory of me and Herpyllis' affection for me, shall look after her in everything, and if she wishes to marry, let her not be given to anyone unworthy of us …
- In addition to what she has already been given, they must give her a talent of silver out of the estate and any three slave-girls she chooses, as well as the slave-girl and slave Pyrrhaeus she already has.
- If she wants to live in Chalcis, let her live in the lodge by the garden, if in Stagira, my father's house.
- Whichever home she chooses, the executors must equip it as they think appropriate, with Herpyllis' agreement …

Diogenes Laertius, *Life of Aristotle* 5.11-14

The will exemplifies the fact that Greek woman could not own property or marry without permission. It does not answer how far these negotiations had been agreed between the parties beforehand (it is worth pointing out that a number of clauses offer considerable flexibility) and raises an issue of considerable importance – the extent to which we should talk about the restriction or protection of women.

3. Lysias: the seduction of Euphiletus' wife

The speaker Euphiletus is defending himself against a charge of murdering the man who seduced his wife.

When, Athenians, I decided to marry and introduce a woman into my household, to start with I acted so as not to interfere with her nor to leave her too much to her own devices to do what she wanted, but I looked after her as I could and kept a reasonable eye on her. When our child was born, I began to trust her and gave her the run of all my property, considering this was the greatest sign of intimacy. In the beginning she was the best of all women – a shrewd, economic housekeeper, looking after everything very carefully. But when my mother died, her death became the cause of all my troubles. For when my wife accompanied her out to be buried, she was seen by this man and eventually corrupted by him. He kept a watch for our slave-girl who did the shopping, made advances through her, and so brought her to ruin.

First, gentlemen, let me give you some details. My house is on two floors, the upper and lower floors being of the same size. The women's quarter is above, the man's below. When the baby was born, its mother suckled it. So that she should not be at risk in descending the stairs when it needed washing, I lived upstairs, the women downstairs. This became so usual that my wife often went down to sleep with the child, to suckle it and prevent it crying. This went on for a long time and I suspected nothing, but was so innocent as to believe my wife was the most chaste woman in the city.

Time passed, gentlemen, and one day I came home unexpectedly from the country. After dinner the child [*downstairs*] started crying and making a fuss: it was being annoyed by the slave-girl on purpose to behave like that. The man was inside. I learned all this afterwards. I told my wife to go down and suckle it to stop it crying. At first she refused, as if thrilled to see me home again after such a long time. But when I grew angry and instructed her to go, she replied 'Yes, so you can have a go at the slave-girl. You pulled her about before when you were drunk.' I laughed at this, but she got up, left, closed the door, pretending to make fun, and drew the bolt. I thought nothing of it and in complete innocence fell happily to sleep after my journey from the country. Towards day she returned and opened the door. I asked why the doors were banging in the night. She said that the baby's lamp had gone out and she had re-lit it from a neighbour's. I said nothing, assuming it to be true. But it did seem to me, gentlemen, that she had put make-up on, though her brother had died only thirty days earlier.

[*Euphiletus now tells how the truth came out. Eratosthenes was having an affair with someone else, who became aware that he was cheating on her. Furious, she sent an old woman to tell Euphiletus that Eratosthenes was having an affair with his wife. Euphiletus forced a confession from his slave-girl, who agreed to help him catch his wife and Eratosthenes in the act.*]

I had a good friend Sostratus. I met him at sunset when he had returned from the country. As I knew that he would find none of his friends at home at that hour, I invited him to dine with me. So he came to my house and we went up to eat. We had a good meal, he left, and I went to sleep. Enter Eratosthenes, gentlemen. The slave-girl wakes me up and says he is inside. I tell her to guard the door, and I leave the house in silence, calling on various friends. Some were at home, others in town. I gathered as many as I could and returned. Taking torches from the nearest shop, we go in. The door had been opened in readiness by the slave-girl. We pushed open the door of the room and the first of us to go in saw him lying beside my wife, those who followed saw him standing naked on the bed.

[*Eratosthenes admits guilt and offers money in reparation, but Euphiletus invokes the law and kills him.*]   Lysias 1.6-24

This passage is striking for its public revelation of the intimate, private details of the relationship between a man and his wife. Men-and-women indoors present a different face to men-and-women outdoors, under the public gaze. It also raises questions about a wife's freedom in the home. Granted this is a law suit – the speaker says what he does because he calculates it will win the sympathy of 500 male jurors over the age of thirty – this is an interesting picture of a Greek wife carrying on an affair in her own home almost literally under the nose of her husband.

4. [Demosthenes] The attack on the farm

The speaker has agreed that he owed Theophemus money, and claims that he had it waiting for him at the bank when Theophemus decided to swoop on his farm and seize goods in lieu. Having taken fifty sheep, a shepherd and a slave out in the fields, they turn their attention to the household:

First they went for the slaves, but they escaped and ran off in different directions. So they approached the house and threw down the door that led into the garden and entered the presence of my wife and children. They proceeded to carry off all the furniture that was still left in the house ... In addition, gentlemen, my wife happened to be in the courtyard eating with the children and with an old nurse of mine, devoted and faithful, who had been freed by my father. She lived with a man when she had been freed, but after he died and she became old and there was no one to look after her, she returned to me. I could not allow my old nurse to live in want. At the same time I was about to sail off on duty, and my wife wanted me to leave a person like this to live with her in the house. There they were in mid-meal when these men leapt in, found them and started seizing the furniture. The rest of the female slaves heard the commotion and locked themselves in the tower where they lived, so the men could not get in there. So they concentrated on removing the furniture from the rest of the house. My wife told them not to touch it, saying that it belonged to her as part of her dowry and that 'You have fifty sheep, the shepherd and the slave, which are worth much more than you are owed' (one of the neighbours had knocked on the door and told her). Further, she said the money was waiting for them at the bank, since she had heard this from me. 'If you wait here,' she said, 'or one of you goes to find him, you shall go back with the money at once. But do not touch the furniture, especially as you have what you are owed.'

[Demosthenes], *Against Euergus and Mnesibulus* 52-7

Again, a lawsuit, and the speaker considers it will help his case to show that his wife is privy to the details all his business affairs, including his finances, and can stick up for herself when alien males barge into her home. Notice also the speaker's compassion for his old female nurse. He clearly thought he would gain credit by describing how he brought her back into the family home.

Rome

1. Pliny: the death of a young girl

It is with the greatest sadness that I write you this letter: the younger daughter of our friend Fundanus has died. I never saw a girl who was more fun, more adorable, more deserving of a long life – or indeed immortality. She was not yet fourteen, but she showed the wisdom of age, the dignity of womanhood, the sweetness of youth – and all with the modesty of innocence. How she clung to her father's neck! How lovingly and modestly she embraced us, her father's friends! How she appreciated what her nurses, teachers and instructors did for her! How diligently and intelligently she read! How sparing and restrained she was in play! How bravely, how patiently, how courageously she bore her final illness! She obeyed doctor's orders, encouraged her sister and father, and even when her strength failed her, she kept going by force of spirit. She held out right to the end, unbroken by the length of her illness or fear of death – and left us all the more reasons to lament her sad loss. It was a grievous and bitter end – the timing even more cruel than death itself. She was engaged to an outstanding young man, the wedding day was fixed, the invitations sent. Now such joy has changed to such grief. I cannot express in words the wound I felt when I heard Fundanus – one grief leading to another – ordering that what was to be spent on clothing, pearls and jewels should now go towards incense, ointment and spices ... he has lost a daughter who resembled him in character no less than in looks and was her father's living image in an extraordinary way.

Pliny, Letters 5.16

We may have problems with Pliny's priorities here. His perception of the young girl is of a young adult. But that was the way Romans thought of children. Pliny was bound to select those details of her existence which would make her seem most like a grown up: it was the highest praise he could afford. There is little sense here that a young girl was of no account in a family's life.

2. A wife's memorial

Furia Spes, freed by Sempronius Firmus, set up this inscription for her beloved husband. We met as boy and girl and from that moment on were bound by mutual affection. I lived with him for too short a time. Our happiness should have continued, but a cruel hand separated us. Sacred spirits of the dead (*Manes*), I beg you to protect the man I love whom I have entrusted to you, to be well-disposed and kind to him during the hours of night, so that I may see him [*in a dream?*] and so that he too may be allowed to persuade fate that I should come to him, gently and soon.

Corpus of Latin Inscriptions 6.18817

It is argued, reasonably, that memorials of this sort often reflect male, not female, priorities. That may not be the case here. The usual male concerns about e.g. status are not in evidence.

3. Pliny: matchmaking

You ask me to look out for a husband for your niece. You were quite right to involve me. You know how much I loved and admired the girl's father Arulenus Rusticus – a fine man – , how much he influenced me in my youth and how he praised me in such a way that I seemed to deserve it. No greater or more agreeable task could be entrusted to me; I could not undertake a more honourable duty than to find a young man worthy to continue Arulenus Rusticus's family line.

It would have been a long search had not the ideal man been ready at hand, almost by fate – Minicius Acilianus. He is a little younger than I am, and he loves me in that friendly way young men love each other, but also respects me as his elder. He wants to be shaped and guided by me as I was by you and your brother. He comes from Brixia [*Brescia*] – my part of Italy, which still keeps and guards the honest frugality and rural simplicity of the old days. His father, Minicius Macrinus, is a leading *eques* [*i.e. businessman, a rank below senator*] with no desire for higher status. The emperor Vespasian chose him to hold the rank of praetor [*which would have entitled him to a seat in the Senate*] but he preferred the quiet life, out of the public eye rather than this political service – or turmoil – of ours. His maternal grandmother is Serrana Procula from Patavium [*Padua*]. You know what Paduans are like: she is a model of strictness even to them. His uncle, Publius Acilius, is a man of exceptional character, judgement and integrity ...

Acilianus himself is energetic, hard-working and very modest. He has distinguished himself in the offices of quaestor, tribune and praetor, so you will not have to campaign on his behalf. He has the looks of a gentleman, a healthy, ruddy complexion, an aristocratic bearing and senatorial elegance. I do not think these features should be overlooked: they are the reward of a bride's virginity. I do not know whether to say that his father is well off: when I think of your priorities, I reckon the subject should be passed over. On the other hand, when I consider the climate of modern opinion and the laws that judge a man's finances to be of first importance [*there were financial hurdles to equestrian and senatorial status*], it did not seem to me this should be omitted ...

Pliny, Letters 1.14

It is usually assumed that arranged marriages were to the girl's disadvantage. But it takes two to make a marriage, and one wonders how Minicius Acilianus reacted to the search. There is nothing in this letter to suggest that the parties involved would have no choice in the matter when it came to making a decision. Again, the public face of a relationship or transaction need not reflect the private, but it is difficult to see any point in Pliny constructing such a loving and reasonable picture of his activity if everyone knew it bore no relation to the reality.

4. Graffiti from Pompeii

Marcus loves Spendusa.
Serena hates Isidore.
Thyas, don't love Fortunatus.
Sarra, you're not acting very nicely, leaving me all alone.
Restitutus has deceived many girls many times.
I have f——ed many girls here.
I came here, I f——ed, I went home.
Let him who loves, prosper. Let him who loves not, perish. And let him who forbids others to love, perish twice over.
Let him who chastises lovers try to fetter the winds and block the endless flow of water from the spring.
Lovers, like bees, lead a honey-sweet life.

Jo-Ann Shelton, As the Romans Did, 120

This is the world of True Lurve, the sort that is endlessly portrayed in Graeco-Roman comedy and love epigram. Try Roman Catullus (first century BC):

My woman says she would prefer to marry no one
Besides me, not even if Jupiter himself were to offer.

So she says: but what a woman writes to her longing lover
Ought to be written on the wind and racing water.

Catullus 70

This world, and that of the aristocratic marriages of the Great and Good, existed side by side as happily then as they do now.

It will be obvious that I have skewed this section in favour of a comparatively rosy view of a woman's existence in the ancient world. I do so because the common assumption is that any woman's life in the ancient world must have been hell.[7] That this was true of many women, I do not doubt. I am sure it was equally true of many men. But poverty and medical ignorance were the main oppressors, neither of them respecters of persons. The defining moment, I think, for male and female alike, was the family you were born into and your general physical condition. If you were born robust and healthy into the aristocratic, wealthy, educated five percent, you would (probably) be fine. If not, a life of unremitting physical hardship and an early death awaited. The following ironic grave inscription tells its own tale:

All a person needs. Bones sweetly reposing, I have no fears of a sudden food-shortage. I do not suffer from arthritis. I am not in debt because I am behind with the rent: in fact, my lodgings are permanent – and free!
Corpus of Latin Inscriptions 6.7193a

We need all the help we can get to understand the private life of people in a world whose sources are so relentlessly male and public. Anyone who has seen the film *The Godfather* would get, I think, some sense of the dynamics of family life and a woman's position in it among the aristocracy of ancient Rome. I end with some extracts from J.K. Campbell's *Honour, Patronage and the Family: a Study of Institutions and Moral Values in a Greek Mountain Community* (Oxford 1964). This anthropological survey of the Sarakatsan people of north-western Greece carried out in the 1950s also gives some sense, I believe, of the functioning of the ancient Greek family:

If a man is nearly all nobility, a natural predisposition to evil is the most striking feature of the female character. She is above all cunning, especially in the sense that her cunning involves the corruption of another, that is the man. She is a constant threat to his honour ... the Devil has a hold over women who are his peculiar emissaries dispatched to provoke men's hearts with sexual passions. Thus the whole burden of the shame of sexual relations is shifted on to the female sex. Since her powers of sexual attraction are of this supernatural order, man in general is unable to resist them ... and once he advances on her, she has not the strength to resist him. In the Sarakatsan view, the power of woman's sexuality, the weakness of her will, and the physical strength of the man, are the important factors involved in sexual activity. It is for these reasons that the individual woman is expected by her kinsmen to have 'shame', in the sense that in speech, gesture, attitude and dress, she must, as far as possible, cloak the existence of this sexuality. For the same reasons that family watches over its women with the greatest care; especially in the case of an unmarried girl, anxious eyes follow her if she must go to the well or collect firewood unaccompanied ...

The wife submits herself completely to her husband because she accepts her position as part of a natural and inevitable order. Her sex is part of her fate. The physical strain of domestic labour under harsh conditions is immense. It is rare to find a woman after four or five years of marriage who retains the least hint of her former comeliness ... but the wife's acceptance of subordination and physical hardship is also made tolerable partly by her relative independence in her own domain, and more particularly by a consciousness of the significance of her position which relative to that of her husband increases in importance with the passage of the years. Therefore a wife accepts her husband's authority, shows respect and esteems him, if he proves able to protect her children and herself and if he uses his power over his family with a measure of justice. The husband reciprocally approves of his wife if she cares for her children with love and faces her physical labours without weakness.

It is only within the privacy and secrecy of the family hut that a man or woman is able to relax, to laugh, to give affection and receive it. The burden of public life is a heavy one. Outside his house a man must be severe and proud. He must strut about like some turkey-cock as if his affairs were matters of abnormal consequence. He must on no account show his emotions unless it be unrestrained anger at some actual or imagined slight. Publicly, he treats his wife and daughters with disdain, barking at them orders in harsh, staccato phrases. An unmarried girl or a wife must walk slowly with measured tread and downcast gaze. Only inside the hut is it possible to abandon these conventional attitudes. After the evening meal, an act of communion to which only a visiting kinsman will be admitted, the whole family, men, women and children, sit or lie round the hearth in no fixed order, laughing, gossiping and asking riddles ... the general tone of the family in assembly is one of the utmost intimacy, solidarity and identification ... it is an atmosphere of easy camaraderie and undemonstrative affection, which is impossible with unrelated persons in any situation, and possible for the members of a family only when they are shielded from the public gaze ...

8

Emperor and Empire

It is not easy to think of the Romans as a modest, self-critical people, but in two respects the description applies.[1] They fully acknowledged both their cultural debt to the Greeks (see p. 19) and the weaknesses of the system of empire they imposed on Europe. The lawyer and politician Cicero declaimed in a case in 66 BC: 'Words cannot express how bitterly we are hated among foreign nations because of the wanton and outrageous conduct of the men we sent to govern them.'[2] The historian Tacitus put the famous complaint into the mouth of the British soldier Calgacus, addressing the Caledonians before battle, '[the Romans] make a desert and call it peace'.[3] This self-criticism did not spring from higher moral values but from self-interest. If the empire was to work, provincials had to be kept happy. It did not serve Rome's purposes for the provinces to be in a constant state of turmoil through bad management.

In a letter *c*. 60 BC to his brother Quintus who was about to start on a third year of tenure as governor of Asia (western Turkey), Cicero gives the following advice. He pinpoints the importance of maintaining a good reputation, which would serve Quintus well on his recall to Rome, of controlling his subordinates (i.e. his staff) and of taking firm action against the bribery and corruption that were so common and to which the Roman courts fitfully responded:

> It is indeed a splendid thing to spend three years in supreme command of Asia without being deflected from the path of honour and self-restraint by any of the temptations your province offers ... what could be more eminently desirable than that your excellence, your restraint and self-control should not be hidden in some corner, but be displayed in Asia before the eyes of our most famous province, for the ears of all tribes and nations to hear of? ...
>
> You must do all you can to make clear that the responsibility you bear for your province to allies, to citizens and to the Roman state is not yours alone, but is shared by all your subordinates ... let it be recognised by your whole province that the lives, the children, the good name and the property of all those whom you govern are very near to your own heart. Finally, ensure that everyone believes that, if word of a bribe reaches your ear, you will take action against the giver as hostile as against the taker. No one will give a bribe when it has been made clear that, generally, those who *pretend* to have your confidence can achieve nothing.
>
> Cicero, *ad familiares* (*To Quintus* 1.1)

But having invoked the priorities of status and self-interest, Cicero now appeals to Quintus' competitive spirit, urging him to show the Greeks who inhabit Asia that Rome has learnt well the lessons of their civilisation:

> [Greeks], the race from which civilisation is believed to have passed to others. We surely ought to give its benefits to those from whom we have received it ... everything that I have achieved I owe to those pursuits and disciplines which have been handed down to us in the literature and teaching of Greeks ... schooled by their precepts, we must wish to exhibit what we have learned before the eyes of our instructors.

The Roman empire was a going concern long before Rome ever had emperors. Sicily became the first Roman province in 241 BC after Rome had defeated Carthage in a dispute over the control of that grain-rich and geographically significant island. By 146 BC Rome had acquired Sardinia, Corsica, Spain, Macedonia (i.e. Greece) and Africa (roughly Tunisia); by 30 BC, Asia Minor (Turkey), Syria, Cyprus, Gaul and finally Egypt were added. It is worth emphasising at once that, in strong contrast to Greeks, Roman had no qualms about offering their precious citizen rights to encourage loyalty to Rome, first among the peoples of Italy, and from the first century BC onwards, outside Italy too (see p. 124).

The start of the Roman empire proper, i.e. an empire run by an emperor, is usually dated to 27 BC, when Octavian, conqueror of Antony and Cleopatra in 31 BC and now sole ruler of the Roman world, took the name Augustus (Greek *Sebastos*, 'revered') and made the political arrangements that restored the trappings of the republic – Senate, consuls and so forth – but drew all real power in his own hands.[4] This required extraordinary cunning, but Augustus was up to it. He was, in contemporary parlance, a master of spin. Historically, Rome feared monarchs and Julius Caesar had been assassinated because he seemed to be assuming monarchical powers (p. 21). Augustus set about persuading the great aristocratic families that things had not changed, that they were as important to the running of the New Order as they had been to that of the Old, that their traditions were not lost, that the republic had not been in vain, that they would be great again and that everything Rome had stood for before the last bloody, suicidal years of the republic would be restored, only better and brighter, and he began dishing out consulships and provincial commands and the other traditional plum jobs to keep them on-side. A brilliant manipulator, he pulled it off – but the *locus* of real power was not in doubt.

This power was expressed as *imperium* – the ancient and traditional right to give orders that was invested in Rome's executive officers (*magistratus*) such as consuls (cf. *impero* 'I order, command').[5] Augustus, ever aware of the niceties of the matter, legislated to ensure that *imperium* over everything officially resided with him. As a result, every ambitious man's career was now in the gift of the emperor: the emperor ultimately became universal patron and final arbiter in everything, even the law. With all power at one man's disposal, *imperium Romanum* begins to be used regularly to describe the new world order. It should really have been *imperium Augusti* – but under the imperial dispensation, Augustus *was* Rome. It should be noted, however, that Augustus never called himself 'emperor', but *princeps* – 'first citizen' (hence 'principate'). This man was an operator.[6]

Up till then, the provinces had served as extensions of Roman power and influence and, in particular, had enriched those Romans who served in them, often by extortion and bribery. But the civil wars fought out in them during the collapse of the republic, as one provincial governor after another declared for this or that side, had shown what a potential danger they were to the centre.[7] Augustus was having none of this. Control of the Roman legions was the bottom line. Augustus for the first time profession-alised the citizen army into a regular force, giving it a clear career structure, and keeping it loyal by generous terms of service and retirement and (most of all) regular pay. That required money, and this was where the provinces came in.[8]

For the next twenty years Augustus spent almost as much time in the provinces as he did in Rome. He completely reorganised and tightened up the direct tax-system into an astonishingly efficient regime, so that money which till then had had a habit of staying in the province flowed regularly, and in quantity, to Rome and especially its armies. Poll-tax and land-tax were the main sources of income, based on regularly revised censuses mapping the physical and human resources of a region. In the Greek east, it was easy to collect because well-organised, accountable cities had long been established there when the Romans took over. In the West, however, there was no urban tradition, let alone democratic self-government. So as Romans provincialised in the West, they established urban building pro-grammes among the communities and set out to win over and train up the local élites to learn their ways and do their bidding in the new urbanised settings. Most élites recognised a good thing when they saw it. *Coloniae* were established (settlements of legionaries) to help other areas develop a sense of urban life.

Here Tacitus describes with his usual dry cynicism how the system worked in Britain:

> To accustom a scattered, uncivilised and therefore combative people to a quiet life of pleasurable ease, Agricola [the Roman governor] gave private encouragement and public assistance to build temples, public squares (*fora*) and mansions, praising the keen and punishing the lazy: competition for honour took the place of compulsion. He educated the sons of the élites in liberal arts, and expressed the view that the British end-product was supe-rior to the Gallic. The result was that those who had rejected the Latin tongue became keen to master it. In the same way our national dress came to be the fashion and the toga seen everywhere, and the British descended slowly into the pleasures of vice – arcades, baths, sumptuous banquets. In

their ignorance they called this civilisation. In fact it was a characteristic of enslavement.

Tacitus, *Agricola* 21

It is important to say, however, that there is no evidence that economic exploitation occurred.

It was not necessarily the case that expansion of the empire automatically resulted in dramatically increased revenues. Every new province (e.g. Judaea in AD 6, Britain in AD 43) brought costs with it, e.g. the garrisoning of legions, which was good business for the local economy but might not swell the imperial coffers by all that much. On the other hand, when the Dacian (Romanian) tribes refused to deal peaceably and consistently with Rome and Trajan decided to bring them to heel (AD 101-107), his victory brought Rome fantastic wealth – about thirty times Rome's annual revenue, if the reported figures for gold and silver bullion are right, and the use of Dacian gold-mines too.[9]

Aware of the need to keep the people happy, Trajan lavished much of this on Rome: months of fantastic free *spectacula* for the people, the construction of his massive Trajan's forum, at 13.6 acres almost as great as all the other *fora* put together,[10] and his public Trajan's baths, all 25.6 acres of them, the size of a small town and requiring a new aqueduct to bring in water 20 miles away that delivered an extra 250,000 gallons a day into Rome.[11] Calculations suggest that about thirteen thousand people would have been involved in constructing these baths, built in a matter of five or six years. About five hundred masons would have been working up the marble. Perhaps two to three thousand ox-cart drivers would have been bringing in the material, causing impossible chaos on the roads, though at least by night (as legislation demanded). Here was job creation on a gigantic scale, its economic benefits filtering down through suppliers, markets, taverns and brothels.

It cannot be emphasised too strongly just how far the Roman empire was in the power of one man. One striking illustration suffices: the Roman historian Suetonius records Augustus' will, and notes that it contained a summary of the state of affairs 'of the whole empire, how many soldiers were under arms and where, how much money there was in the public purses and what revenues were owed. He also added the names of the freedmen and slaves from whom the full accounts could be demanded.'

This is simply extraordinary: no one in the whole of Rome, certainly not the Senate, knew the financial and military position of the empire – only Augustus and the officials that he kept round him. Indeed, during an earlier serious illness we are told that Augustus had to sketch the position out hastily on the back of an envelope in case he dropped dead and left everyone in the dark. Then consider who these officials were – not the Roman great and good but slaves and freedmen. Here is another major change in the running of Rome. Under the republic, the Senate house and

Roman forum were the heart of Rome's body politic (see p. 52). Backstairs intrigue there certainly was, but politics was a matter of open senatorial debate between aristocrats, and public involvement through voting in the colleges. Not under the emperors. The centre of power shifted away from the forum to the Palatine hill (or wherever the emperor's private apartments happened to be) and to the emperor's court, *aula*, a Latinised form of a Greek word meaning the royal palace of Greek kings. Here, surrounded by family, close friends and trusted advisers, many of them slaves or freed ex-slaves, the emperor took the decisions that counted.[12]

This is one of the reasons why histories of the imperial period (like those of Tacitus and Suetonius) are so full of anecdote, rumour and gossip. In a world where decisions were taken behind closed doors, they became an important source of evidence. As the historian Cassius Dio (*c.* AD 164-229) points out:

> Formerly, everything was brought to the Senate and the people, even if events happened some way away. Because of this, everyone knew about them and many wrote about them, so that the truth of events, however much coloured by fear and favour, friendship and enmity in some authors, could be found in the works of others writing of the same events, and in public records. But after this time, most things that happened began to be kept secret and were concealed, and whatever did become public was not trusted because it could not be verified. The suspicion is that what was said and done was controlled by those in power and their associates.
>
> Cassius Dio, *Roman History* 53.19

'Rumour' in Tacitus' hands in particular is rhetorically used to the most deadly effect, almost as an ironic comment on the state of the (un)availability of information under the emperors. Consider his typically slippery account of the death of Augustus in AD 14 and the accession of Tiberius, a critical moment in the imperial project (see note 4). Augustus had chosen his grandson Agrippa as successor-elect, but Augustus' wife Livia would have none of it: Agrippa was banished, so that Tiberius, her son by a former marriage, would succeed. Tacitus suggests – hedging his account – that Augustus arranged a secret reconciliation with Agrippa, that Fabius Maximus stupidly blew the gaff on the trip, was duly punished, and Livia moved swiftly to make sure nothing like it could happen again, meanwhile summoning her son Tiberius back from his trip to Illyricum. I italicise the words that create the air of doubt and mystery:

> Augustus' health now took a turn for the worse, and some *suspected* his wife [Livia] of foul play. For a *rumour* had got about that, a few months earlier, Augustus, confiding in a *chosen few*, had gone with a single companion, Fabius Maximus, to visit Agrippa; that there were tearful scenes and signs of affection on both sides and *hopes* that the young man would be restored to his ancestral household; that Maximus had told his wife Marcia about it, and that she had told Livia; that Augustus got to know of the leak and soon after,

when Maximus was dead (*perhaps* by suicide), that Marcia had been *heard* at the funeral lamenting and accusing herself of responsibility for her husband's death. *Whatever the facts* of the matter, Tiberius had hardly set foot in Illyricum before a letter from his mother ordered him home and it is *not at all clear* whether, when he reached Italy, he found Augustus *alive or dead*. For Livia had efficiently sealed off the house and streets with her guards, and optimistic bulletins were announced at intervals, until *the steps dictated by the situation* had been taken and a single report was made that Augustus was dead and Tiberius in control.

Tacitus, Annals 1.5

Observe how, by the suggestive collocation of rumour, possibility and innuendo, Tacitus creates an overwhelming impression that Livia had done away with Augustus to ensure Tiberius' accession, but without ever quite saying so.

Perhaps the most extraordinary feature of the imperial court is the work-load placed on the emperor's shoulders. It is easy to imagine him, surrounded by squadrons of officials, concentrating on the big picture, making masterful policies to expand the empire here, contract it there, and leaving the bits and pieces to his staff. Not so. The fact is that the emperor had very little by way of a civil service at his disposal at all. Further, very few emperors seem to have had anything remotely resembling a 'policy' for the empire. The day-to-day responsibility for running the provinces lay with the provincial governors and their local staff, and they got on with it (the intelligent emperors took great care in appointing efficient, non-corrupt governors). With the exception of Augustus, and perhaps Hadrian, evidence for active rather than reactive policy-making across the empire is negligible. As long as the provinces were at peace and the money was coming in, the emperor was happy. So what did the emperor *do*? Was life as an emperor in fact all orgies and bloodbaths?

For some it seems to have been,[13] but the typical reality is rather different. There is a wonderful story told of Hadrian. On tour in the provinces and hurrying to a meeting, he was stopped by a woman in the street. Shaking her off, he said he was too busy to listen to her. 'Then don't be emperor' came back the reply. Hadrian stopped and listened. The terrible truth is that, when emperors were not touring the provinces sorting out problems, they seem to have spent most of their time answering letters and listening to petitions. The rule for provincials seems to have been – if you have a gripe, and the local authority won't fix it, write to the emperor. He'll get it sorted. And he usually did.[14] After all, the emperor ultimately carried the can: he was the final arbiter of the law and dispenser of justice.

Seneca, adviser to the emperor Nero, gives some idea of what the pressure was like when he writes:

So many thousands of people have to be given audience, so many petitions have to be dealt with; such a crush of matters coming together from the whole world has to be sorted out, so that it can be submitted in due order to the most eminent *princeps*.

When Julius Caesar was assassinated in 44 BC, he was carrying a bunch of written petitions in his hand, and the conspirators gathered round him with an oral one for the release of Metellus Cimber from exile (Caesar was unpopular with some of the people because instead of watching the Games he used the time to reply to correspondence).

To give some idea of the triviality of the concerns that got as far as the emperor, here is a reply by Marcus Aurelius to a woman who married her uncle forty years ago and wants the children legitimised:

> We are moved by the length of time during which, in ignorance of the law, you have been married to your uncle, and the fact that you were placed in matrimony by your grandmother, and by the number of your children. So, as all these considerations come together, we confirm that the status of your children who result from this marriage shall be as if they were conceived legitimately.

Trivial to the emperor, crucial to this woman. The emperor replies in person to her. These are the nuts and bolts of empire.

The demands on the emperor's time were overwhelming, and none of the replies happened automatically: in the absence of a civil service, only he could respond. He was expected to write his own speeches, judgements, and letters and when he went on tour of the provinces, papers and embassies followed him. Under such pressure, even the most gracious emperor could crack. Here is a letter from Pliny the younger, governor of Bithynia (in Asia Minor, northern Turkey), to his emperor Trajan. Pliny had been chosen by Trajan to sort out some particular financial problems that beset the province, and we possess a raft of letters from him on various subjects, with Trajan's replies, the most famous being the correspondence on the treatment of Christians.[15] But here Pliny seeks advice on a somewhat less pressing matter and Trajan's reply is curt:

Pliny to Trajan
When people come of age, marry, enter public office or dedicate a building, it is usual for them to invite all the local senators and even quite a few ordinary people to distribute presents of one or two *denarii* [say £10 or £20]. I would appreciate your advice on whether this should be allowed, if at all. My own view is that invitations of this kind are sometimes permissible, especially on ceremonial occasions, but the practice of issuing thousands or more seems excessive, and could be regarded as a form of corruption.

Pliny, *Letters* 116

Trajan to Pliny

You are right to fear that issuing invitations could lead to corruption, if the numbers are excessive and people are invited on an official basis rather than individually, as personal friends. But I chose you to make your own judgements about how to control the behaviour of the provincials, and to make your own decisions about what is necessary for their own peace and security.

Pliny, *Letters* 117

The underlying rebuke is unmistakable.

If the aristocracy was happy, the finances secure, the army loyal, the provinces at peace and the emperor's court on top of affairs and alert to what was going on, it was only left to the emperor to win the affection of the people of Rome. Bread and circuses, in the poet Juvenal's telling phrase, were the traditional recipe for success (he might have added 'and public utilities', to take Trajan's example quoted above), and the emperors supplied them. As the orator Fronto says, 'the people of Rome are held fast by two things above all, the corn-dole and shows, and the success of government depends on amusement as much as on serious things'. Augustus' *Res Gestae*, 'My Achievements', his own fascinating account of his reign, records the following details:

I gave three gladiatorial games in my own name and five in that of my sons and grandsons; at these games 10,000 men took part in combat. Twice in my own name and a third time in that of my grandson I presented to the people displays by athletes summoned from all parts. I produced shows in my own name four times and in place of other magistrates twenty-three times ... I gave beast hunts of African beasts in my own name or that of my sons and grandsons in the circus or forum or amphitheatre on twenty-six occasions, in which about 3,500 beasts were destroyed. I produced a naval battle as a show for the people at the place across the Tiber now occupied by the grove of the Caesars, where a site 1,800 feet long and 1,200 broad was excavated. There thirty beaked triremes or biremes and still more smaller vessels were joined in battle. About 3,000 men, besides the rowers, fought in these fleets.

Augustus, *Res Gestae* 22-3

The main reason the people adored Nero was that he was a man after their own heart: he was a showman *manqué*, and loved to perform himself on stage, singing and acting, and to take part in Games (especially driving chariots). 'Dead – and what an artist' were his last words as his regime collapsed around him, the army, the provinces, the aristocracy, even his own court turned against him, the finances in chaos, and only the people on his side.

There is no point in drawing up a balance-sheet of the rights and wrongs, benefits and disadvantages of empire. One's judgement will depend on where one directs one's gaze. Who will reconcile a Calgacus with a Cicero? At one level the empire could be said to have been most influential in providing a unified and broadly peaceful world within a single legal and educational framework (at least for the wealthy) in which Christianity could spread – for good or ill. But as Richard Jenkyns points out,[16] the empire's combination of autocracy with the principle of world-wide citizenship and the idea of the rule of law has also provided a crucial model for the large-scale organisation of peoples ever since, from the Catholic Church (with its Pope, bishops and canon law) and Charlemagne to the British empire.[17] Indeed, if one includes Roman republicanism in the equation (see p. 52), one can fairly say that the Romans have for two thousand years provided the West's preferred national as well as imperial model of government.

This is what makes Roman politics so endlessly fascinating. To end, I quote here a letter, dated 17 March 44 BC (two days after Julius Caesar's assassination), from Decimus Brutus to his friends Brutus and Cassius, leaders of the anti-Caesar conspiracy (Decimus was governor-designate of a province in Gaul, and was in Rome but not among the assassins). Hirtius and Marc Antony were the pro-Caesar consuls at the time of the assassination. It is clear that the conspirators thought killing Caesar would solve the problem and nothing more was required (translated by L.P. Wilkinson):

Our situation is as follows. Hirtius was at my house yesterday evening. He made it clear to me what Antony's intentions were – evil and treacherous in the extreme; he had said that he could not let me have my province, and that he did not think any of us could safely remain in the Capitol in view of the unrest among the troops and the masses. I am sure you will realise that both these contentions are false and that the truth is to be found in what Hirtius made clear, namely that Antony is afraid that, if our position received even moderate support, there would be no part for *them* to play on the political stage.

In this awkward situation I decided to request a nominal mission abroad for myself and our colleagues, by way of finding a decent excuse for leaving Rome. Hirtius promised to obtain this, but I am not confident that he will; there is so much arrogance and hostility towards us in the air. And even if they grant our request, I think that before long we shall find ourselves declared public enemies or outlaws.

You know what I want to advise? We must yield to fate. I think we must clear out of Italy and emigrate to Rhodes or somewhere. If things get better, we can return to Rome; if no worse, we can live in exile; if worse, we can have recourse to extreme measures. Here perhaps you may ask, why wait for the last stage rather than make an effort of some sort now? The answer is that we have no rallying-points except Sextus Pompey [in Spain with troops] and Caecilius Bassus [who lead a successful revolt against Caesarians in Syria, with Parthian help], who will gain in strength, I expect, when the news about Caesar arrives. It will be time enough to join them when we have found out how strong they are.

On behalf of yourself and Cassius I will give any undertaking you wish: Hirtius insists that I do so. I must ask you to answer this letter as soon as possible since I have no doubt he will let me know about my request by ten o'clock. Please say where we can meet, that is to say, where you would like to come.

Since my last conversation with Hirtius I have decided to ask for a state-provided bodyguard while we are in Rome. I don't expect they will agree: we would be putting them so very much in the wrong. But I thought I ought to make any request I considered fair.

Cicero, ad familiares 11.1[18]

9

The English Vocabulary

The impact of the Greek and Latin languages on basically Germanic English has been very considerable.

On the evidence of the concordance, Shakespeare wielded a vocabulary of some 29,066 different words. But that total depends on what you mean by a 'word'. These days we count e.g. 'gone', 'goes' and 'going' as one word, 'go' (known as a 'lexeme', a unit of meaning regardless of any different forms it may possess). On that count, Shakespeare's word-count comes down to nearer 20,000. Since the total English vocabulary at the end of the Renaissance was about 200,000 lexemes, this is a very large active vocabulary, but Shakespeare's range would be far larger today, given the increase in number of words in the English lexicon and the communications' explosion. A recent sampling exercise carried out in association with an office secretary, business woman and lecturer revealed that they had an active vocabulary (i.e. lexemes they used) of 31,500, 63,000 and 56,250 respectively.[1]

The total English vocabulary is very hard to calculate. The 1992 *OED* lists some 500,000 words. But a million insects have been described, and a few million more await description. Add in flora and fauna, and the problem compounds. Given the extent to which Latin and Greek are used to construct the technical vocabulary, one could easily, if absurdly, claim that the English language was 90 per cent Latin and Greek.

For everyday purposes, words derived from Greek, Latin, or Latin via French, make up about half our vocabulary. For educational purposes, however, that percentage can rise. The core conceptual vocabulary of the disciplines represented in the curriculum ranges from 67 per cent of Graeco-Latin words in logic and mathematics to 86 per cent in aesthetics.[2] This is not surprising. Many Graeco-Latin words were specifically introduced into the language during the Renaissance to enable English to deal with the new concepts implicit in these fast-developing subjects. By contrast, Graeco-Latin words make up a very small percentage indeed of the vocabulary of, for example, children's books, or the primary school class or the tabloid soccer report. In these areas, Anglo-Saxon rules supreme.

The story of how English speakers arrived on these shores and how the language became so rich in Latin and Greek is straightforward enough. In AD 410 the Roman empire in the West collapsed and Roman legions departed Britain, leaving the indigenous Celts behind. Enter, then, the original Englishmen in the wake of departing Romans – that is, Frisians (from north Holland), Saxons (from north Germany) and Angles and Jutes (from south and north Denmark), all speaking a form of German. So English is a Germanic language. These invading Germans called the indigenous British Celts *wealas*, 'foreigners' (hence 'Wales', where many of the Celts fled), and the Celts called the Germans 'Saxons', whatever their actual tribe. By the sixth century AD, however, these 'Saxons' are regularly being called *Angli* in our Latin sources (in AD 601 Aethelbert, king of Kent, is named in Latin *rex Anglorum*), and *Anglia* becomes the Latin name for the country. This is the source of Old English *Engle*, and the language, *Englisc* (*sc* pronounced *sh*). From about AD 1000 the country is called *Englaland* ('land of the Angles'), whence 'England'.

The Germanic invaders had already had contact with the Romans before they came to England, and there are about two hundred words of Latin origin in the Anglo-Saxon they brought with them. These include words that were to become today:

Wine (Latin *vinum*), wall (*vallum*), street (*strata*), cheese (*caseus*), cheap (*caupo*, 'innkeeper'), mile (*mille*), pound (*pondo*, lit. 'by weight'), mint (*moneta*, from the temple of Juno Moneta in Rome, where money was minted), sack (*saccus*), sock (*soccus*), pan (*patina*), peas (*pisum* – originally in English a collective singular 'pease', from which 'pea' was formed, as if 'pease' was plural), inch (*uncia*), pepper (*piper*), beer (*bibere* 'to drink').

There were a few of Greek origin too, again coming into Anglo-Saxon via Latin: butter (Greek *bouturon*, Latin *butyrum*), dish (*diskos, discus*), mint (the herb) (*minthê, mentha*), devil (*diabolos* 'slanderer', *diabolus*), priest (*presbuteros* 'elder', *presbyter*); 'church' was taken over by Saxons directly from the Greek (Greek *kuriakon* 'the Lord's *sc.* House', late Greek *kurikon*, Saxon *cirice*). The Latin for 'church' was *ecclesia* (cf. Fr. *église*, It. *chiesa*).

Note: from now on, Anglo-Saxon will be called Old English (OE) and all dates will be AD, unless otherwise indicated.

The arrival of Christian missionaries under St Augustine in 597 to convert the Anglo-Saxons brought an influx of Latin and some Greek words into OE, most of them connected with the Church:

We find from Latin: mass (*missa*), altar (*altar*), preach (*praedico*), verse (*versus*), epistle (*epistula*), plant (*planta*), lily (*lilium*), pike (*picus*), provost (*praepositus*), cat (*catta*), noon (*nona* 'the ninth hour'), pear (*pirum*), creed (*credo*), disciple (*discipulus*). From Greek words taken over by Latin, we find: school (Greek *scholê* 'leisure', Latin *scola*), apostle (*apostolos* 'sent out', *apostolus*), acolyte (*akolouthos* 'follower', *acolitus*), hymn (*humnos* 'song', *hymnus),* deacon (*diakonos* 'servant', *diaconus*), bishop (*episkopos* 'overseer, attendant', *episcopus*), psalm (*psalmos* 'plucking', *psalmus*), angel (*aggelos* 'messenger', *angelus*), martyr (*martus* 'witness', *martyr*), charity (*kharis* 'grace, reciprocity', *caritas*), demon (*daimôn* 'divinity', *daemon*), paradise (*paradeisos* 'garden', *paradisus*), choir (*khoros* 'chorus', *chorus*), grammar (*grammatikê* 'to do with letters', *grammatica*). [3]

The Viking invasions, beginning in 787 and continuing spasmodically for the next two hundred years, also left their mark on the English language. Draw, for example, a line from London to Chester: north of that is the Danelaw, where it was agreed Vikings could settle, and note the huge number of towns with names ending in '-by' = farm, town (e.g. Grimsby) – almost entirely restricted to the Danelaw area -, '-thwaite' = clearing (Applethwaite), '-thorp' = village (Althorp) and '-toft' = homestead (Lowestoft).

For our purposes, however, the main interest of this period lies in the translations of Alfred, King of Wessex (849-899). Observing the steep decline in education and therefore in Latin learning, presumably due to the Viking invasions, Alfred determined that the way back lay in the translation of Latin texts into English. He arranged for Bede's great *Ecclesiastical History* to be translated, and himself translated Boethius, St Augustine and some Psalms. His thinking is recorded in the preface to his translation (*c.* 890) of Pope Gregory's *Pastoral Care*:[4]

> I wondered why the good, wise men who were formerly found throughout England did not wish to translate any part of those [Latin] books into English. But I immediately answered myself, and said 'They did not think men would ever become so careless and that learning would decay like this; they refrained from doing it through this resolve, namely they wished that the more languages we knew, the greater would be the wisdom in the land.' Then I recalled how the Law [=Old Testament] was first composed in the Hebrew language, and thereafter, when the Greeks learned it, they translated it all into their own language, and all the other books as well. And so too the Romans, after they had mastered them, translated them all through learned interpreters into their own language. Similarly all the other Christian peoples turned some part of them into their own language. Therefore it seems better to me ... that we should turn into the language that we can all understand certain books that are the most necessary for all men to know ... After that one can instruct in Latin those whom one wishes to teach further, and wishes to advance to holy orders.
>
> Alfred, *Pastoral Care*

The period known as Middle English (ME) runs from *c.* 1150-1450. This is the moment of cataclysmic change in the English language: the invasion in 1066 of William Duke of Normandy, and the imposition of French as the language of administration (for which Latin was also extensively used), law, education,[5] Church, and literature. Not till 1362 was English used in Parliament, itself a good French word, from *parler* 'to speak'. The effects of this change on English in the early years are hard to determine, since

French is almost completely dominant in surviving texts. So ME starts (somewhat indeterminately) somewhere in the twelfth century. English documents start to emerge in the thirteenth century. In the fourteenth century we have *Piers Plowman* and *Sir Gawain and the Green Knight*, and with Chaucer (*c*. 1345-1400) comes the full flowering of the new English.

The spelling and vocabulary of English were deeply affected by the Norman conquest. French spelling conventions replaced English in words such as *cwen*, which became *queen*, *sercle* which became *cercle*, and *k/c* which became *ch* (hence kirk/church). As for vocabulary, perhaps some 10,000 French words entered English in the ME period – almost all, inevitably, based on the Latin brought by Julius Caesar's conquest of Gaul in the 50s BC, from which French had developed during and after the Roman empire.

Here are some French loan words, all originally Latin, those with asterisks taken into Latin from Greek:

Constable, court, government*, liberty, parliament, peasant, prince, revenue, statute, tax, tyrant*; accuse, arrest, assault, convict, crime, decree, depose, evidence, fraud, heir, indictment, inquest, judge, libel, perjury, prison, punishment, verdict; abbey, anoint, baptism*, cathedral*, charity*, communion, convent, creator, crucifix, faith, heresy*, homily*, mercy, miracle, religion, repent, saint, salvation, schism*, theology*, vicar, virgin, virtue; anatomy*, calendar, clause, copy, gender, geometry*, gout, grammar*, logic*, medicine, metal, noun, pain, physician*, plague*, pleurisy*, poison, pulse, sphere*, square, stomach*, surgeon*, treatise.

Many straight Latin loan words also entered the language at this time, mostly from professional and technical vocabulary. These include:

Law and administration
Arbitrator, client, conspiracy, conviction, custody, homicide, implement, legal, legitimate, memorandum, pauper, prosecute, summary, suppress, testify.
Science and learning
(Greek words borrowed by Latin are asterisked) Allegory*, comet*, contradiction, diaphragm*, discuss, equator, essence, explicit, formal, history*, index, intellect, item, library, ligament, magnify, mechanical*, prosody*, recipe, scribe, simile.
Religion
Collect, diocese*, immortal, incarnate, infinite, missal, pulpit, requiem, scripture, tract.
General
Admit, adjacent, collision, combine, conclude, contempt, depression, distract, exclude, gesture, imaginary, include, incredible, individual, infancy,

interest, interrupt, moderate, necessary, nervous, ornate, picture, private, quiet, reject, solitary, spacious, subjugate, substitute, temperate, tolerance.

Some idea of the impact of this massive new vocabulary can be gathered from the prologue to Chaucer's *Canterbury Tales*: in 858 lines, there are nearly five hundred French loan words. We now find the linguistic phenomenon known as 'etymological doublets' emerging.[6] French derives from vulgar Latin. By the medieval period, this Latin had undergone very considerable transformation in becoming French. It was this French that William the Conqueror imposed on England. But French also borrowed directly from classical and late Latin in the medieval period, as did English – and these borrowed Latin words were, of course, unchanged from their original forms. Thus Latin *fragilis* emerges in English as 'frail', via Old French 'fraile', and again directly from Latin as 'fragile'. Latin *traditio* becomes (via French 'traison') 'treason' and directly, 'tradition'. Latin *pauper* becomes 'poor' (via 'pauvre') and directly, 'pauper'. Latin *securitas* becomes surety and security. There is even an etymological triplet: Latin *ratio* gives us 'reason' (via 'raison'), 'ration' (Latin, but with a French suffix) and 'ratio' (pure Latin).

By the Renaissance (*c.* 1450-1650), a language recognisable as modern English has formed. This, after all, is the world of Shakespeare (1564-1616) and the Authorized Version of the Bible (1611). It is at this time that Latin and Greek words are directly adopted *en masse* in order to meet the new intellectual interests flooding into the country from the continent. Quite apart from the renewed interest in the classical world (prompted by the arrival of Greek manuscripts from Byzantium into Italy from the thirteenth century onwards), great strides were being made in science, medicine and the arts, the Americas were being opened up (Columbus 1492) and Copernicus was re-organising the solar system (1543). Soon Aristotle, Hippocrates, Galen and Ptolemy would be replaced as supreme arbiters of the physical, scientific and medical worlds (see Chapter 14), but the new intellectual revolution needed new vocabulary and it was still felt that Latin and Greek were the best sources for it. From this period we welcome (words of Greek derivation asterisked):

Adapt, agile, alienate, allusion, anachronism*, anonymous*, appropriate, atmosphere*, autograph*, capsule, catastrophe*, chaos*, climax*, contradictory, crisis*, criterion*, critic*, disability, disrespect, emancipate, emphasis*, encylopedia*, enthusiasm*, epilepsy*, eradicate, exact, exaggerate, exist, explain, external, fact, glottis*, harass, idiosyncrasy*, larynx*, lexicon*, malignant, monopoly*, monosyllable*, obstruction, pancreas*, parasite*, parenthesis*, pathetic*, pneumonia*, relevant, scheme*, skeleton*, species, system*, tactics*, temperature, tendon, thermometer*, tibia, tonic*, transcribe, ulna, utopian*, vacuum, virus.

Not that the new vocabulary was universally welcomed. John Cheke was a brilliant classical scholar, appointed first Regius Professor of Greek at Cambridge in 1540 when Greek as a subject was still in its infancy. He inveighed against the pollution of English in his letter to Sir Thomas Hoby, 16 July 1557: 'I am of this opinion* that our tongue should be written clean and pure*, unmixed* and unmangled* with borrowings of other tongues, wherein if we take not heed by time, ever borrowing and never paying*, she shall be fain to keep her house as bankrupt*. For then doth our tongue naturally* and praisably utter her meaning, when she borroweth no counterfeitness* of other tongues to attire* herself withal.' I pedantically asterisk those words of non-Germanic origin.

Indeed, strenuous efforts were made to match the new vocabulary with alternatives from the old. Thus, in 1573, Ralph Lever proposed a new series of delightful non-Latinate terms for the study of logic – 'endsay' was proposed for 'conclusion', 'ifsay' for 'condition', 'naysay' for 'negation', 'say-what' for 'definition', 'shewsay' for 'proposition' and 'yeasay' for 'affirmation'. Such debates, which continue to this day, were ancient even then: Greeks and Romans had argued the toss over precisely the same issues 1,500 years earlier (see Chapter 10).

Words of Latin and Greek derivation have continued to trickle into the language since then, according to need. Most of them are technical. There is no reason why they have to be Latin or Greek, of course; but since the technical vocabulary has historically been Latin and Greek, continuity seems advisable.

All of which brings us back to education. The Graeco-Latin vocabulary listed above – there are thousands more such words one could add – reads like a handbook of the language of secondary and higher education. To simplify a complicated issue,[7] the child who moves from the basically Anglo-Saxon of primary education to the increasing Graeco-Latin of secondary and higher education without some means of coming to terms with this radical change in vocabulary will find problems. It would be agreeable to argue that all children should learn Latin and Greek to help them over this 'language barrier'. But children from linguistically rich backgrounds will make the transition with ease anyway, as will those whose school itself offers a linguistically rich environment. It is a matter of ensuring that words that seem 'difficult', whether Graeco-Latin or not, become a natural and inevitable component of a child's vocabulary as early as possible.[8]

Vocabulary, however, is only one aspect of the Graeco-Latin contribution to our language. Our very understanding of how language works has its origins in Greek and Roman thought, as the next chapter makes clear.

10

The Language of Grammar

As well as using languages that had a profound effect on the English vocabulary, Greeks and Romans established the traditional terminology and to some extent the working concepts by which language has been analysed ever since. Even the invention of modern linguistics has not entirely displaced this mighty legacy. In constructing a vocabulary for thinking about language, the ancient world also established an equally influential concept of linguistic education, whose echoes remain with us today, for good or ill (there is a time chart listing the people mentioned in this chapter on p. 97).

The fifth-century BC Greek intellectual Protagoras first classified nouns as masculine, feminine and 'things' (*skeuê*). Aristotle observed that many nouns classified as 'thing' (e.g. *paidion*, 'boy') were in fact masculine or feminine. By the first century BC, *oudeteron* 'neither, neuter' was in use, as was *koinon* ('common') and *epikoinon* (one gender, used of both sexes, the origin of our 'epicene'). Aristotle[1] defined particle (which also includes preposition), 'name' (noun, pronoun, adjective and probably adverb), conjunction and verb (distinguishing present and past tenses), and talked also of vowels, consonants, syllables, inflections (the changing endings of a word), subject and predicate and even 'utterances', a sentence or group of words producing a collective meaning (here he adds significantly 'there can be an utterance without verbs'). But he does not name the different inflections.

It was the Greek Stoic philosophers (third century BC onwards, see Chapter 13) who, with enormous range and subtlety, began to develop this basic analysis into the system we know today.[2] For example, sounds were discussed ('air articulated and set in motion by thought' said Diogenes of Babylon, *c*. 240-152 BC). Dionysius of Halicarnassus describes *m* as pronounced with the 'mouth pressed together at the lips' and the breath 'partly through the nostrils'. Length of syllables was analysed. Tenses were categorised as future, present or past, and past was sub-divided into perfect, imperfect, pluperfect and 'aorist' (*aoristos*, literally 'undefined' in relation to the perfect-imperfect, i.e. the 'plain' past – to put it very crudely, not 'I have played' or 'I was playing' but 'I played'). Verbs were analysed by 'voice' – active, passive or neither (i.e. 'middle' or reflexive); alternative systems described verbs as transitive or intransitive; and 'moods' were recognised (indicative, imperative, subjunctive, optative). By the time of the second-century BC Greek grammarian Dionysius Thrax ('from Thrace' – his work survives[3]), eight parts of speech had been defined – noun (which included adjectives), pronoun, verb, adverb, article, participle, preposition and conjunction; nouns were divided by their inflections into cases – nominative, vocative, accusative, genitive, dative; and into number – singular, plural and (in Greek only) dual.

This terminology was all originally Greek, but when Roman grammarians joined in the fun in the second century BC (p. 20), they invented grammatical terms by analogy with the Greek, and these are the origins of our terms. Thus:

Greek	Latin	English
onoma 'name'	*nomen*	noun
rhêma 'what is said'	*verbum*	verb
epi-rrhema 'in addition to what is said'	*ad-verbium*	adverb
ant-ônumia 'in-place-of noun'	*pro-nomen*	pronoun
sun-desmos 'binding together'	*con-iunctio*	conjunction
pro-thesis 'placing before'	*prae-positio*	preposition
metokhê 'sharing' (i.e. the function of a verb and noun/adjective)	*participium*	participle

Adjectives were eventually given a category of their own, as a sub-class (*adiectiva* 'added on') of noun. Interestingly, Roman grammarians, who knew perfectly well that Greek had a definite article 'the' (*ho hê to*) but Latin did not, still talked about Latin as if it did, on the grounds that the science of grammar, being the logical analysis of categories, demanded it (they tended to use *hic haec hoc* 'this' in its place).[4] On the same grounds they talked of subjunctive and optative moods, of which again the latter occurs in Greek but not Latin.[5]

Our case names too derive from Latin, though Greeks, of course, had got there first.[6] Aristotle's word for 'case' was *ptôsis*, 'falling, modification', whence Latin *casus* (*cado* 'I fall') and so 'case'. This 'falling' image was taken literally: the ancients envisaged the nominative, *nominativus*, the 'naming' case (or subject of a sentence) as 'at the top', and the other cases falling away from it sideways (whence Greek *engklisis* 'leaning' = *declinatio*, 'declining').[7] The genitive, *genitivus* 'giving birth', was the equivalent of Greek *genikê*, 'generic' (represented by English 'of'); the dative, *dativus* 'giving', from Greek *dotikê* 'giving' (English 'to' or 'for'); and accusative, *accusativus* 'accusing', from *aitiatikê* 'produced by a cause, effected' (the direct object). The dreaded ablative case, *ablativus*, 'that from which something is taken away' (English 'by, with or from') was unique to Latin and is first mentioned by the first-century AD professor Quintilian.[8] The

Roman antiquarian Varro (116-27 BC) calls the ablative the 'sixth case' or the 'Latin case'.

But 'grammar' in our sense was not all that was collected by the ancients under the heading of *grammatikê* (Greek *gramma* 'letter', Latin *grammatica*).[9] Varro defined it as general knowledge of literature, with four functions – reading, writing, understanding and evaluating, or (as explained in a different source) reading, explaining, emending and judging. Dionysius Thrax produced six functions – reading verse, explanations of poetic figures, of rare words and of obscure references, etymology, inflections and finally (the grandest discipline of all) criticism.[10]

This definition reflects the huge range of the ancients' interests in language. Intensive work, for example, was done in Alexandria on Greek dialects, foreign words, and technical vocabulary (e.g. fishermen's terms and cookery) and long lists were compiled, Aristophanes of Byzantium producing a most stimulating one of 'words suspected of not having been used by the ancients'. But as far as Greek went this was not mere compilation for its own sake. These lists were needed. The literary language of Homer and classical Greece had over time diverged further and further from the spoken language. How could it be understood without help? It is somehow comforting to find that Greeks of the second century BC needed to check the meaning of words in Homer as often as we do.

Etymology too was of considerable interest to early Greek thinkers, and significant names were common in Homer and tragedy. The Trojan hero Hector, for example, called his son Scamandrios (after the river Scamander) but 'everyone else called him Astyanax' (*astu* = city, *anax* = chief), and Homer now thoughtfully explains 'because Hector alone protected Ilium'.[11] Plato's dialogue *Cratylus* (early fourth century BC) is entirely devoted to etymology and takes the form of a discussion about the relationship between language and reality. Cratylus argues that words and names are 'natural', applied to things because that is what the things really *are*: etymology (Greek *etumos*, 'true, real'), in other words, gives a true account of the essence of the thing to which it is applied. Hermogenes, on the other hand, argues that, far from being natural or true, words are merely arbitrary sounds applied to things by convention or agreement.

Socrates now takes over. He agrees with Cratylus to some extent, producing an amazing list of outrageous etymologies that 'explain' the thing they refer to. For example, the Greek for 'Zeus' in the accusative case is *Dia*. The Greek word for 'through, because of' is *dia*. Ah, says Socrates: everything in the world happens 'because of' Zeus. This is etymological drivel – and if Plato did not know it was, he comes up with a host of other examples which he certainly did.[12] On the other hand, Socrates also agrees with Hermogenes to the extent that words are not *perfect* representations of reality (otherwise one could not distinguish between the word and the thing). So, Socrates concludes, words, though helpful, are not the best guide to understanding the real world.

Roman grammarians in the second century BC took up the Greek torch with tremendous gusto. Varro in his twenty-five volume *de lingua Latina* (Books 5-10 survive in part) is a shining example of the passion with which they set to work. One particular argument to which Romans responded related to the concept of the 'purity' of language. There is a fine story in Aulus Gellius (b. *c.* AD 125) about Pompey.[13] Preparing to consecrate his Temple to Victory in 55 BC, he could not decide how to describe himself on the accompanying inscription: should he be consul *tertium* ('for the third time', *tertium* accusative, expressing time 'throughout', i.e. consul throughout the whole of the year) or consul *tertio* (the ablative *tertio* expressing time 'when', i.e. consul in the year). He consulted all the leading professors, and they all gave different answers, so he went in despair to Cicero to make the final decision. Cicero, keen not to hurt professorial feelings by adjudicating for one side or the other, cut the Gordian knot and suggested he write *tert.* Gellius goes on to report that when the wall containing the inscription fell down and was rebuilt, the number of the third consulship was indicated by III.

For Greeks too the issue of linguistic purity was pressing. In the diversified world of the fifth-century BC city-state, the Greek language was expressed in many different dialects, taken all over the Mediterranean by colonisation. But when King Philip II's all-conquering Macedonian court adopted Attic Greek (the dialect of Athens) in the fourth century BC, Attic, which already enjoyed high prestige as the *literary* language of the Greek world, gradually became standard throughout the Greek-speaking world. So it was this dialect that was taken east by Alexander the Great to be spoken in quite new places. What was the literary and intellectual élite in different parts of the world – many of whom would not have had Greek as a first language – to make of this? How could they be certain they were speaking, but much more important writing, it correctly? What were the educational implications? *Hellênismos*, a Greekness 'faultless in respect of rules and without careless usage' became a priority for them. The Greeks even had a word for 'speaking incorrectly' – *soloikos* (cf. our 'solecism'), said to derive from the Athenian colonists of Soloi in Cilicia (southern Turkey) what had forgot how to talk proper.

No surprise, then, that the concept of 'purity' was picked up by Romans in relation to their own *Latinitas* – to ensure, for example, that the standards set by the Ciceros and Virgils were maintained and, as the empire grew larger and the spoken and written languages diverged, to identify some common baseline for the educated, literary élite. Then again, the Latin language was changing fast under Greek influence (we have already considered its new grammatical terminology). How should one write and spell and protect it from unhealthy foreign influences in a great cosmopolitan city like Rome? It is important to emphasise here that we are not talking about everyday spoken Latin (or Greek) but about the formal language that was written and spoken on public occasions. This highly

Time Chart

Greek	Roman
fl. c. 720 Homer	
c. 490-420 Protagoras	
429-347 Plato	
384-322 Aristotle	
356-323 Alexander the Great	
(Hellenistic period)	
300 Stoicism invented by Zeno	
c. 280 Alexandrian Museum founded	
c. 257-180 Aristophanes of Byzantium	
c. 240-152 Stoic Diogenes of Babylon, visited Rome 156-155	
c. 170-90 Dionysius Thrax, taught in Rhodes	
146 Greece becomes Roman province	146 Greece becomes Roman province
	116-27 Varro
	106-43 Cicero
	100-44 Julius Caesar
31 Hellenistic period ends	70-19 Virgil
fl. 7 Dionysius of Halicarnassus, lived in Rome	
	AD 14-37 Tiberius Emperor
	AD 41-54 Claudius Emperor
	first century AD Remmius Palaemon
	b. *c.* AD 35 Quintilian
c. AD 101-177 Herodes Atticus	b. *c.* AD 70 Suetonius
second century AD Apollonius Dyscolus, lived in Alexandria; short visit to Rome	b. AD 125 Aulus Gellius
	fourth century AD Donatus
	AD 486 End of Roman empire in West
fifth century AD – Roman empire in East centres round Byzantium	fifth/sixth century AD Priscian taught Latin in Byzantium

literary language is what counted for Rome's writers, the educated élite, and explains why the Latin (and Greek) that survives today is of such high quality (as if, in AD 4000, all that survived of English up till AD 2000 were to be Shakespeare, Milton, Pope, Gibbon, Keats, Hazlitt, Waugh and

Orwell). It is a very different medium from the language of the man in the street, as we can tell from e.g. graffiti, other remnants of everyday ('vulgar') Latin and indeed modern Italian. If you wind back modern Italian in accordance with rules of linguistic development, you end up with vulgar, not classical, Latin.

Julius Caesar himself in the 50s BC contributed to the debate about literary purity, writing two books on word-formation while crossing the Alps to return to his army in Gaul.[14] This work was entitled *de analogia*, and it disguises an important debate that had by then polarised discussions of language and still does. Two schools of thought about the nature of language had sprung up, both of Greek origin. One was the 'Alexandrian' commitment to 'analogy' (*analogia* 'regularity'), which claimed that language was a convention, should therefore be subject to conventional rules, and should therefore admit only regular, logical formations. Here is an irregular formation: grammarians should throw it out and replace it with a regular one. The other school preferred the Stoic theory of 'anomaly' (*anômalia*, 'exception'), arguing that language was capricious and unpredictable in the same way as nature itself, but since it was a system of signs hiding an underlying system connected with the expression of thought, it could not be changed in the name of mere logical formalisation.[15] The debate still has a familiar ring.[16]

Translation too was an issue, especially for Romans.[17] In a sense, their whole culture was an intellectual response to, i.e. 'translation' of, Greek culture (see pp. 18-22). One of the first works of Latin literature was Livius Andronicus' translation of Homer's *Odyssey* (see Chapter 2, note 6). In his *de rerum natura* the first-century BC Lucretius was still expressing concern about whether the Latin language could rise to the demands of describing the nature of the universe (he need not have worried). As we have seen, Latin grammarians invented a complete new grammatical terminology based on Greek. Quintilian (X.v.2) recommends translation as an excellent way to acquire facility in writing, pointing out that Cicero translated Xenophon and Plato. This was how Cicero came to invent Latin philosophical vocabulary by lifting words wholesale from the Greek and transliterating or translating them straight into Latin, e.g. *qualitas*. Horace argues against too literal translation ('do not try to render the original word-for-word like a slavish translator', *Ars Poetica* 133) and St Jerome, quoting approvingly from Horace, recommended that 'sense was transferred into sense, not words into words' (*Letters* 57.5). These principles informed translation all the way down to Dryden, who distinguished between translation as metaphrase (word-for-word), paraphrase (keeping the sense) and imitation (modernising and adapting).[18]

These are a few of the intense debates about language that raged around the Graeco-Roman world from the second century BC onwards, and on which later grammarians like Apollonius Dyscolos, Donatus and Priscian built their hugely influential grammars. Priscian in particular was notable for the first systematic treatment of syntax that we know of from the ancient world. Donatus and Priscian between them became *the* authorities for the teaching of grammar and Latin in western medieval Europe, and their influence can still be observed.

However, they both drew on a common source, and this looks to have been Remmius Palaemon, a freed slave of the first century AD, whose Latin grammatical handbook is the first to be attested, though it survives only in fragments. Hats off, then, to Palaemon, but keep everything else firmly on – the Roman historian Suetonius (b. *c.* AD 70) says that 'he was notorious for every sort of vice and ... the last person to whom the education of boys or young men should be entrusted'.[19]

Which brings us neatly to the ancient teaching of grammar. Here, too, a tradition was established with a long and glorious history which has even had to be re-invented today in phonics, the system of teaching reading that was at the heart of ancient primary education.

Greek children of the Hellenistic period learnt first the letters of the alphabet, in four lines of verse (iambic pentameters, like the dialogue of Greek tragedy, letters italicised):

est' ('there is') *alpha* , *bêta, gamma, delta* t' *ei* te kai (t', te, te kai = 'and')
zet', êta, thêt', iôta, kappa, lambda, mu,
nu, xei, to ('the') *ou, pei, rhô,* to *sigma, tau,* to *u,*
paronta ('being present') *phei,* te *khei,* te *tôi* ('with') *psei,* eis ('up to') to *ô.*

Roman teachers invented games to encourage children to learn – alphabet cakes, moveable wooden letters and so on. The wealthy Greek sophist Herodes Atticus (*c.* AD 101-177) helped his dim son learn the alphabet with twenty-four slaves, each one named after a letter.

Next came syllables, first two-letter syllables in correct sequence – e.g. *ba be bê bi bo bu bô, ga ge gê gi go gu gô* up to *psa pse ... psô*, each letter being named before it was pronounced ('*bêta alpha ba*'). Three-letter syllables followed (*ban ben bên* etc.), and so on and on. The syllables mastered, the children then moved on to words, first those with one syllable, then two etc., with many strange sounding words thrown in for practice, e.g. the (apparent) illness *knaxzbi* and the possibly medical term *phlegmodrôps* (shades of school spelling tests involving well-known Californian plants like Eschscholtzia, named in 1821 after J.F. v. Eschscholtz). Syllables and words thoroughly mastered, the children were now allowed to read passages of continuous prose, the words in the earliest passages split up by syllables. Since Greek, like Latin, was written with no punctuation or gaps between words, this was by no means an easy exercise and the children needed all the help they could get. Recitation, singing and learning by heart of passages were commonplace. Writing was taught by the same sequence. It goes without saying that the Romans adopted this form of primary education almost wholesale. And so the first steps to literacy were taken.

Greek education remained broadly based – the three Rs, music, and gymnastics dominated. Greek higher education could involve rhetoric, philosophy, medicine, science and mathematics. In theory, Roman education covered literary subjects – grammar, rhetoric and dialectic (logic) – and then the mathematical subjects – geometry, arithmetic, astronomy and musical theory – but in practice it remained predominantly literary. Higher education concentrated on the art of persuasive public speaking, the *sine qua non* of success for the young Roman for whom the traditional career paths of law and politics beckoned.[20] What was common to the literary studies of both Greeks and Romans was that specific authors and their standard works (the 'canon') were selected for study, mostly poetry and mostly from their respective 'classical' periods. Language was not regarded as a living, changing organism, but an eternally fixed entity whose rules, based on long-dead authors, had to be learned almost like a science.

Here is an example of the way the first line of Virgil's *Aeneid* should be taught according to Priscian:[21] 'I sing of battles and the man who first from Troy's shores ...':

arma virumque cano Troiae qui primus ab oris
Arms man-and I-sing Troy's who first from shores

Scan the line.
arma vir/umque ca/no Troi/ae qui/ primus ab/ oris
How many caesuras?
Two.
What are they?
The penthemimera and hephthemimera [= fifth and seventh syllables].
Which is which?
The penthemimera is *arma vir/umque ca/no* and the hephthemimera is *arma vir/umque ca/no Troi/ae*.
How many 'figures' [i.e. half-feet] has it?
Ten.
Why?
Because it is made up of three dactyls and two spondees [Priscian seems to have forgotten the last spondee].
How many parts of speech are there?
Nine.
How many nouns?
Six – *arma, virum, Troiae, qui, primus, oris* [remember that nouns and adjectives were not differentiated].
How many verbs?
One – *cano*.
How many prepositions?
One – *ab*.
How many conjunctions?

One – *que*.
Study each word in turn. Let us begin with *arma*. What part of speech is it?
A noun.
What is its quality?
Appellative.
What kind is it?
General.
What gender?
Neuter.
How do you know?
All nouns ending in -*a* in the plural are neuter.
Why is *arma* not used in the singular?

And so on. One can see now what sort of grisly effect the ancient definition of 'grammar' and 'grammatical' priorities had on school teaching. Our own system of linguistic training, however, with its abhorrence of anything remotely technical, delivers in this respect an equally short-sighted education to our young.

Education in the ancient world sounds like hard work. Nothing wrong with that. But if the educators were hard men, and many seem to have been, it does not mean they did not have high ideals. Here Quintilian describes the good teacher:

> His first priority must be to treat his pupils as if he were their parent, and to consider that he is in the position of those who have handed their children over to him. He must have no vices himself nor tolerate them in others. He must not be strict and humourless, or free-and-easy and over-familiar: the one breeds hatred, the other contempt. His conversation must concentrate on what is good and honourable; the more sound advice he gives, the less he will need to punish. Rarely angry, but never ignoring what needs correction, he must be clear in his teaching, hard-working, and firm without browbeating. He must happily answer questions, and question those who remain silent. In praising his pupils' work (= their recitations), he must be neither grudging nor effusive: the one will put them off, the other encourage complacency. In correcting where necessary, he must not be sarcastic, let alone abusive; for the teacher who criticises his pupils as if he hates them puts many off the commitment to study ... pupils who are taught properly love and respect their teacher: it is impossible to say how much more willingly we copy those whom we like.
>
> Quintilian, *Institutio Oratoria* II.ii.5-8

A brief coda. It is said with painful regularity that claims about the usefulness of Latin in helping one understand English are false: Latin, with its quite un-English case-system and word-order, is a rotten model on which to understand the mother tongue. This, at one level, is so obviously true that it is hardly worth saying. But it is not the point. The issue is, not how closely the Latin model fits the English model, but what Latin tells you about language. In other words, how good a meta-language, or general example of language, is Latin? Is it better than any other?

I can give no answer to the last question, knowing only a limited range of European languages. But Latin strikes me as exemplary precisely *because* it is so different from English. It yields meaning only after intense linguistic analysis at a number of different, mostly alien, levels (case and word-order being the most alien). That grappling with linguistic concepts, through a language whose vocabulary has so much in common with English anyway and which itself provides the language of grammar, provides a superb grounding for understanding language generally. For many people, even those who learned Latin only to a very basic level, this has been Latin's prime benefit. Whether it was right to *justify* the teaching of Latin on those grounds is a different matter: but it does not affect the argument about the actual consequences of learning Latin for many people.[22] The fact that some people hated Latin and others gained their understanding of language by other means merely demonstrates, if it needed demonstration, that there are many ways to skin a cat. We all know that.

Epic Influence

Greeks and Romans established literary standards that dominated western Europe till the nineteenth century. The opening of epics offers a clear
illustration of the development of one aspect of that tradition. We begin
with the start of Homer's *Iliad* (c. 720 BC), the first words of western
literature. The broad context is the Trojan War, fought between Greeks
and Trojans for the return of Helen, the Greek king Menelaus' wife. But
Homer begins most unexpectedly (note: bold indicates features that will
be discussed):

> The **wrath**[1] – **Sing**, **goddess**, [the wrath] of Peleus' son Achilles,
> Accursed [wrath], **that** placed **unnumbered agonies** on the Greeks,
> And dispatched to Hades **many mighty** souls
> Of heroes, and made them prey for dogs
> 5   And a feast for birds, and **Zeus's plan** was fulfilled,
> From when the two **first** split in **conflict**
> [i.e.] The son of Atreus [Agamemnon], lord of men, and godlike Achilles.
> **Which**, then, of the **gods** brought the two together to fight?
> Leto's and Zeus's son [Apollo]. For he, **angered** at the king,
> 10   sent an evil plague throughout the army, and the people perished ...
>
> Homer, *Iliad* 1.1-10

The poem has a subject, announced in the first word – the wrath of the
Greek hero Achilles – and the 'goddess' (i.e. the Muse, goddess of memory[2])
is asked to sing it. This wrath was, we learn, destructive not of the enemy
Trojans (who are not mentioned in the proem) but, amazingly, of Achilles'
own side, the Greeks (1-5). Already the poet is announcing the abnormality
of Achilles. But it was all divinely ordained by Zeus (5), and triggered by
a conflict between Achilles and Agamemnon, leader of the Greek army
besieging Troy (6-7). Which god started this conflict? Apollo, who sent an
evil plague on the army ...

Now compare the opening of the second work of western literature,
Homer's *Odyssey* (c. 700 BC):

> The **man** – **tell me, Muse** of [the man] of many turns, **who** very
>   far/**much**
> Was **driven**, when he had sacked Troy's holy citadel.
> **Many** men's cities he saw, and knew their minds,

> **Many agonies** he **suffered** at **sea** in his heart,
> 5   Trying to win **his life and return** of his companions.
> But even so he did not save his companions, though desiring to:
> For they destroyed themselves by their own recklessness,
> Fools, who [consumed] the cattle of Hyperion the sun
> Consumed. And **he** removed from them their day of return.
> 10   From some point, goddess, daughter of Zeus, tell us these things too.
>   Then all the others, as many as escaped steep death,
> Were at home, having escaped war and the sea.
> **Him alone** [Odysseus], yearning for his return and his wife,
> Did the lady nymph **Calypso** keep …
>
> Homer, Odyssey 1.1-14

The broad context is the return of the Greeks from the Trojan War, after Troy had been sacked and Helen won back. The subject announced again in the first word is 'the man', and again the Muse is asked to sing it. Which man, we wonder? He was a man who travelled far and wide, suffered much, and lost his companions *en route* home from Troy. It is stressed, though, that it was the companions' fault – they ate the cattle of the Sun God Hyperion. The Muse is asked to pick up the story somewhere or other, and off we go – at the moment when all the other Greeks had returned safely home, but this man alone was being held back by the goddess Calypso. Who *is* he? He has not in fact been named – but presumably listeners would have guessed by now.

It is at once apparent that these two preludes or proems (Greek *prooimion*, 'prior to the song') have much in common: a significant first word ('wrath', 'man'), an appeal to a 'goddess' or 'Muse', a request for her to 'sing' or 'tell' the story, a relative clause ('the wrath … which', 'the man …who'), the 'agonies' that resulted, which are 'unnumbered' and 'many', and the causative influence of gods (Zeus and Apollo in the *Iliad*, Hyperion, Calypso and – as emerges slightly later – Poseidon's hatred of Odysseus in the *Odyssey*) and of men (the quarrel of Achilles and Agamemnon, the folly of Odysseus' companions).

These two proems established the pattern for epic beginnings. Virgil's *Aeneid* (19 BC) continues and develops the tradition:[3]

> **Arms** and the **man I sing**, **who first** from the shores of Troy
> And, fate's exile, came to Italy and the Lavinian
> Shores, a man much **buffeted** on land and **sea**
> By the might of the **gods**, because of cruel **Juno's** unremitting **anger**,
> 5   and **suffering much** in war as well, **till** he should **found a city**
> and bring his gods to Latium; from which [arose] the Latin race,
> the Alban fathers and high walls of Rome.
> **Muse**, review the **reasons** for me, by what insult to her divinity
> Or in what grief the queen of the gods forced a man known for
>   **righteousness**
> 10   to become involved in **so many disasters**, to enter upon **so
> many labours**. Is there **so great wrath** in the hearts of **gods**?

There was an ancient city (Phoenicians colonised it) ...
Virgil, *Aeneid* 1.1-12

Virgil begins with key words – 'arms' (compare the warlike *Iliad*) and a 'man' (compare the *Odyssey*). But 'I' (Virgil) sings the tale in the first line, not the Muse or the goddess. She makes her grand entry in 8, for reasons that will soon emerge. There follows the epic relative ('the man who ...'), and observe that, as in the *Odyssey*, the man is not named in the proem. But he 'first' came – the significant moment is identified by Virgil as it was in the *Iliad*, in the 'first' time Achilles and Agamemnon came into conflict. Aeneas is a traveller – he came to Italy (2) but 'much buffeted' (3) and 'suffering much' (5), with 'so many disasters ... and labours' (10). Odysseus too was a traveller, 'much driven' (1) and seeing the cities of 'many men' and suffering 'many agonies' (4). Aeneas' troubles were caused by the gods (4) – specifically, Juno, queen of the gods, who was 'angry' with him (4, 11), as Hyperion was with Odysseus' men and Poseidon with Odysseus. 'Anger' is an established epic motivator, as we also know from the *Iliad* (1, 9). Aeneas has a mission – to found a city (5), not, like the Greeks, destroy one. Odysseus has one too – to recover a city, i.e. to return home safely (5). Virgil at once indicates that Aeneas succeeds (6-7) in his mission – Virgil here looks beyond the end of the *Aeneid* – but Homer simply foretells the loss of Odysseus' companions, which occurs half way through the *Odyssey*. Achilles' mission does not emerge in the proem of the *Iliad*. He does not have one.

The Muse appears at 8. Her job is to expand on the reasons for Juno's anger, already indicated at 4. Since only a god can know the mind of the gods, it is logical for Virgil to call on the Muse at this point. In 1, Virgil himself can 'sing' the story because it is Roman history. Everyone knows it. But the detail of a goddess' motivation cannot be guessed; it has to be vouchsafed to humans by the Muse, who knows (note 'to me', 8, and cf. 'to me' at *Odyssey* 1). So Virgil here appeals to the Muse for an explanation of the divine anger, in the shape of a series of questions put to her (cf. the question at *Iliad* 8). One more point, before the story begins: Aeneas is a man famous for his *pietas*. 'Righteousness', 'respect for gods and family' are not the terms in which Homeric heroes were touted. The proem finished, off we go into the story: 'There was an ancient city ...'

Over a millennium and a half later, in 1674, Milton published his twelve-book *Paradise Lost* (a ten-book version had appeared earlier, in 1667: note that Virgil's *Aeneid* is in twelve books, both Homer's in twenty-four). This was an epic. Milton knew how epics began:[4]

> Of **man's first disobedience**, and the fruit
> Of that forbidden tree, **whose** mortal taste
> Brought **death** into the world, and **all our woe**,
> With loss of Eden, **till** one greater man
> 5   Restore us, and regain the blissful seat,

Sing, heavenly muse, that on the secret top
Of Oreb, or of Sinai, didst inspire
That shepherd, **who first** taught the chosen seed,
In the beginning how the heavens and earth
10   Rose out of chaos: or if Sion's hill
Delight thee more, and Siloa's brook that flowed
Fast by the oracle of God; I thence
Invoke thy aid to my adventurous song,
That with no middle flight intends to soar
15   Above the Aonian mount, while it pursues
Things unattempted yet in prose and rhyme.
And chiefly thou O Spirit, that dost prefer
Before all temples the upright heart and pure,
Instruct me, for thou know'st; thou from the first
20   Wast present, and with mighty wings outspread
Dove-like sat'st brooding on the vast abyss
And mad'st it pregnant: what in me is dark
Illumine, what is low raise and support;
That to the height of this great argument
25   I may assert eternal providence,
And justify the ways of God to men.
    Say first, for heaven hides nothing from thy view,
Nor the deep tract of hell, say first **what cause**
Moved our grand parents in that happy state,
30   Favoured of heaven so highly, to fall off
From their creator, and transgress his will
For one restraint, lords of the world besides?
Who first seduced them to that foul revolt?
The infernal serpent; **he it was**, whose guile...

Milton, *Paradise Lost* 1.1-34

The structure of Milton's argument in this mighty opening is as follows:

1-6: the heavenly Muse is summoned to sing of the fall of Adam, the first man, the expulsion from Eden and man's eventual restoration by 'one greater man', Jesus.

6-10: this Muse is described as being the inspiration of Moses (8, 'that shepherd') who from the top of Mt Horeb or Mt Sinai (the Bible cannot make up its mind which, *Deut.* 4.10, *Exod.* 19.20: Horeb is a spur of Sinai) received the ten commandments and then taught the chosen people of Israel ('seed') how God created the world, out of 'chaos' (10).

10-16: the Muse is now offered an alternative, possibly preferable (11), New Testament location, on Sion hill (10), i.e. Mt Zion in Jerusalem, where Solomon's temple stood, and beside which ran the stream serving the pool of Siloam (11), where Jesus cured a blind man (*John* 9.7). One remembers that Milton was blind (cf. 'dark', 22). Milton will be happy to draw his inspiration from there (12-13) for what is going to be a brand new type of epic (14-16).

17-26: but the Holy Spirit, which needs no temple, will be Milton's chief inspiration, because it was actually present at the creation (19-22) and indeed, was the very agent of creation (22).

27-34: Milton now demands to know how it all started. Who was responsible? It was the serpent.

This is all quite wonderful (the mighty copulation visualised at 20-2; that 'illumine' 23; the magnificent momentum of it all, and thrilling climax). But we are here not as scintillating literary critics but as dull, plodding classicists, and it is time conscientiously to tick off the references. It is at once apparent that Milton is playing off the classical against the biblical. He admits as much at 14-16. The Aonian mount is Mt Helicon in Boeotia, a seat of the ancient Greek Muses (Boeotia's primitive name was Aonia). Above the grove of the Muses was Hippocrene ('horse-fountain'), an inspirational fountain created when the mythical horse Pegasus, who attempted to fly up to Mt Olympus, struck the ground with his hoof (modern Kriopigádi, near the top of Helicon). It was here that the epic poet Hesiod received his calling to compose his *Theogony* ('Birth of the Gods').[5] Milton's song is going to 'soar above' that mountain, its stream (cf. Siloa's brook at 11-12), and those classical gods, dealing with matters 'unattempted yet in prose or rhyme' (16). This biblical epic will cap anything the pagans can offer.

Milton in fact overtrumps the classical with the biblical throughout the proem. The Muse at 6 is 'heavenly' because Milton is playing on Urania, the goddess of astronomy in the classical tradition, a name derived from Greek *ouranios*, 'heavenly'. The point is that the classical muse lives on a mountain. Milton's lives in heaven. That Milton plays on Urania here is indicated when he summons her again but denies her pagan connections:

> Descend from heaven Urania, by that name
> If rightly called thou art, whose voice divine
> Following, above the Olympian hill I soar,
> Above the flight of Pegasean wing.
> 5 The meaning, not the name I call: for thou
> Nor of the muses nine, nor on the top
> Of old Olympus dwell'st, but heavenly born ...
>
> Milton, *Paradise Lost* 7.1-7

Milton refashions Urania to Christian use (and compare 3 'above the Olympian hill' with 1.15, and the reference to Pegasus in 4 with the Hesiodic connection elucidated above). So, to revert to *PL* I, she sings from sacred Old Testament sites like Horeb and Sinai to ancient biblical heroes like Moses, and from New Testament sites, like Mt Zion and Siloa, where (perhaps) she helped inspire Jesus' healing of the blind. But even she cannot do it all. At 17, Urania herself is demoted in favour of, or perhaps refigured into, or even reinforced by, the Holy Spirit – a purely biblical concept, of whose biblical origins there is no doubt (19-22).

Then again, consider the theme. Achilles' wrath, Odysseus' return, even the founding of Rome, pale by comparison with the fall of man, initially favoured by heaven (30) but seduced into catastrophic transgression and revolt (31-3). Far from being a matter of death (*Iliad*) and agonies (*Iliad, Odyssey*) for a few Greeks, or suffering, disaster and labours for Aeneas, *PL* will describe how death itself was brought into the world in the first place, bringing with it not 'innumerable agonies' (*Iliad*) but '*all* our woe' (3), and how man's final salvation was at last achieved through 'one greater man' (4). Milton's theme is 'eternal providence' (25), not some temporary Greek or Roman disaster; far from merely identifying what god or man did what to whom in the course of an essentially human adventure, Milton will 'justify the ways of God to men' (26) – an undertaking far greater than, for example, merely founding the Roman race (*Aeneid* 5-7).

Finally, the pagan epic poet commanded the presence of the Muses because it was the poet's job to sing the past and the Muses' job to transmit the truth about the past, via the poet, to the people. Milton too summons the Muse and Holy Spirit, but the relationship is a more complex one. For Milton, 'the upright heart and pure' is the strict condition of the Muse's inspiration; instruction (19) and illumination (23), as well as information, are what he seeks to achieve his ends.

This then is a thoroughly Christianising opening, challenging the pagan at almost every point. But for all that, it is impossible to miss the classical element in Milton's great proem. 'Of man's ...' reminds us of *Odyssey* 1 (note Milton does not name 'the man' either); 'first' of *Aeneid* 1; 'disobedience' and its disastrous consequences of *Iliad* 1-5, also replete with death and woe; 'tree, whose mortal taste ...' exemplifies the relative clause typical at the start of a proem (*Iliad* 2, *Odyssey* 1, *Aeneid* 1); 'till' in 4 presents us with a glorious future beyond the scope of the present epic, as it does in *Aeneid* 5; 'Sing, heavenly Muse' is pure classicism, and we have already observed how Milton appropriates and reforms this Muse for his Christian purposes.

A further note is worth adding here. For all Urania's Christianity, she still visits the mountain tops and brooks (Oreb, Sinai, Siloa's brook), like the good pagan Muses we saw in Hesiod; and indeed, Milton's long hymn in honour of her and of the Holy Spirit (6-22) is not merely a Christianising redefinition, but is also intended to trump the long hymn in honour of the Muses that starts Hesiod's *Theogony* (1-115). Hesiod's pagan Muses, too, tell 'how at first gods and the earth came to be' (108), as Milton's Urania does at 9-10, except that Milton's Muse heretically tells him 'how the heavens and earth/Rose out of chaos'. This is not biblical: *Genesis* 1.2 tells us that the earth was without form and void, and was created out of nothing. Has Milton been remembering his Hesiod, where 'In the beginning was Chaos' (*Theogony* 116)?

We move on. Like Virgil, Milton distinguishes between history (Adam and Eve 1-5), which Urania can sing, and the deeper mysteries of eternal providence and justification, 'the ways of God', for which the Holy Spirit's help is needed (22-6). Finally, 'Say first, what cause' (27-32) is a series of questions straight out of *Aeneid* 8-10, and the straight question with straight answer, 'Who first ...? The infernal serpent' (33-4), is pure *Iliad* (8-9).

Milton knew precisely what he was doing. At *PL* 9.13-24 he argues that his theme is 'not less but more heroic than the wrath/Of stern Achilles ... /or rage/Of Turnus [Aeneas' enemy in the *Aeneid*] ... /Or Neptune's ire [*Odyssey*] or Juno's [for Aeneas]' and hopes that his 'celestial patroness' (the Muse), who visits him nightly and 'dictates to me slumbering', will help him rise to the task. But it is noticeable how few modern commentators on *PL* seem to realise just how rich this interaction is between the classical and the biblical.[6]

The proem to *Paradise Regained* continues Milton's pagan, in this case Virgilian, connection:

> I who erewhile the happy garden sung,
> By one man's disobedience lost, now sing
> Recovered Paradise to all mankind ...
>> Milton, *Paradise Regained* 1.1-3

The earliest surviving manuscripts of Virgil's *Aeneid* open that epic not with *arma virumque cano* but *ille ego qui quondam* ...:

> I am he who once tuned my song on a slender reed [a reference to
>   Virgil's first work *Eclogues*]
> and, leaving the woods, forced the neighbouring
> fields to obey the worker, however greedy –
> a work most pleasing to farmers [his second work, *Georgics*]; but
>   now of Mars' shuddersome
> *arma virumque cano* ...
>> Virgil, *Aeneid* 1

Since Virgil's work was always referred to in the ancient world as his *arma virumque cano*, not his *ille ego qui quondam*, these lines, whoever their author is, do not form the opening of the *Aeneid*. But they frequently appear in seventeenth-century texts of Virgil, and Milton is referring to them here. Note in Milton, and compare with Virgil, 'I', 'who', 'erewhile', 'sung', 'now'; and 'happy garden' is a clear Virgilian pastoral touch.

All of which things having been said, one is now in a position to enjoy a little fun with spoof epic openings. Here is Canto I of Pope's *Rape of the Lock* (1711) ('rape' derives from Latin *rapio* 'seize', but the sexual implications remain). Robert, Lord Petre, had cut a lock of hair off Arabella Fermor, also known as Belle (in the poem, she is called Belinda; Pope plays on 'belle' in the opening lines). This had caused the two previously friendly families to fall out, and Pope's friend John Caryll, who had been Lord

Petre's guardian, suggested in a letter that Pope poeticise the incident (they were all well-known to each other). Pope agreed, recording in a letter that Caryll 'desired me to write a poem to make a jest of it, and laugh them together again. It was with this view that I wrote the Rape of the Lock.'

All the reflexes of an epic proem are here – the mighty themes, the Muses, the series of questions, the search for causes, the rage, the instant plunge into the story with 'Sol ...' – but all deliciously trivialised and diminished (the reference to Sol is surely a sly dig at Homer's rosy-fingered dawn):[7]

> **What dire offence** from am'rous **causes** springs,
> **What mighty contests** rise from trivial things,
> **I sing** – this verse to Caryll, **Muse**! is due;
> This ev'n Belinda may vouchsafe to view:
> 5   Slight is the subject, but not so the praise,
> If she inspire, and he approve my lays.
> **Say what** strange **motive, Goddess**! cou'd compel
> A well-bred Lord t' assault a gentle belle?
> Oh **say what** stranger **cause**, yet unexplored,
> 10   Cou'd make a gentle belle reject a Lord?
> In tasks so **bold**, can little men engage,
> And in soft bosoms dwell such **mighty rage**?
> **Sol thro' white curtains shot** a tim'rous ray ...
> > Pope, *Rape of the Lock* 1.1-13

Classical influences do not make poetry better or worse. Ignorance of those influences, however, diminishes our understanding and enjoyment of the poetry, whether it is good or bad.

But 'influence' is not just a matter of references. It is a matter of the whole shape and structure of the language itself. Take a few lines from Pope's *Moral Essays: Epistle to a Lady*, 231-4. I print the first line word for word down the page, adding comments:

> *Pleasures* [noun or verb? Wait.]
> *the* [An odd start. Plough on.]
> *sex* [Means 'women' in Pope. This is sounding lubricious. Hang in there.]
> *as* [What *is* going on?]
> *children* [*Pleasures the sex as children* ...? Sounds like a job for the social services.]
> *birds* [*Pleasures the sex as children birds*? Or the Crown Prosecution Service.]
> *pursue*

Ah. The main verb. Light dawns. Make 'the sex' (women) the subject of the sentence and we get: 'Women pursue pleasures as children [pursue] birds.'

The displaced word-order ('pleasures' is object, not subject), the ellipse (we have to provide 'pursue' with the 'as children birds' clause), the balance ('pleasures' object, 'the sex' subject, as 'children' subject, 'birds' object: this ABBA arrangement is called 'chiasmus'), the comparison ('as children'), the antithesis ('women' and 'pleasures' *vs.* 'children' and 'birds'), the whole sentence in baffling suspense and tension until the verb at the end unlocks it and meaning floods in – this is pure Latin.

Continue:

> *Pleasures the sex, as children birds, pursue,*
> *Still out of reach, yet never out of view,*

These phrases qualify 'birds/pleasures' and form a doublet: note the anaphora 'out of', 'out of', with antithesis of 'still' and 'never', 'reach' and 'view'.

> *Pleasures the sex, as children birds, pursue,*
> *Still out of reach, yet never out of view,*
> *Sure, if they catch, to spoil the toy at most,*

'Sure' refers to 'children/women'; 'catch' requires the object 'birds/pleasures'; 'the toy' = 'birds/pleasures'.

> *Pleasures the sex, as children birds, pursue,*
> *Still out of reach, yet never out of view,*
> *Sure, if they catch, to spoil the toy at most,*
> *To covet flying, and regret when lost.*

'Flying' = 'the birds as they fly, out of reach' (ellipse); 'when lost' = 'the birds' (ellipse). Note the balance and antithesis of 'covet' and 'regret', 'flying' and 'lost', this time in ABAB formation.

Observe now the balance of the first two and last two lines:
Line 1 = main verb + 'as' clause; line 2 = a doublet qualifying 'pleasures/birds'.
Line 3 = adjectival clause + 'if clause'; line 4 = doublet qualifying 'the sex/children'.
Equally, observe the triplet of lines 3-4: '... to spoil ...'/ 'to covet ...', '[to] regret'.

The balance, antithesis, and ellipse; the rhythmic sequence and intricate build-up of clauses in varying patterns; and the development of the image with minute point-by-point comparison between 'women/children' and 'pleasures/birds' – this level of density and detail of pointed shaping and structuring is utterly Latinate. If such intense rhetorical control is not to taste, there is at least something to be gained by understanding how Pope is going to work and appreciating the skill with which he does it.

The above analysis merely scratches the surface, of course. Pope is writing English, not Latin. The practised literary critic will soon be lost from view as he digs deeper and deeper into it, the occasional shovel of mixed substrate sailing through the air the only indication of his heroic subterranean exertions. Nevertheless, surface work is an essential preliminary to a full understanding of the art of Pope, and all other classicising poets.

Standing on Orders

Envisage 'classical architecture' and one probably thinks of a rectangle of white, battered, marble columns – in other words, a Greek temple. But there was more to a Greek temple than that (Fig. 2). First, the columns were topped with capitals that supported the entablature, on which the roof was fixed. Second, the columns surrounded a sort of shoe-box (*cella*). This shoe-box was entered by a lockable door. This was where the statue of the divinity, and sometimes also state treasure, was kept.[1] Third, the ridge-tile roof ended in a triangular gable at each end. These gable ends could be filled with sculpture (undecorated temples outnumber decorated): the technical term for this gable end is 'pediment'. Most temples are now a sequence of battered columns, because the roofs fell in or were removed long ago, leaving the construction open to the elements.[2]

The triangular pediment placed above the columns at either end of a temple is an important marker of the 'classical', but the columns them-selves are the real marker. Columns *are* classical architecture. Or rather, certain styles of column are – in particular the Doric, Ionic and Corinthian (Fig. 3).[3] This chapter is going to concentrate on those three styles and show how they have been used, first in the Graeco-Roman world, and then, after the Renaissance had revived interest in the theory and practice of classical architecture in the West, nearly all over the world. This, inciden-tally, is a highly traditional way to approach classical architecture. Nearly

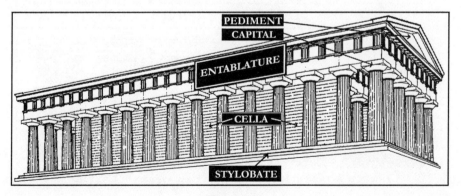

Figure 2

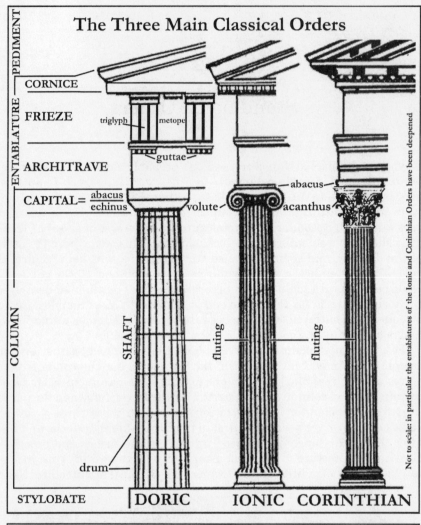

The Three Main Classical Orders

PEDIMENT

CORNICE

ENTABLATURE

FRIEZE — triglyph — metope

ARCHITRAVE — guttae

CAPITAL = abacus / echinus — volute

abacus

acanthus

COLUMN

SHAFT

fluting

fluting

drum

STYLOBATE

DORIC — IONIC — CORINTHIAN

Not to scale: in particular the entablatures of the Ionic and Corinthian Orders have been deepened

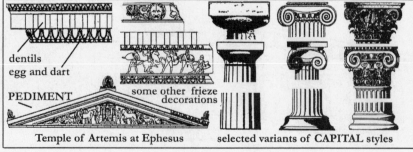

dentils
egg and dart

PEDIMENT

some other frieze decorations

Temple of Artemis at Ephesus — selected variants of CAPITAL styles

Figure 3

all introductions to the subject, starting with the Italian Sebastiano Serlio's in the sixteenth century, begin this way.[4]

A brief word on technicalities. After the sixth century BC, Greek columns were made of individual stone drums, dowelled together one on top of the other.[5] The drums were cut roughly to size at the quarry (as were e.g. marble blocks for statues – marble is softer when first cut),[6] then dressed on site, the flutes being added when the column had been securely put up (to flute it earlier was to run the risk of needing to replace the whole drum if it was badly handled and e.g. chipped during erection. This is why some buildings appear unfinished: the money ran out, and the fine finishing, including rubbing and polishing, was always the last thing to be done when everything was securely in place). Drums were lifted into rough position by block and tackle, and crowbars nudged them into their final resting place.[7]

There are inescapable restrictions on a structure held up by columns. First, the columns have to support the roof. To do so, the columns need a 'bridge' of some sort running around the top of them on to which the roof can be fixed. This bridge is called the **architrave** (Fig. 3, and compare the complete entablature of Fig. 2) and consists of individual stone blocks. Clearly, the wider the gap between the columns that needs bridging, the bigger the **architrave** has to be in order to carry the weight of the roof. So the space between the columns is controlled by the size and strength of the **architrave**. Second, lacking flying buttresses, such a structure will be easily pushed outwards if the *overall* weight placed on it is too great (that is why there is a shoe-box inside the temple: it has a vital structural function – to bear the massive weight of a roof made of terracotta tiles, or in the case of e.g. the Parthenon, marble). Third, there is a limit to the number of storeys that free-standing columns can securely support.[8]

These limitations are important, and presented a major problem to the Romans who, as usual, took over these Greek orders and used them for their own purposes (see p. 19).[9] To put the matter simply, Greek columns were the aesthetically pleasing means of physically holding up the roof of a public building like a temple or a stoa/colonnade, bringing light and shade and therefore coolness into an enclosed space (Fig. 4). They were beautiful and functional. But Greeks did not construct multi-storey buildings of the gigantic size that Romans did. Greek theatres, for example, were scooped out of hillsides, their stadiums set into terrain already well-suited to the purpose. The Romans, captivated by the glory of Greek architecture, therefore faced a problem. Columns were *the* way to express fine public architecture.[10] But how do you build a Colosseum out of columns?

The answer, of course, is that you don't. You dig huge foundations of concrete and travertine (a hard stone, one of the two main natural Roman building materials); and you build up the main structure out of a travertine framework, with internal facings made of the other common material,

Figure 4

volcanic tufa (soft and easily dressed but liable to weathering). But how do you let the light in? This is the big Roman break-through: light is let in not through columns, but through a continuous series of arches ('arcading').[11] This is structurally a vital breakthrough: an arch is far stronger and far lighter than an architrave. But the Romans make of it an aesthetic breakthrough too. This is not any old arcading: this is arcading *decorated with columns*.[12]

Consider the Colosseum (Plate 6). The orders ascend the building: Doric/Tuscan at the bottom, then Ionic, then Corinthian, and at the top some sort of composite column.[13] Not one of them serves any structural function. They are all there for visual pleasure. Also, not one of them is a free-standing column either. In the lower three levels, the columns are 'engaged' – i.e. they are columns sawn in half (as it were) and stuck onto a flat surface. The technical term is 'pilaster'. On the top level, the pilasters are not even round: they are flat. They are also much taller than the other three levels, and frame small square windows, not arches.

Now look at the arches, drawn in close-up (Fig. 5). First observe the way the pedestal on which the pilaster stands responds to the sill to which it is attached: the lower moulding of the pedestal matches the footing of the sill, and the pedestal ends flush with the sill top. The base of the column 'sits' on the sill, and the Ionic column (note the volute capital) rises to its entablature – a sort of architrave, frieze and cornice look-a-like, 'support-

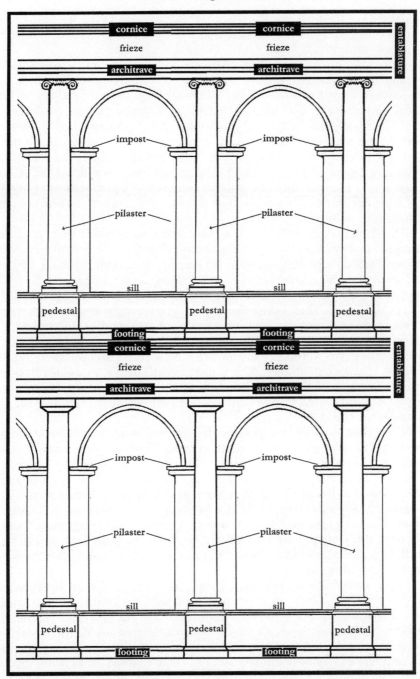

Figure 5

ing' the next storey. I use the inverted commas advisedly. Columns must *support* things. That is their function. If they do not support things (and these columns do not) they must *look* as if they do.

Now examine the arch, rising from its impost just over half-way up the columns to its height a little way below the architrave. The arch and impost are doing the work of supporting this gigantic building. The physics must be right. But the point is that physics (function) and aesthetics go hand-in-hand. The arch + columns ensemble also *looks* right. In other words, the architect has not just slapped on the columns as an after-thought ('Pretty it up a bit, Brian, there's a good lad. You know, few columns. Them, what do you call them, them Ironic wossits, innit? Class, they are.'). He has thought how to combine a functional arch with a pleasing decoration of columns that respects the proportions and rhythms traditional to them.

The Roman triumphal arch is the direct descendant of this simple design. Observe the Arch of Constantine (Plate 7). Four Corinthian col-umns, each on a pedestal, rise to an entablature, each carrying a figure. Where is the architrave? Nowhere. Or rather, each column is topped with a piece of stone that *looks* like an architrave, but does not span the gap to the next column. This is pure decoration. The columns divide the arch into three sections, a central arch (the largest) and two smaller side arches. The keystone, or highest point, of the central arch reaches the bottom of the entablature; the keystones of the two side arches reaches the top of the impost of the central arch. The arches are all of the same height-width ratio. This compact and pleasing design was adapted by Renaissance architects to Church fronts – the central arch forming the nave, the two side arches the aisles.

This, then, is the first half of the Roman revolution. The second is concrete, an even greater contribution to architectural development. Con-crete, *opus caementicum*, was a form of mortar (lime, sand and water), but with the sand consisting of volcanic dust called *pozzolana* (*pulvis puteo-lanus*, because it was used first at Puteoli, near Naples). This not only gave the mortar greater strength; it also became cohesive without the need for the water to evaporate out, and so could be used under water too. Volume for volume, concrete weighs less than stone, so puts less strain on a building, needs less buttressing and can roof a larger space. It can also be more easily shaped.

The result of this technological breakthrough is vaults, cross vaults and domes.[14] It is difficult not to overestimate the significance of this revolu-tion. For the architect, it meant a liberation from the tyranny of rectangles and the solid masonry out of which they were created. A heady world of suggestive and illusionary interior curved space (with supporting columns, of course) was now available to him. The consequences were utterly dramatic. A quite unfair comparison will make the point. Here is the inside of a standard Roman villa (Plate 8). There is no curved space in sight. Like nearly all architecture before the arch and concrete, it is pure shoe-box. Now observe the (reconstructed) interior of the *basilica nova* (started AD 307) (Plate 9(a)). The arch + (Corinthian-composite) columns form dominates, each column topped by a 'pointless' architrave + frieze + cornice, the whole rising to a complex, cross-vaulted ceiling. It is noticeable that another vital, richly columned architectural form is prefigured in this 'basilica'-style building, i.e. the Church (Plate 9(b), cf. Plate 9 (c)) – a central nave flanked by aisles on either side. The face of western architecture has been changed for ever.[15]

We now wind forward a thousand years to sixteenth-century Italy. It is important to stress that the Roman revolution has not been forgotten in the interval. But Christianity has been dominant, cultural and economic circumstances have changed, and the morality and expense of lush, complex, pagan architecture perhaps called into question.[16] Consider, for example, the chaste, almost spiritual interior of S. Maria Novella (after 1279) (Plate 10). Here is the refined basilica style, the march of columns along the central nave guiding the eye unerringly to the altar at the end. The arcading is still there – arch + columns – along the aisles, and the columns support the vaults above, but what etiolated columns they are, their almost mock decoration nodding insipidly to their glorious ancestors. But the Renaissance is round the corner, and the rediscovery and re-justification of the classical. A key player here is the first-century BC Roman architect Vitruvius.

Vitruvius' ten-book *de architectura* on architecture, building and engineering was the only architectural treatise to survive from the ancient world. It was wholly disregarded at the time when it was produced, but when it was rediscovered during the Renaissance hunt through the libraries for all things classical, it became the key text for Renaissance architects. It was translated into French in 1539, German in 1548 and Italian in 1521, 1536, 1556, and 1590. Vitruvius defines his basic principles by stating that 'architecture depends on order, arrangement, proportion, symmetry, propriety and economy'. His aim is to show that architecture is at heart a mathematical science. So when he describes how to build a temple, he argues that there should be a degree of controlled commensurability between the parts and the whole, on the analogy of the human body. This approach becomes even more holistic when Vitruvius tries to show that the rules governing architecture are the same as those governing all the other arts, human behaviour and even indeed the cosmos.[17] He identifies three major styles of column – Doric, Ionic and Corinthian – and goes into considerable detail about their proportion, decoration and integration. The unit of measurement is the column diameter. So the column's height, spacing with other columns, base height, capital height and so on are expressed in terms of column diameter, e.g. the height of Doric columns is seven times their thickness, of Ionic and Corinthian, nine times their thickness, and so on. These 'rules', ignored by

Vitruvius' contemporaries, were fallen on eagerly by Renaissance and later architects and theorists of the classical style.[18] No one followed the rules slavishly, but they gave an authoritative starting point to the debate about the new, classicising direction architecture was taking, while Vitruvius' holistic approach, relating architecture to behaviour and the structure of the universe, helped supply the moral basis for the enterprise.

Nowadays there is no city in the western world[19] that does not reflect the Graeco-Roman architectural achievement, as reinterpreted from the Renaissance onwards. Resisting the temptation to fill the rest of the book with the visual evidence, I select Palladio's Church of the Redeemer, Il Redentore in Venice (after a design by Palladio in 1576),[20] (Plate 11). It is hard not to hug oneself with pleasure as one sees what Palladio has done with these ancient forms. A flight of stairs leads up to an entrance (A) of the arch + pilaster type – note impost and keystone – with a small, plain entablature + pediment. This is framed within a larger unit (B): four pilasters (the inner two round, the outer two flat) + entablature + pediment, together forming the main front of the Church, whose width the steps span. Now look to either side of that front, and we see Palladio has constructed another similar, but half 'hidden', lower unit (C): four pilasters (all flat) + entablature + pediment. Observe that the base of this pediment is at the same level as the base of the pediment over the arch. Now go further back and one has what looks suspiciously like a hidden repeat sequence: a roof *looking* like a pediment (with three figures attached to the line of the 'cornice'), (B1), but of exactly the same width as the main front (B); and behind that a lower hidden unit, (C1), of exactly the same width as (C), but with a much larger entablature, to bring the base of its pediment up to the level of the base of the entablature of B1. Above it all rises a magnificent dome. We wonder if Palladio is trying to outdo Hadrian's miraculous Pantheon, with its Greek temple front and stupendous dome larger than St Paul's or St Peter's, and holding the world record for a concrete span till the CNIT building in Paris in 1958 (Plate 13).[21] Palladio's interior is equally miraculous (Plate 12).

13

Stoics and Epicureans

Two philosophies were developed in Athens in the late fourth and third centuries BC that were to have a powerful influence upon Roman and later, including scientific, thought. Stoicism was the brainchild of Zeno, a Greek from Cyprus, who came to Athens in 313 BC. It acquired its name from the *stoa* (long, pillared portico: see p. 116) where he taught.[1] The Greek Epicurus invented Epicureanism. He was born on the island of Samos and in 306 BC bought a house in Athens with a garden which became the headquarters of Epicureanism (when ancient writers talk about 'the garden', this is the philosophy they mean).[2]

These two philosophies share three features common to much ancient philosophy. First, philosophers work by establishing an hypothesis and seeing what they can deduce from it. The idea of experimentation to check if the hypothesis or any of its conclusions was correct was not known to them (see Chapter 14). Second, they are ethical: they aim to show adherents what the good life is and, at the practical level, how to lead it. Third, they are holistic: that is, they derive their views about how the good life should be led from their views about the material construction of the universe. Of course, the ancients knew nothing about the actual make-up of the physical world. There were as many theories as there were exponents. Consequently, they carefully chose their notions of the physical world to support their ethical teachings.

For Stoics, all reality is material.[3] The universe is the result of the active principle, God, influencing passive matter. God in this case is as material as matter, and was identified by Stoics with heavenly fire or *pneuma*, 'breath, spirit', a sort of fiery air.[4] God is mixed with matter throughout the universe (cf. Wordsworth's *Tintern Abbey* with its 'sense sublime/Of something far more deeply interfused ... a motion and a spirit that impels/All thinking things, all objects of all thought,/And rolls through all things'). In a sense, then, the universe is God and God is the universe. Since ancients believed that reason (*logos*) was the highest faculty to which man could aspire, God must be rational (i.e. one can give an account of him). Since God is everywhere in the universe, the universe too must be rational. But God is present throughout the universe in different ways, most importantly, in our soul, which is the part of us that shares in the divine spirit or *pneuma*: in other words, our soul is the divine within us.[5] Given that humans have powers of reason, then, the purpose of life must be to exercise the reasoning faculty, our highest faculty, so as to align our soul as closely as possible with the divine. That will ensure true happiness.[6]

This raises a serious problem. Plato had explained behaviour by positing an irrational element to the soul, and thought of existence as an eternal struggle between the rational and irrational within us. Philosophers like Aristotle and Epicurus had agreed with him. But if our soul is the 'divine *pneuma*' within us, as Stoics argued, without an element of irrationality in it, how can we be anything other than rational? Their answer was that reason itself can be perverted. They used the image of a walker and runner to explain. Both walker and runner have good reasons for acting as they do. The difference is that the walker is in complete control of his movements. He can stop, turn, reverse, at will. But a runner, who is doing the same thing only faster, does not have such control. Reason, in other words, varies between healthy and unhealthy states, and this can cause us to make unsound judgements.

So, for example, if we are tempted to steal, that is not a matter of desires or needs beyond our control. We judge that (say) a Mars Bar is worth having. We judge that it is worth the risk required to have it free. We therefore take steps to get it. But at every stage we have the power to take a different decision. In other words, emotional responses like desire, anger, etc. are nothing but bad decisions. If we were more rational, we would not submit to them. Consequently, we are responsible for our own lives. Every decision we take is up to us. We can choose to live in accordance with the divine, natural world, be rational and therefore happy; or we can choose the opposite. We must, in other words, live in a state of permanent self-examination if we are to be happy, functioning and useful humans. Never has 'Know thyself' meant so much as it did in Stoic philosophy.[7]

There are, however, further problems. Since God as *pneuma* infuses the universe, he must therefore control everything. Since his laws are divine, and so exception-free, his will must be done all the time. Fate, therefore, or providence, rules our lives, and Stoic philosophy is teleological: life has a purpose. This therefore is a deterministic world: there is no escape from its iron grip.[8] But if that is the case, how can human action be free, and how can everything be our responsibility, 'up to us'? As with their use of the image of the runner and the walker, Stoics turned to analogy to tackle the problem. Imagine, says the Greek Stoic Chrysippus, that you throw a cylindrical stone down a slope. You cause it to move; but once it hits the slope, it starts to roll headlong, taking on its own movement. You do not bring that movement about. It is brought about because, being that shape, it has that capacity. So fate sets us going, but the impulses of our own minds and our actions are governed by the mental 'shape' we possess. In another image, a dog is imagined, tied to a wagon by a leash. It is fate (teleology) that he travels with the wagon from A to B. But he can travel willingly and enjoyably, in accordance with reason, or he can squirm and struggle and have a miserable time of it, against reason. It is up to the dog.

Happiness, then, depends on living one's life rationally, in accordance with reason/fate/providence/God. But what did it mean to live 'rationally'? Briefly, to live ethically. The Greek *êthos* means 'character', and for Greek philosophers, happiness did not depend on doing right actions, but on being the right sort of person. Only that would make you truly happy. For a Stoic, that meant being virtuous, or good; this would result in living the best life, rationally, according to nature. Virtue for a Stoic depends on *oikeiôsis*, 'appropriation, making something one's own' (the opposite would be 'alienation'). As one grows up, one begins to see that it is natural and advantageous to seek some things and avoid others, and virtue is growing into an awareness of and appropriating such observations, making the right selections among this variety of external goods. Absolute goodness is the only ultimate target: the other apparent goods of human existence like health or wealth or status should be, or at least should become, 'matters of indifference'. Some, like health, may indeed be preferable to others ('preferable indifferents'), but should never be pursued for their own sakes. Whether one achieves one's selection is not important: it is selecting rightly that is the vital thing. Cicero comes up with the image of the spearman or archer. The important thing is to aim to hit the target. If you do hit it, that is a bonus. If you do not, no matter: your selection of ends in view was right, and that is what counts.[9] This logic led Stoics to believe that there were times when it was right to commit suicide.

This all sounds horribly rational and calculating. For example, a Stoic would attempt to save a child from a house-fire not for the sake of the child but because it was a virtuous thing to do. If he failed, he would feel no remorse. First, he had done the right thing – how could one feel remorseful about that? Second, death is just one of those things, neither good nor bad in itself. Third, it must have been fated anyway. In mitigation, one can fairly point out that the Stoic does not act differently from any other normal human being in the circumstances; and, after all, it is only his internal mental state that is different from that of others – surely his own business. None of this prevents him from being sympathetic to another's loss: sympathy is one of those responses one can select.

Stoic belief that God/*pneuma* was in everything, everywhere, produced one very important result. As we have seen, the Stoic appears to be a cold, unsocial animal, concerned only with ensuring his own happiness by exercising virtue, i.e. making the right selection of external goods. But Stoics did believe in the *universality* of divine providence and thought that humans naturally developed from instinctively wishing to benefit only their own children, family and friends into wishing to benefit humanity at large. From this it is a short step to thinking in terms of world-wide citizenship and of a law of nations. As Cicero argues:

First of all the world was made for the sake of gods and humans, and whatever there is in it was prepared and devised for the enjoyment of humans. For the world is, as it were, a common home of gods and humans, or the city of both groups; for only those who have the use of reason live by law and right.

Cicero, *On the Nature of the Gods* 2.154

The concept of a world family whose welfare it is everyone's duty to promote goes far beyond anything found in Greek philosophy. For example, Stoic teaching argued that it was a duty to treat slaves well: as humans, they too shared in the divine *pneuma*. But this did not lead them to conclude that slaves should be freed. There was, to the Stoic, no need for that. The slave's mind was free, even if his body was not. He was therefore in the same position as everyone to select virtuously from among any external goods he might come across.[10]

The consequence is that Stoics took a full part in public life and politics (Seneca the younger, the millionaire poet, playwright and Nero's guide in his early years, is a good example). Further, it may not be mere chance that Romans slowly widened the scope of citizenship as their power grew, and eventually made citizenship for all free peoples a reality under the emperor Caracalla in the third century AD, though by this time citizenship did not carry with it the benefits of voting and exemption from taxes that it once had.[11] The *ius gentium*, 'law of nations', also became a reality as a result of Roman legal thinking.

For Epicurus, humanity is plagued by one central obsession – the fear of death. To escape this domination, we engage in all sorts of distractions: we seek for power, fame, honour, fortune, glory, reputation. The result is that life is hell. Epicurus therefore studies the nature of the world in order to find grounds for removing this debilitating fear. He is looking to do two things: first, to show that the gods have no interest in us and do not control either nature or us; second that we do not survive death and therefore have nothing to fear in the afterlife. In this way, the central obstacle to our happiness will be removed.

Epicurus looked to the atomic theory of matter to prove his thesis. This theory had been invented by Democritus in fifth-century Athens to deal with the philosophical problem of change.[12] This was an age-old problem. Thales, for example, thought the basic principle was water, Heraclitus that it was fire. But how did these turn into wood, flesh, stone? The problem was given a deadly new twist by Parmenides. To put it crudely, he argued that if something is, it is: it cannot suddenly not be, or be something else. So: a tree *is* a tree. It cannot be not-tree. On those terms, change is impossible. But Parmenides could see this did not work. If you set fire to a tree, it became not-tree. It changed. Indeed, as he looked around, he could see the whole world changing, all the time. Given that this could not possibly be the case, since he had proved change was impossible, Parmenides came up with a thunderbolt of a solution – our senses must be deceiving us.[13]

Greek philosophers were stunned by this conclusion, but could not see a way round it. They therefore invented the atomic theory to counteract it. They argued that, whatever was happening in the world of the senses, no change was in fact occurring below the level of sense-perception. This was because the world was made up of atoms (literally 'uncuttables'), matter that we could not see, but which never changed. The world in all its diversity was created by the various ways these unchanging atoms grouped themselves.

Epicurus, then, argues that the world consists not of *pneuma* but of indivisible atoms and void. These atoms move downwards through the void at constant speed, but swerve unpredictably from time to time. This causes them to collide with other atoms and thus form themselves into clumps – matter.[14] Further, Epicurus argues that everything is made up of these atoms – man, his soul, even the gods. This now leaves the way open for Epicurus to argue that, since we and our souls are nothing but atoms, then at death we and our souls dissolve and return to the great atom pool in the sky. So there is no afterlife, and nothing to fear in death.[15] As for the soul, Epicurus agrees there is such a thing but believes it has nothing to do with the gods or reason: it simply transmits sensations from the body to the mind, and impulses from the mind to the body (e.g. to the limbs, to move).

The question Epicurus now has to tackle is whether the gods take any interest in us. That they do not, he argues – or rather his disciple Lucretius argues – is proved by the observation that the world is full of imperfections, e.g. crags, bogs, seas, blazing heat, freezing cold, intractable earth, wild beasts, disease, death.[16] If men worship the gods, it is only because they have had visions of powerful, immortal beings in their dreams (which at least proves the gods exist); or because they want to explain celestial phenomena and natural disasters like earthquakes. Lucretius continues:

> Miserable race of men, that attributes such acts to gods and such bitter anger! What grief they produced for themselves, what wounds for us, what tears for our children! It is no piety to be seen, head veiled, turning towards a stone, to approach every altar, to lie prostrate on the ground, to stretch out one's palms before the shrines of the gods, to spatter the altars with the blood of animals and heap prayer on prayer, but rather, to be able to contemplate everything with a mind at peace.
>
> Lucretius, *On the Nature of the Universe* 5.1194-1203

Further, if gods really are gods, they must be perfectly happy. Why on earth in that case should they wish to create the world in the first place, let alone interest themselves in us? The conclusion must be that the world was not even created by the gods: it was born and will die, as a necessary consequence of being created by chance out of atoms. But the gods will not suffer this fate. First, they inhabit the *intermundia*, a place set apart, where nothing touches them:

> The Gods, by right of Nature, must possess
> An Everlasting Age, of perfect Peace:
> Far off, remov'd from us, and our Affairs:
> Neither approached by Dangers, or by Cares:
> Rich in themselves, to whom we cannot add:
> Not pleas'd by Good Deeds; nor provok'd by Bad.
> Earl of Rochester, translating Lucretius, 1.44-9; cf. 3.18-22

Second, the atoms out of which gods are made are extremely fine and subtle, and they seem to be constantly replaced and renewed by a fresh stream of atoms. One scholar has drawn a useful comparison with a waterfall.[17] Gods may, therefore, be atoms, but they are so constituted as to make death an impossibility for them.

Having established that the gods have no concern for us and that there is no afterlife, Epicurus now has to tackle the ethical problem of what the good life is and how we can lead it, and like the Stoics, Epicurus believes that what counts is the sort of person you are. His theory derives from his beliefs about hedonism (Greek *hêdonê*, 'pleasure'), i.e. that absence of physical and mental pain is the key to happiness. The word is *ataraxia* 'freedom from anxiety'.[18] This does not mean eternal self-indulgence. A hangover is painful. Nor does it mean eternal asceticism, out of fear that pleasure may turn nasty on you. What one must do is avoid desire for anything that causes anxiety, especially anything that has no limits, like wealth or status, because these will never satisfy you. To help the budding Epicurean, Epicurus defines desire in three categories:

1. Natural and necessary (sub-divided into necessary for happiness, for freedom from disturbance and for life), e.g. food, drink, sex, and absence of anxiety.
2. Natural and unnecessary, e.g. specific types of food and drink.
3. Unnatural and unnecessary, e.g. fame, power.

The ultimate aim, in fact, is to become like the gods – self-sufficient, undisturbed and unaffected by anything.[19]

The implication of Epicurus' philosophy is that life has no awesome, ultimate purpose. Unlike Stoicism, therefore, life for an Epicurean is non-teleological. It has no aim, no greater end in view. One lives, free from anxiety, and dies. That is that. Not that life is pre-determined. The unpredictable atomic swerve of the atoms in the soul means that we have freedom of will (there is much controversy about how Epicurus thought this actually worked). But life is a pretty passive business for Epicureans. Inevitably, it raises all sorts of questions about life in society. For example, justice for Epicureans has no absolute existence in its own right, except as a series of mutually expedient agreements between people to provide against the infliction or suffering of harm. If it brings pleasure or absence of pain to break the law, why not go ahead and break it? Epicurus replies as follows:

> Injustice is not an evil in itself but only in the fear attendant upon the suspicion that those appointed to punish such offences will spot them. It is not possible for the man who secretly breaks any part of the social contract to remain confident that he will not be discovered, even if he has escaped a thousand times to date. For it will remain unclear if he will be detected until the day he dies.
>
> Diogenes Laertius, *Life of Epicurus* 151

But followers of Epicurus will not involve themselves deeply in society. Withdrawal from public life and the affairs of the majority to a life in a community of the like-minded is the way to happiness (the contrast here with Stoic public involvement is strong). This can be interpreted as selfishness. Lucretius almost seems to be gloating when he says:

> Sweet it is, when the winds are whipping up a storm on the great ocean, to watch someone else's struggles – from the land. Not that another's distress gives pleasurable delight, but because it is sweet to realise from what dangers you yourself are free.
>
> Lucretius, *On the Nature of the Universe* 2.1-4

But he does not gloat. He merely reflects on the pleasures that adherence to Epicurus' doctrines bring. It is a pleasure Lucretius clearly wants to spread and it clearly gives pleasure to do so: why else should Lucretius have written his great epic? The second-century AD essayist Plutarch even said it was an Epicurean view that it is more pleasant to give a benefit than receive one – true altruism.[20] (Aristotle reaches the same conclusion by a different, more Greek, route, arguing that the man supreme in virtue prefers to benefit others because it will confirm how great he is). Epicureanism, in other words, did not necessarily result in a wholly self-centred existence.[21]

This brief sketch of some of the two philosophies' main doctrines hides a mountain of debate, both ancient and modern. Cicero, for example, attacked both schools, holding generally to the Sceptic position invented by the Greek Pyrrho about the same time as Stoicism and Epicureanism that since we cannot know anything, we must suspend judgement and regard traditional beliefs and customs as the best guide. Epicureans thought this far too anxiety-provoking. Stoics counter-argued that it was impossible to lead a normal life unless you made *some* judgements. Sceptics came back by arguing that they did make judgements but reached decisions about what *seemed* to them to be the case. The 'plausible impression'was what counted, and this appeared the best way to lead the tranquil existence. And so the arguments trundled gently around.

These quasi-theological systems have induced strong reactions down the ages.[22] Early Christians, for example, fiercely rejected Epicurean views of the mortal soul, a material universe lacking 'spirit', and divine disinterest in humanity. But the Epicurean idea of membership of an alternative, closely-bonded community, withdrawn from society, was congenial to them, especially when the Church was being persecuted. Otherwise, for fifteen hundred years Epicurus was seen (quite unfairly) as nothing more than a reprobate who advocated the gratification of sensual desires. His main impact on later thought was in the seventeenth century, when his atomic theory caught the imagination of scientists and can be said to have laid the basis of modern science (see p. 133).

Christian thinkers, though utterly rejecting Stoic materialism, found much more acceptable the Stoic view that the universe was a matter-spirit duality, that divinity interfused it, and that man should try to be virtuous and at one with God. They also paid careful attention to Stoic theodicy, i.e. their attempts to explain why a good God should allow evil in the world. In fact it is noticeable during late antiquity, as Christianity spread, both that pagan philosophers became more religious, and Christians became more ready to listen to them.[23] Pagan thinkers like Plotinus, for example, began to talk in terms of the soul's transcendental progress to knowledge of the divine (rather as Plato had in the fourth century BC) and to pay less, if any, attention to cult, myth and ritual, which formed the heart of pagan religion. Again, Stoic thinkers, like the Jews and early Christians, had no time for the veneration of images.[24] The point is that Christian thinkers respected their classical education (see p. 24). They wanted to find a compromise between it and their revealed religion that would make Christianity acceptable to pagan thought.

It was to Platonism that Christians turned to make the bridge. Platonic thought centres round the idea that this world is good, but transient: there is a reality above and beyond it to which we can all aspire, and to which we should dedicate our lives. This reality is the Good, and any goodness we correspondingly find in our transient world derives from it. The search for it is arduous and demanding, but rewarding: the nearer we approach to understanding the Good, the more fulfilling our lives will be. This is only a very partial description of what Plato stood for, of course,[25] but represents the area of Platonic thought to which Christians thought they could attach their lifelines. If the Christian God becomes the Good, much else about Christian life and belief, *mutatis mutandis*, falls into position. Christians could then tack on some pragmatic Stoic views about the soul, God and the virtuous life being one, and present a package that would make sense to pagan thinkers without wholly violating Christian doctrine.[26]

For all the technical debates, however, Stoic and Epicurean theories about how life should be led form the most significant part of their work, and their precepts and ideas ring as freshly today as ever. I end the chapter with a random collection of *aperçus*:

Get used to the belief that death is nothing to us. All good and evil are in the perception, but death is the deprivation of perception. So the right understanding that death is nothing to us makes this mortal life enjoyable, not because it makes life eternal, but because it removes the fear of death. There is nothing fearful about life to the man who truly understands that there is nothing fearful about not living. So that man is a fool who says that he fears death, not because it will distress him when it comes, but because it distresses him now, in the prospect.

Diogenes Laertius, quoting Epicurus' letter to
Menoeceus, *Life of Epicurus* 124-15

Remember that the future is not ours but not completely not ours, in order not to count upon it as a certainty, nor despair of it as not a certainty.

Diogenes Laertius, letter, *Life of Epicurus* 127

We do everything to this end, to be free of pain and fear. Once we have attained this, the tempest of the soul is laid.

Diogenes Laertius, letter, *Life of Epicurus* 128

The beginning [of pleasure] and a very great benefit is good sense. Good sense is more valuable even than philosophy, because all the other virtues derive from it: it teaches that a life of pleasure is impossible to lead if it is not also sensible, honourable and just; nor is it possible to lead a sensible, honourable and just life without it also being a life of pleasure. For the virtues and the life of pleasure grow together, and there is no life of pleasure without them.

Diogenes Laertius, letter, *Life of Epicurus* 132

[The man who does not fear death] mocks at Fate, which some introduce as master of everything, by pointing out that some things happen of necessity, others by chance, others through our own agency. He sees that necessity destroys accountability and that chance is random; but what we do is our own free choice, and it here that praise and blame are naturally attached.

Diogenes Laertius, letter, *Life of Epicurus* 133-4

Why, mortal, is death so great a thing to you that you should indulge in such excessive grief over it? Why lament and weep over death? If life was good to you, and its blessings have not drained away, as if from a leaky bucket, and perished unenjoyed, why not retire from life satisfied, as a guest from a banquet, idiot, and calmly seize a rest free from all cares? But if everything you have gathered has been wasted and lost and life is a burden, why seek to add more, which will only be stupidly lost again and perish unenjoyed? Is it not better to make an end of life and its toil?

Lucretius, *On the Nature of the Universe* 3.933-43

The man bored with staying at home often abandons his great house and suddenly returns again, because abroad makes him feel no better. He races off to his house in the country, driving his horses at speed, as if he were going to help fight a fire there. As soon as he steps over the threshold, he yawns, or sinks into a heavy sleep and seeks oblivion, or dashes off back to the city again. In this way each man seeks to escape from himself; yet for all that he still clings unwillingly to the person he cannot escape from, and hates himself, because, being sick, he can find no cure for his illness.

Lucretius, *On the Nature of the Universe* 3.1060-70

Do not ask things to happen as you wish, but wish them to happen as they do happen, and your life will go smoothly.

Epictetus, *Handbook* 8[27]

Remember that you are an actor in a play, which is as the author wants it to be: short, if he wants it short; long, if he wants it long. If he wants you to act a poor man, a cripple, a public official, or a private person, see that you act it with skill. For it is your job to act well the part assigned to you; but to choose it is another's.

Epictetus, *Handbook* 17

You are a little soul, carrying a corpse.

Epictetus, *Handbook* 26

No man is free who is not master of himself.

Epictetus, *Handbook* 35

The noblest way to avenge yourself is not to become as they are.

Marcus Aurelius, *Meditations* 6.6[28]

Remember that the power that pulls our strings is that which is hidden within us: that is the source of our action, and our life, and that, if one may say so, is the person himself.

Marcus Aurelius, *Meditations* 10.38

If the light of the torch shines forth without ever losing its radiance until it is extinguished, shall truth, justice and temperance be extinguished in yourself before you reach the end?

Marcus Aurelius, *Meditations* 12.15

14

Breaking the Ancient Stranglehold

The classical world exerted an intellectual grip on the West for about fifteen hundred years (till, let us say, the sixteenth century). It is fashionable in some quarters to blame the Greeks and Romans for this, as if it is their fault that the people who succeeded them believed so much of the nonsense they came up with. Two things need to be said. First, and very briefly, the German tribes that dominated Europe after the fall of the Roman empire (see p. 22) brought no new intellectual apparatus with them to bear upon the Christian-classical cultural world. They were overwhelmed by and acquiesced in that achievement.

Second, when the intellectual world did begin to shift from the sixteenth century onwards, it was to some extent because a technology was being harnessed in a way that had not occurred to earlier generations. Medieval alchemists, attempting to transform base metals into gold and silver, based their theories on sound Aristotelian principles but needed to *do* it, not merely philosophise about its possibilities. They brought about considerable advances in the understanding of chemical processes and the development of apparatus to help distil and analyse substances. Proponents of magic, convinced of the sympathy and affinities between the animate and inanimate world, investigated the properties of e.g. stones, plants, liquids and magnets. Then again, cartography, astronomy and surveying provided new models of measurement; mathematical theory was applied to perspective and so to technical drawing, architecture and warfare (gunnery and fortifications); clocks were built and instrument-making generally moved forward. When in Italy the sense began to develop that nature was a sort of mechanism, and needed therefore to be dismantled if it was to be understood, the demand for seriously accurate mathematical instrumentation and exact measuring techniques was set in train. Most critical of all, perhaps, was Columbus' discovery that there was more to the world than the ancients ever dreamed of. This revelation that the Greeks, Romans and the Church were not all-knowing, even about *this* world, came as a thunderbolt.

Of even greater importance, however, was the extraordinary intellectual leap that brought the new technology into play so successfully. The thinkers of the ancient world worked on the principle of deduction from hypothesis. One observed the world, drew up a hypothesis on the strength of that observation, and possibly from the comfort of one's armchair, with the help of a bottle of scotch and a large cigar, deduced what followed from it. That is a principled and rational procedure – indeed, the foundation of rational thinking because it assumes the world is rational and explicable – but what it omitted was the stage which enabled one to test one's hypotheses and conclusions. It omitted, in other words, experimentation.

When Thales claimed the basic 'principle' of the world was water, when Heraclitus argued that it was fire, when ancient doctors talked in term of health depending on the balance of four humours, they argued their cases, in public, with tremendous intensity and no holds barred. Such free, open debate, with no limits on what could be said or thought, was of great cultural significance. But the debates were philosophical (one would almost say theological) in character. The ancients argued about the nature of the world on the strength of long-held assumptions and what their eyes could see, in purely philosophical terms – like oppositions (hot *vs*. cold, dry *vs*. wet, etc.), analogy (e.g. the cosmos is like a state, where 'justice' keeps things in balance),[1] induction, deduction, logical impossibility and probability. But as you cannot set up an experiment to test the existence of God or the nature of the Trinity or the innate goodness or evil of man,[2] so you cannot say much that is seriously useful about the nature of the world without ever submitting your arguments to the test of experiment. By that, I do not mean testing to see if something works (ancient technologists did that all the time) or testing to see if an experiment will support one's hypothesis – Greeks occasionally did that[3] – but, first, testing and rejecting and re-resting hypotheses on the basis of experiment till an answer, whatever it is, emerges, and, second, asking questions the answer to which (whatever they are) experiment will reveal. Aristotle asserted that everything consisted of earth, air, fire and water. Why did he not test the hypothesis, or even ask 'in what proportion'? It would have been perfectly simple.

It may seem odd that, given what the ancients did achieve intellectually, the experimental method did not occur to them. Some argue that they just did not have the technology. This is not true. Babylonians had earlier shown what could be done technologically,[4] with astonishing brilliance. As for Greeks and Romans, one does not sail a ship, drain a mine, blow glass, fire a pot, plough a field, build a temple or produce tools and fine tableware ware without considerable technological awareness. Greeks even produced gadgets. Take the astronomical 'computer' found off Anticythera, complete with toothed gearing.[5] Perhaps designed for astrological purposes (no sailor needed such a device), it is of a complexity identical to Mohammed Ibn Abi-Bakr's astrolabe of AD 1022.

One can try other explanations: the absence of teams of scientists working on the same problems, lack of easy communications, the inability to reproduce experimental apparatus (one can bet there was only one Anticythera machine), or a way of thinking about the world that privileged mind very firmly over matter. But the problem of understanding why the ancients did not develop the experimental method is, in fact, largely *our* problem. The experimental method is something we so take for granted that it is impossible to imagine a time when it was not received practice. But the fact is that, with axiomatic reasoning (which the Greeks did invent), the experimental method is the greatest intellectual break-through ever compassed by man. As Einstein pointed out, it is amazing that it was done at all. So when Aristotle says that he proved by experi-ment that, when sea water evaporated, it became fresh, and then claims, absurdly, that the same was true of wine, our reaction tends to be 'Aris-totle? *The* Aristotle? What's up with the ninny?' But it is not what was wrong with Aristotle. It is what was triumphantly right about sixteenth-century Europe.

This was indeed a brave new world. Science finally broke with philoso-phy and established its own stunning rationale. Mind-sets were changed for ever, and the foundations of western thought, secure for some fifteen hundred years, were comprehensively destroyed in the course of a few hundred years, with powerful ramifications for the Church too, which by a process of compromise and assimilation had reconciled itself to many aspects of the classical understanding of the physical world.

It must be stressed, however, that this stunning revolution did not happen overnight. The weight of authority behind the Christian-classical world-view was enormous. Take Aristotle's theory of matter and change. His aim was to explain why matter looked and felt as it did, i.e. what its tangible, sensible properties were, and he rejected any theory that de-pended on a form of matter below the level of perception. So he rejected atomism in favour of the theory that matter consisted of the four elements earth, air, fire and water. Further, each of these was a combination of two of the four qualities hot, cold, dry and moist (e.g. fire = hot + dry, etc.). Changes in these created change in matter (so one thing can change into another – the principle behind alchemy). So much for the earth: but heavenly bodies were quite different. His reasoning went: the heavenly bodies move in perfect circular motion. The four elements, however, do not: earth and water fall down, fire and air move up. Of course it is possible to force them in different directions, but heavenly movement is not forced, but natural. Therefore, heavenly bodies are made up of a different sub-stance. Aristotle called it *aithêr*.

Even in the seventeenth century, if the master said it, it must be true, and many used the new experimental techniques to try to demonstrate that Aristotle was right. When other explanations were offered, battle was fiercely joined. The French Jesuit Pierre Gassendi (1592-1655) was instru-mental in breaking the Aristotelian mould. He became fascinated by Epicurus, Lucretius and the atomic theory of matter (espoused by Francis Bacon, 1561-1626, before him), and wrote a series of commentaries on the issue, duly modified and accommodated to Christian teaching, as the best way of investigating nature. This work came to the attention of scientists including Robert Boyle (like Newton, a keen alchemist), whose work on gases had convinced him that Aristotle's theory of matter was nonsense.[6] The psychological resistance to the atomic theory was strong, but Boyle and others saw its potential to explain how the world worked, and adopted it keenly. Their explanation of the functioning of atoms was wrong (kinetic theory awaited the nineteenth century), but the early atomists' work can now be seen as a defining moment in modern science. Soon the theory that matter consisted of 'minute particles' became received wisdom, and translations of Lucretius all the rage (the first by Thomas Creech, 1682). In 1803 John Dalton (1766-1844) founded modern atomic theory with a series of statements about chemical combination, many of which Epicurus would have applauded, e.g. elements consist of individual small particles (atoms); atoms can neither be created nor destroyed.[7]

Again, medical theory over two thousand years old still held good in the seventeenth century. If Hippocrates laid the foundations of that theory in fifth-century BC Greece,[8] the lasting structure raised on that base was designed by the Greek doctor Galen (AD 129 – *c*. 200). Trained in the school of hard knocks as a gladiator physician in Asia Minor, he ended up as court physician to the emperor Marcus Aurelius in Rome. He took Plato, Hippocrates and Aristotle as his intellectual mentors, expanding on their work in practical and theoretical areas in anatomy, physiology, pathology, pharmacy and dietetics. He was also a philosopher of some note. All this, added to his religious attitudes and belief in teleology, turned him in the middle ages into a figure as untouchable in medicine as Aristotle and Plato were in philosophy.

The result was that in the seventeenth century Galen's theory of the four 'temperaments' (hot, moist, cold and dry) and four 'humours' (blood, phlegm, yellow bile and black bile) still dominated medical thought.[9] Thus men were hot and dry, women cold and moist. Psychology danced to the same tune. Excess of blood made one sanguine (Latin *sanguis*, 'blood'), excess of phlegm 'phlegmatic' (Greek *phlegma* 'heat, fire'), excess of bile (Greek *kholos*) 'choleric'. Illness and health depended on maintaining a balance in the temperaments and the humours. Too hot, you took remedies that were cold – and so on. Causes were attributed to location, the atmosphere, or the wrath of God. It was all complete nonsense, an unscientific world knowing nothing of bacteria or viruses or any of the data we take for granted today. But one cannot blame Galen if no one had been able to do any better. It was not till 1878 that Pasteur unveiled his germ theory of infection;[10] viruses were first isolated in 1884.

Likewise, according to Galen, there were two types of blood. Venous blood, originating in the liver, encouraged growth, and was expended in providing it; arterial blood, originating in the heart and being mixed with spirit (*pneuma* – see p. 121), gave life and spread to all parts of the body, where it too was expended. In other words, blood did not circulate, but moved outwards from its source through the body, where it was used up. Nor did the heart drive the blood through the arteries: the arteries' own 'pulsative faculties' squeezed it out into the system. Renaissance doctors were not wholly happy with this description. For example, the Belgian doctor Vesalius (1514-1564) dissected bodies to check Galen's findings. He was most reluctant to say Galen was wrong when he found discrepancies, but was eventually forced to – and was roundly attacked for it (must have been something wrong with the corpse, commented one doctor).[11] Vesalius justified himself by saying that he was reviving true Galenic medicine, as against badly translated, text-based learning. William Harvey (1578-1657) finally put all the clues together and published his *de motu cordis* ('On the motion of the heart') in Latin in 1628, demonstrating the circulation of the blood. But he still believed that the blood had Galenic properties, being 'full of spirit' and 'alimentative', and that it returned depleted to the heart in order to 'recover its perfection' and be recharged with these properties before being pumped out again. As the Sun was to the world, he said, so the heart was to the body – a truly Aristotelian way of looking at things.[12]

So too in all areas of new thought at this time, the most brilliant advances were made without immediately demolishing the ancient view of the world. When, for example, in 1543 Copernicus put the sun, not the earth, at the centre of his solar system, the remaining planets were still embedded on the rims of homocentric, crystalline spheres that carried them in regular, circular motion through the heavens, an idea Eudoxus had prescribed in the fourth century BC and Aristotle had developed. When Columbus sailed west to discover the New World, he did so knowing what he ought to find, namely, that the land mass of the world was much greater than the seas. Aristotle had said so, and so had Esdras in the Apocrypha, claiming only one seventh of the world was sea. Columbus was therefore delighted to conclude from the waters flowing out of the Orinoco in Venezuela that a huge land-mass must lie to the south.

The story of Ptolemy's maps neatly summarises the theme of this chapter. The second-century AD astronomer and geographer Ptolemy had collected a vast amount of information about the size, location and often fantastic inhabitants of the then known world (i.e. a territory whose outer limits were defined by Spain, Britain, across Germany to south Russia, India and Sri Lanka, and back west to Arabia and the northern half of Africa). It included exciting places like magnetic islands that would extract all the nails from passing ships. This information was converted into maps in Byzantium in the thirteenth century and translated into Latin in the fifteenth. No smart home was to be seen without one. A lot of it was wrong (not surprisingly, it led Columbus to believe he had reached Asia, not the Caribbean), but Ptolemy himself admitted that geography was an inexact science, and modern geographers set to work to correct and augment it. Anywhere marked *terra incognita secundum Ptolemaeum*, 'unknown territory according to Ptolemy', begged for exploration.[13]

The point is that fresh work had to start somewhere. It could only start from what people knew: and what they knew was what the ancients had told them. It is not surprising, then, that the dramatic scientific and medical advances of the sixteenth and seventeenth centuries did not in a single instant explode the accumulated 'wisdom' of two thousand years. Until the Renaissance, we can say that western man had gone about as far as he could in producing a model of the world with the two tools at his disposal – the rational mind and the observing eye. Science, in other words, was essentially the handmaid of philosophy. It says something for the satisfying explanatory power of the ancient model, and/or the influence of the Church, that it lasted so long and required such a superhuman effort to replace it. The ensuing technological and experimental revolution was to offer tools for the hand, eye and mind to work with that would have left the Aristotles and Galens of the ancient world green with envy. It was a revolution classical Greeks would have recognised and applauded. Had they too not submitted the received ideas of their world to precisely the same sort of examination, with equally startling results?[14]

APPENDIX 1

The Pronunciation of Latin and the Spelling of Greek

As I learned from my *QED: Learn Latin* series in the *Telegraph* papers,[1] the pronunciation of Latin arouses fierce passions. Many readers told me that no one knew how it was pronounced, and then fiercely asserted that Latin *v* was pronounced as English 'v', not 'w'. Others said that Latin *in caelis* 'in the heavens' should be pronounced 'in chayleess', not (as I had recommended) 'in kyleess'.

As I indicated in Chapters 9 and 10, arguments about pronunciation and grammar are thousands of years old. Modern pronunciations of Latin exist for a variety of reasons. There is the old French pronunciation, dating back to AD 1066. After William's conquest, Latin was taught with a French pronunciation. Hence *gens* 'tribe' was pronounced 'jens', *iustus* 'just' was pronounced 'justus', *Cicero* (hard c) as 'Sisero'. Then there is the revised pronunciation of the great Dutch scholar Erasmus, published in 1528, expounded in an agreeable discussion between a bear and a lion. This never fully caught on, but was itself subject to corruption because of the change of pronunciation in English: thus in the course of the Great Vowel Shift, long *i* ('ee') became pronounced as in 'wine'. Then again, there is church pronunciation, which is nothing but the modern Italian that Pope Pius X tried to impose on the Church in 1912 (hence 'chayleess').

The debate has surfaced intermittently on and off, but was finally laid to rest in 1965 when W.S. Allen, Professor of Comparative Philology at Cambridge, published his definitive *Vox Latina: The Pronunciation of Classical Latin* (Cambridge 1965, revised 1989). He concludes: 'The degree of accuracy with which we can reconstruct the ancient pronunciation varies from sound to sound, but for the most part can be determined within quite narrow limits.' The evidence is impressive and wide-ranging. Here are a few examples and the conclusions they lead to:

1. Writers talk about how the language sounded. Thus the grammarian Terentianus Maurus talks of the vibrating sound the Latin *r* produced, and the satirist Lucilius says that *r* sounds like a growling dog. This means we should trill *r* (as Scots do) in Latin, thus distinguishing between *pacis* 'of peace' and *parcis* 'you spare'.
2. The transliteration of Latin into other languages yields important results. We know that ancient Greek *k* was pronounced hard. So when Latin *Cicero* appears in Greek as *Kikerôn* and not *Siserôn* (the -*ôn* ending is a Greek termination), we can be certain that Latin *c* was pronounced hard. In time, it softened (Latin for 'hundred' *centum* becomes French *cent*), but our evidence suggests this did not happen till *c*. AD 500.
3. Metres helps the argument. Take the pronunciation of Latin *v*. 'Wood', *silva*, appears occasionally in verse as three syllables. If *v* was pronounced 'w', this

would explain things ('sil-oow-a'); with *v* pronounced as 'v', *silva* could never be scanned as three syllables. Then again *Valerius* appears transliterated into Greek as *Oualerios*, suggesting the 'w' sound; and a Latin grammarian argued that when you said *tu* ('you' singular) and *vos* ('you' plural) in Latin, your lips pointed at the person you were addressing. This would happen only if *v* was pronounced 'w'. So however much the words may sound to us like characters from the Seven Dwarfs, Julius Caesar did indeed say 'wayny, weedy, weeky' (*veni, vidi, vici* 'I came, I saw, I conquered'). Over time *v* changed its sound, and a Latin grammarian of the second century AD tells us it was pronounced 'with friction'. That suggests it was now sounding more like 'v'.

4. Inscriptions are extremely informative, especially when they are illiterate. For example, we find *in pace* 'in peace' written *im pace*, and *in balneo* 'in the bath' as *im balneo*. So it looks as if Romans slurred 'n' to 'm' before a 'p' or 'b'. Even more surprising, we find *ignes* 'fires' written as *ingnes*, and there is other evidence to suggest that 'gn' was pronounced 'ngn'. So *magnus* 'large' sounded roughly like English 'ha*ng*nail'.

5. Spelling conventions also help. *Consul* 'consul' was often written *cosul*, and when Romans abbreviated it, they wrote *cos*., not *con*. or *cons*. So 'n' was probably not pronounced before 's'. Further evidence is supplied by ancient Greek, which writes the Latin name *Hortensius* as *Hortesios*; and we hear of aristocratic Romans such as Cicero preferring to drop *n* before *s* and saying e.g. *foresia* ('public matters') not *forensia*. Cf. modern Italian 'bride', *sposa*, from Latin *sponsa* ('spouse').

No language stands still. Ancient English was no more pronounced like modern English than Latin was like modern Italian or ancient Greek like modern Greek (on which, see W.S. Allen, *Vox Graeca* [third edition, Cambridge 1987]). On the other hand, one is free to pronounce a foreign language according to the conventions of the mother tongue (we do not pronounce the capital of France as the French do, nor 'Cicero' as the Romans did). The pronunciation of Church Latin is now traditional. If it bears no relation to classical Latin, so what? But if one wants a common pronunciation, then classical Latin as described by Professor Allen offers a standard, in the same way that a Frenchmen's French, rather than Sir Edward Heath's, does for that language.

The spelling of ancient Greek proper names in English causes similar problems, because Greek proper names have been adopted into English in their Latin forms, Latin having been the language of English education for so long. For example, Plato is the latinised form of Greek *Platon*, Apollo of *Apollon*. The examples in the table opposite indicate the basic rules of the Latinisation of Greek.[2] The Greek is exactly transliterated, and the Latin equivalent given in the next column.

Even so, that is not the end of the story, because English has its own conventions as well, which control the final English form of the Latinised Greek word. For example, Greek *Korinthos*, Latin *Corinthus*, but English Corinth; Greek *Athenai*, Latin *Athenae*, but English Athens; Greek *Aristoteles*, so Latin, but English Aristotle, and so on.

Greek	Latin	Notes
Thoukudidês	Thucydides	Greek *ou* becomes Latin *u*; Greek *u* becomes Latin *y*, in certain circumstances[3]; Greek *k* becomes Latin *c*.
Aiskhulos	Aeschylus	Greek *ai* becomes Latin *ae*; Greek *-os* ending becomes Latin *-us* ending.[4] Thus Greek *Epikouros* becames Latin *Epicurus*.
Ilion	Ilium	Greek *-on* ending becomes Latin *-um*.
Akhilleus	Achilles	Greek *-eus* ending becomes Latin *-es*.
Phoibê	Phoebe	Greek *-oi* can become Latin *-oe*.
Peirênê	Pirene	Greek *-ei* can become Latin *-i*.

APPENDIX 2

The Rationale for Classics in Schools[1]

1. Introduction

Go to any party, say you teach classics, and someone will announce that Latin and Greek are dead languages and therefore useless. But if Latin and Greek are dead languages, then Mozart is dead music and Shakespeare is dead poetry, and are they not pretty useless too?

To put the case in a nutshell: Classics justifies itself by what it has to offer. It is either valuable in itself, or it is nothing. Classics in translation in particular complements and enriches the humanities curriculum – English, History, Modern Languages and the Arts – by providing historical foundations for and 2,000-year-old perspectives and insights into the cultural issues with which the humanities engage, and is accessible to the most and least able.

2. Definitions

By 'Classics' we mean Latin and Greek (studied as languages), and Ancient History and Classical Civilisation (studied in translation), available at GCSE and A level. Study of the Greeks and Romans is available at Key Stage 2 (ages 7-11) and Key Stage 3 (ages 11-14).

3. Justification

Any attempt to justify the study of a subject runs the risk of the counter-challenge 'Does not subject X do the same?' An excellent recent publication, for example, argues that 'Classics is good to think with'.[2] Indeed it is, but so are Maths and History, the sceptic will reply.

The argument from 'relevance' is also difficult, prompting the question 'relevant to what and to whom?' The answer depends on one's values, interests and purposes. The study of Shakespeare, for example, is 'irrelevant' to becoming a lawyer, but does that mean people wishing to become lawyers are wasting their time studying Shakespeare? Besides, to say that classics or Shakespeare is irrelevant to anyone's experience is to ignore the fact that reading *creates* experience.

The temptation, then, is to whip up a snowstorm of justifications, in the hope that one or two will settle. For classics, it has been claimed that it e.g. teaches English grammar and spelling and provides a rich and stimulating linguistic environment; helps pupils learn other languages; makes good puzzles; encourages logical thinking; develops intellectual rigour; is not a soft option; is interdisciplinary; is multi-cultural; offers breadth and balance; introduces pupils to a common cultural heritage; helps pupils understand modern society by making them think about past societies; and so on.

Classics does deliver these benefits, of course, but so do many other subjects. The danger of this approach is that utility becomes the sole criterion of educational value. If utility is then restricted to social utility, literature comes to be judged by its capacity to massage the reader's conscience. Any tract against slavery is thus automatically better than any work of ancient literature (which takes slavery for granted), as if moral edification were an index of aesthetic or cultural merit. The approach also offers hostages to fortune, since in the eyes of critics the bad reasons will always leap off the page at the expense of good (see p. 146).

The purpose of this rationale is to identify the unique value of classics.

4. Classics in translation: history and culture

Our past was shaped by Europe, the Church and Graeco-Roman culture (see especially Chapters 13 and 14). The technological and scientific revolution of the seventeenth century began to change all that. An ancient Greek transported into the sixteenth century AD would find the world strange but not incomprehensible; transported into the third millennium, he would think he was dreaming, or had gone mad. The temptation for us to throw away 2,000 years of history in the face of this tremendous revolution is powerful. The modern world is so different from the past that the past can have nothing to say to us.

Cannot the past just be interesting? Certainly the past has nothing to say about the technological aspects of the modern world where the major changes have taken place. One searches Sophocles in vain for insights into the advantages of digital over analogue communication systems. But there is more to life than technology, and if one thinks that literature, politics, art, architecture, design, religion, language, law, philosophy, medicine, education, myth, historiography, morality, relationships, values, freedom, war, society, culture, and nature (to take a few examples) are worth discussing in other than technological terms, Greeks and Romans actually got all these discussions going as far as the West is concerned over 2,000 years ago.

Classics in translation, making the subject available to everyone in a way that it was not in the past, introduces all these topics, but seen through entirely different eyes, in the detailed study of Greek and Roman history and civilisation.

5. Latin and Greek

There are three reasons why the ancient languages are rare in schools. The first is educational: the schools judge their pupils will profit nothing from the study. The second is economic: in a time of falling budgets and government-imposed curricula, there is no room on the timetable, and even if there were, finances would not permit them. The third is cultural: simple prejudice.

There is little one can do about prejudice. It is a form of ignorance, unforgivable in educators, usually arising from some unhappy past failure or disinclination. It did for Socrates and it bids fair to do for Latin and Greek too. The economic arguments are not insurmountable. Lamentably, they are often nothing but a disguise for prejudice. But where there is a will, there is a way, and there are plenty of grant-giving bodies on the scene.[3] The educational arguments must be tackled here:

- One cannot beat the heady aesthetic, cultural and intellectual experience of reading the real thing in the original – everything from Homer and the Greek tragedians to Catullus, the New Testament and the simplest inscription.
- A heavily inflected language radically different from English illustrates the variety of ways that humans can express themselves, as well as demanding closeness and accuracy of linguistic observation.
- The study of a past, alien culture in an alien language makes intense demands on the intellect, imagination and capacity to understand.

Then consider the spin-offs:

- As exemplars of how language works (i.e. as meta-languages), Latin and Greek help us understand how our own, or any, language works, and develop other useful skills.[4]
- By mastering a vocabulary which provides English with most of its vocabulary of secondary and higher education, pupils increase their chance of success in school and their pleasure in life. The richer the language, the richer the existence (see p. 92).

6. Some misconceptions

Latin and Greek are suitable only for the linguistically able

This is probably true for those studying the subjects to GCSE and A level. They thus cater for the gifted. But modern courses are so constructed that in the early years all pupils can profit from the linguistic advantages that some study of the languages can bring. This is especially true of the new primary school Latin course by Barbara Bell, *Minimus* (Cambridge 1999), designed for all abilities.

Latin and Greek take too long to learn

In the past one did undergo an interminable linguistic grounding before reaching the real thing. This had very considerable benefits for those able to take advantage of them, but many pupils abandoned the languages before meeting the ancient world in any other than a narrowly linguistic sense. This is no longer the case. Modern Latin and Greek courses have been as much influenced by new methods of learning languages as have modern languages, and teach the ability to read and understand the languages more efficiently than in the past.

Latin and Greek are élitist exercises, divorced from the real world

See pp. 145f. for an answer to the 'élitist' issue. As for the 'real world', most school subjects bear no relation to it. One of the main purposes of the ancient languages is to open pupils' eyes to the existence of radically different, but highly articulate, languages and worlds 2,000 years old. The more divorced the languages are from everyday experience, the better, as long as they are not divorced from the ancient world too (the criticism that could be made of past courses, with their concentration on ditches, arrows, roses, poets and farmers, though their passion for slaves, girls and queens was politically well ahead of their time. As pure technical training in language, however, they were unmatched, and a joyful experience for those who liked that sort of thing).

Studying Classics does not lead to a job

What does? Many of those studying even for a vocational degree, e.g. law, do not end up in the career for which it was designed. The facts are as follows:

- No subject, unless vocational, automatically opens up or restricts job prospects.
- Nearly 40 per cent of jobs are not subject-specific.
- Most employers look for a flexible work-force: they emphasise skills like the ability to communicate, co-operate, lead, work on one's own, re-learn, re-train and so on.

In other words, a classicist is on the same footing as everyone else who has not studied a vocational degree subject. Careers advisers who suggest otherwise do not understand today's world of work.

Classicists of my acquaintance have gone into marketing, retail, personnel, hospital management, the wine trade, prison service, computing, banking, city head-hunting, opera, insurance, accountancy, the law, publishing, journalism, book-binding, dogs' homes, hospital management, British rail, advertising, auctioneering, the Church, teaching and so on. See Appendix 3, note 6.

To put it briefly: schools are selling their pupils short culturally, historically, aesthetically and linguistically if they do not engage them with the world of the ancient Greeks and Romans.

APPENDIX 3

Primal Scream

'Classics' derives from *classis*. This word was used to mean one of the five property groups into which Servius Tullius, the sixth king of Rome (578-535 BC), divided the Roman people for tax purposes; then a body of citizens summoned for military purposes, a levy; and then the specialisation of this usage into the most common meaning, 'fleet'. *Classicus* meant 'belonging to the highest class'; in Aulus Gellius XIX.viii.15 it is used for the first time of literature, referring to a *scriptor adsiduus*, 'an authoritative writer', who is an orator or a poet, and *e cohorte illa antiquiore* 'from that earlier cohort [of such writers]'. The *scriptor classicus* is contrasted with a *scriptor proletarius*. There is a lot of class in classics. But 'class' is a double-edged sword, and classics has been on the receiving end of the sharp edge of that sword for too long.

One can see why. In *Four Lectures on the Advantages of a Classical Education as an Auxiliary to a Commercial Education* (1846), Andrew Amos quotes a physician, a Dr Armstrong, who 'recommends reciting Greek as an excellent mode of strengthening the chest'. He writes:

Read aloud resounding Homer's strains
And wield the thunder of Demosthenes.
The chest so exercised improves its strength
And quick vibrations through the bowels drive
The restless blood, which in inactive days
Would loiter else in unelastic tubes.

Well, yes. Or then again, no.

Then take Lord Macaulay. Here is a man who records that in India in 1835 he read 'Aeschylus twice; Sophocles twice; Euripides once; Pindar twice; Callimachus; Apollonius Rhodius; Quintus Calaber; Theocritus twice; Herodotus; Thucydides; almost all Xenophon's works; almost all Plato; Aristotle's Politics, and a good deal of his Organon, besides dipping elsewhere in him; the whole of Plutarch's Lives; about half of Lucian; two or three books of Athenaeus; Plautus twice; Terence twice; Lucretius twice; Catullus; Tibullus; Propertius; Lucan; Statius; Silius Italicus; Livy; Velleius Paterculus; Sallust; Caesar; and lastly Cicero. I have, indeed, a little of Cicero left; but I shall finish him in a few days. I am now deep in Aristophanes and Lucian.'

Yet what sense did he make of this admirably voracious reading? Not much. Here in an essay on the Athenian orators Macaulay takes us back to Athens in the 'time of its power and glory':

A crowd is assembled round a portico. All are gazing with delight at the entablature: for Phidias is putting up the frieze. We turn into another street:

a rhapsodist is reciting there: men, women and children are thronging round him; the tears are running down their cheeks; their eyes are fixed; their very breath is still; for he is telling how Priam fell at the feet of Achilles and kissed those hands – the terrible, the murderous – which had slain so many of his sons. We enter the public place: there is a ring of youths, all leaning forward, with sparkling eyes, and gestures of expectation. Socrates is pitted against the famous atheist from Ionia, and had just brought him to a contradiction in terms. But we are interrupted. 'Room for the Prytanes.' The general assembly is to meet. The people are swarming in on every side. Proclamation is made: 'Who wishes to speak?' There is a shout and clapping of hands: Pericles is mounting the stand. Then for a play of Sophocles: and away to sup with Aspasia. I know of no modern university which has so excellent a system of education.

At any moment one expects an invasion of Spartans led by Julius Caesar to save the Roman empire from the Vikings ('Gee, Marco Polo', said Charlemagne ...). It is gibberish. Phidias was a sculptor, not a builder. *Stoa* is the Greek for 'portico', and metopes would be less misleading than frieze. Rhapsodists no more sang in the street then than Pavarotti does now. Socrates appears to be an evangelist, though there was no category of 'atheist' in fifth-century Athens and no dialogue in which Socrates debates the existence of the gods. The Assembly appears to be meeting when a drama festival is on, and a play by Sophocles seems to be on in the evening, as if we were in Drury Lane (plays were put on once, in competition, three tragedies + satyr play, during the day). Sup with Aspasia and you had better make sure Pericles is there too or risk a thick ear: unless Macaulay is referring to Aspasia when she was (rumour had it) a whore.

There is no doubt that absurd claims have been made for education in classics, resulting in the sort of quasi-mystic, a-historical tosh that Dr Armstrong and Lord Macaulay came up with. But that world is long dead, and I get rather tired when it is resurrected and used to belabour the study of the classical past. In the *Independent on Sunday* for 21 July 1991, for example, the distinguished journalist Neal Ascherson launched a scathing attack on Latin which concluded 'Latin is part of England's fake heritage, part of that pseudo-ancient landscape which I call Druidic. And it should be left to fall down'.[1]

His argument is familiar enough. If Latin teaches you about the structure of language, Russian would do that better (he found Greek more 'modern').[2] Latin demands conformity to rules and therefore produces only people subservient to authority. Latin is supposed to produce 'classical values' in the learner – virtue, self-abnegation, balance – but all that means is swallowing uncritically the Roman empire's sentimental myths about itself. Latin is not a 'universal language' but 'exclusive, esoteric, the private code of a privileged class'. It performs 'a rite of exclusion for those outside, a ceremony of submission for those inside'.

Mr Ascherson was at Eton and learned Latin for ten years and Greek for seven, and Etonians are notorious for believing that the only way things can be done is the Etonian way. But it was prejudice that did for Socrates, and it is Etonian prejudice of Mr Ascherson's kind that continues to threaten to do for classics as well. His whole argument is in fact one massive *ignoratio elenchi*. For it has nothing to do with whether Latin is worth studying or not. If Latin was used to create privileged and exclusive circles at Eton, that says nothing about the subject but everything about the way it was justified and taught. If teachers at Eton used Latin to induce 'subordination of the will on a mental barrack-square', that is not the subject's fault. If Latin was justified by bad arguments, you cannot blame Latin for that. Mr Ascherson even blames Latin for the fact that he did not learn Slavic languages. Blame the curriculum at Eton, please. One could submit maths, physics, history, any subject you care to mention, to an identical attack.

Mr Ascherson, in other words, has confused the subject-in-itself with the banal and snobbish ideology with which it was in his view invested by staff at Eton forty years ago. Latin, for him, is still a ten-year period of unquestioning mental subordination directed at inculcating obedience, encouraging superciliousness and imparting classical values.[3] It demands the 'internalising of a vast web of rules and regulations'. It produces only clerks.

It is as if Mr Ascherson had learned medicine under Dr Mengele and is calling for it to be banned because he can see no other rationale for or way of teaching it. The fact that there are any number of bad reasons for learning Latin does not preclude the existence of good ones. If it is possible to teach Latin badly, it is also possible to teach it well. An academic discipline, cannot be 'good' or 'bad' *per se*: in that respect Latin, like Greek, physics and even geography,[4] remains morally neutral. The fact that the Open University receives about 700 applications a year from adults wishing to begin Greek, and a considerable demand (as yet unmet) to continue with it, must tell one something. Indeed, the Open University starts teaching Latin in the year 2000. It takes no Spurinna picking through the entrails to predict it will receive thousands of applications. Perhaps the OU should issue a health warning that the students are all about to be turned into obedient, supercilious clerks. People who, against all the odds, study Latin and Greek today will be astonished that someone like Mr Ascherson still believes his experience to be the norm.

There are as many reasons for wanting and not wanting to learn Latin and Greek as there are (non) learners. I have over a thousand letters from those who used the 'QED: Learn Latin' and 'Eureka: Learn Ancient Greek' courses I devised for *The Sunday Telegraph* and *The Daily Telegraph* (see Reading List) explaining what the languages have meant to them. 'Improving my English' or 'learning more about words' are not arguments I would use to justify the teaching of Latin, but there is no 'correct' argument. That is what these readers have got out of Latin and Greek. Take it or leave it.

What really gets up classicists' noses, however, are bad arguments for *not* studying the subject. Mr Ascherson's charge of 'élitism' is one.[5] 'Irrelevance' is another. 'Irrelevance' to *what*, however? It cannot be to getting a job.[6] If 'the past' is irrelevant, then farewell history and every other humanities discipline. 'But they are dead languages' is another. No, merely immortal. And they are not dead, just not spoken. That does not make them dead, any more than Chaucer or Shakespeare are dead literature. 'They take too long to learn' is another. That all depends on what you mean by 'learn'. How long is a piece of string? How long does it take to 'learn' physics? One can spend a lifetime on physics as one can on Greek. Or one can spend two weeks on Greek at an intensive summer school and start battling through the Greek New Testament. There are quicker ways of learning Latin than ten years at Eton. These claims, in fact, are all enormously feeble, almost dishonest, excuses. I much prefer straight assertions like 'I can't see the point', 'I have better things to do', 'Languages bore me', 'I am no good at languages', and 'I do not care about history'.

We are past the days when it was assumed that there was a fit between running a profitable cotton mill and penning Greek iambics on the theme of the Calydonian boar.[7] We do not appear to be past the days, however, when the sort of prejudice that did for Socrates bids fair to do for a crucial part of our intellectual and cultural history – a history that becomes more, not less, important as the years go by.

The great Michael Faraday, it is said, having given a demonstration of electro-magnetism, was asked by Gladstone 'But what use is it?' Faraday replied that he did not know, but guessed that Gladstone would one day be able to tax it. Gladstone, a classicist, asks a question about use. Faraday, a scientist, cannot answer it. It is a telling, and historically *typical* exchange. Up till the invention of technology, science was always 'useless'. Socrates tells us that as a young man he was very excited by questions about the nature and origin of the universe, but eventually concluded they were pointless. The big question was – how should we lead our lives? Petrarch, the fourteenth-century poet, scholar and father of the Renaissance, made the same point with exquisite clarity in ridiculing a scholastic opponent:

> He has much to say about animals, birds, and fishes; how many hairs there are in a lion's mane; how many tail feathers there are in a bird; with how many arms a squid binds a ship-wrecked sailor; that elephants copulate from behind and grow for two years in the womb ... What is the use, I pray you, of knowing the nature of beasts, birds, fishes and serpents, and not knowing, or spurning, the nature of man, to what end we are born, and whence and whither we pilgrimage?
>
> Petrarch, *On His Own Ignorance*

The dichotomy Petrarch imposes is false – just because we know about beasts and birds does not prevent us also asking questions about the meaning of life. Further, science and technology have revolutionised the way we live and understand the world – there can be no question of ignoring them now. Indeed, intellectually we have never lived in more exciting times, and they are exciting precisely because the pace of change is so fast and full of promise and the problems associated with it so demanding of response, and because modern communications open up the debate, for the first time in human history, to everyone.[8] Whatever else our society is doing, it is not intellectually stagnating.

But the ethical, philosophical and human problems arising from the intellectual revolution do not go away – they multiply – and the question about how best to live one's life remains to be answered. Nor does one have to answer in Petrarch's religious terms and speculate about metaphysical journeys. The value of living – one's personal richness of life and usefulness to others – is just as valid a conceptualisation.

Some would argue for a moratorium on virtually all technical development (bar medical and environmental problems) while we try as humans to make up for the reaction-deficit to everything that has happened and assimilate scientific advance into our ways of thinking about human priorities. I profoundly disagree. Problems are there to be solved. We do not grow if we do not push ourselves to the limit. But if public problems require public solution, we cannot answer questions about the value of life in any other way than privately.

Here we need all the help we can get, and it seems to me transparent that the richer our understanding of the human condition, the richer and more satisfying our lives will be. If that is right, we are mad to jettison the perspectives of the past. Plato may not solve all, or probably any, of our problems (if he could, we would be in real trouble). That does not matter. There are thousands of years of human experience there on a plate. All we have to do is reach out and take it.

We rightly put enormous energy into preserving for future generations a healthy physical environment. There is a cultural environment too – what humans have thought and done. The fifth-century Greek historian Herodotus, as usual, got it right. He prefaces his magnificent history of the wars between Greeks and Persians (490-479 BC) with the words:

> Herodotus from Halicarnassus [west coast of Turkey] composed this history so that time will not obliterate men's achievements and the great and wonderful deeds of Greeks and non-Greeks alike will not go unrecorded ...
>
> Herodotus, *Histories* 1.1

We cannot get too much greatness and wonder, past or present.

APPENDIX 4

Useful Facts and Sources

Roman numbers[1]

- I = 1, V = 5, X = 10, L = 50, C = 100, D = 500, M = 1000. The origins of this system are debated.
- One adds or subtracts to form intervening numbers. The general rule is that if the smaller number is to the left, subtract (IX = 9), if to the right, add (XI = 11). But inscriptions prefer the additive method, e.g. IV = IIII, XXXX = XL, sometimes to extremes, e.g. IIIIII for VI = 6 and XXXXXX for LX = 60.
- A system of bars indicating 'multiply by' were used for very high numbers. Thus $\underline{} = x\ 1{,}000$ (so $\overline{V} = 5{,}000$) while $\overline{\sqcap} = x\ 100{,}000$ (so $\overline{\sqcap V} = 500{,}000$).

Roman money

as is the lowest unit of money.

2½ *asses* = 1 *sestertius* ('sesterce'), symbolised by HS (originally IIS = 2 + half, *semis*). *Sestertius* derives from *semis tertius*, i.e. the third [whole unit is] half.

4 *sestertii* = 1 *denarius*.

25 *denarii* = 1 *aureus*.

I sometimes think of the *sestertius* as something between £1 and £10, but that simply illustrates how impossible it is to apply contemporary values.

Roman measure

1 *pes* (foot) = 296 mm. (11.65 inches). It was usually divided into twelve *unciae*, 'inches'.

5 *pedes* = 1 *passus* (pace).

125 *passus* = 1 *stadium*.

1000 *passus* = 1 mile, derived from *mille passus* (1480 m.; 1618½ yards).

Greek money

Obol[os] is the lowest unit of money.

6 *oboloi* = 1 *drakhma* lit. 'handful'.

100 *drakhmai* = 1 *m(i)na*

60 *m(i)nai* = 1 talent.

These are related to the weight of the coins. On the Attic standard, an obol is about 0.72 grams, a drachma 4.31 grams, a mina 431 grams (about 1 lb), a talent 25.86 kg (about 60 lb).

Abbreviations of names[2]

- An aristocratic Roman male usually had three names, e.g. **Marcus** (*praenomen*, individual name) **Tullius** (*nomen*, the clan name) **Cicero** (*cognomen*, the family name). So **Gaius** (individual name) **Iulius** (of the Julian clan) **Caesar** (family).
- To these could be added honorary titles, e.g. **Magnus** 'the Great', like Pompey, or **Africanus** 'African' (for outstanding military service there), like Scipio.
- If you were adopted, you took the name of your adopter, adding **-ianus** to your clan or family name. Thus the first Roman emperor **Gaius Octavius** [no *cognomen*] was adopted by Julius Caesar and so became **Gaius Iulius Caesar Octavianus** – adding **Augustus** in 27 BC (see p. 78).
- Women had no *cognomen* and only rarely a *praenomen*.

A. = Aulus, C. = Gaius, Cn. = Gnaeus, D. = Decimus, K. = Kaeso, L. = Lucius, M. = Marcus, M'. = Manius, Mam. = Mamercus, P. = Publius, Q. = Quintus, S. (Sex.) = Sextus, Ser. = Servius, Sp. = Spurius, T. = Titus, Ti. (Tib.) = Tiberius.

The Roman calendar[3]

- The Roman calendar originally followed the ten-month farming year, beginning in March and ending in December (i.e. with an uncounted gap in our January and February) – hence Septem-ber 'seven', Octo-ber 'eight', Novem-ber 'nine', Decem-ber 'ten'. January and February were added, it seems, from 153 BC (from then on consuls are listed as entering office on 1 January).
- Renaming months was a popular political pastime: thus July (originally *Quintilis*, 'fifth') was renamed after Julius Caesar, and August (*Sextilis* 'sixth') after Augustus.
- The calculation of days of the month was a matter of counting *backwards*, *inclusively*, from the three fixed days: the Calends (*Kalendae*) the 1st, Nones (*Nonae*) the 5th, and Ides (*Idus*) the 13th (in March, July, October, May, the Nones fall on the 7th day, and the Ides on the 15th). *Prid.* = *pridie*, the day before.
- Thus Roman days are described as 'the Xth day (*diem*) before (*ante*) the Kal./Non./Id. of the month', e.g. *prid. Kal. Iun.* = 'the day before the first of June' (May 31st), *ante diem* (*a.d.*) *III Kal. Iun.* = 'the third day before the first of June' = May 30th (counting inclusively, i.e. May 30th, May 31st, June 1st).
- The years were not regularly calculated *anno urbis conditae* 'in the year of the city having-been-founded' or *ab urbe condita* 'from the city-having-been-founded' (A.U.C.) because Romans could not agree when Rome was founded. The traditional date 753 BC (by our calculation) was one of a number on offer between 759 and 748 BC. Romans usually dated by the name of the consuls of the year ('in the year of X as consul'). Consuls started in the year the republic was founded, in 509 BC, and we have complete consul lists from 509 BC to AD 541.
- Greeks dated years either by the presiding archons (state executives, 'in the archonship of X') or less precisely by Olympiads, the four-year periods between the Olympic Games, which started in 776 BC ('in the eight Olympiad').

The Roman day

- Romans divided the day into twelve equal portions (*horae*, whence 'hours') from sunrise to sunset.

- Each *hora* varied in length according to the time of year, from 45 minutes to 75 minutes.
- According to Pliny the elder, Rome's first sundial was constructed in 293 BC.
- Hours of equal, constant length were invented by cosmographers and astronomers.
- Greek astronomers followed the Egyptian practice of dividing the day up into 24 equal hours, but the Babylonian practice of dividing each hour up into sixty equal units.
- Medieval astronomers adopted this practice, whence our system of hours and minutes.

The Roman epigrammatist Martial describes the typical day for us, work being crammed as far as possible into the hours of brightest light:

> The first and second hours summon those visiting their patrons,[4]
> The third keeps the barristers busy till they're hoarse,
> Rome keeps men busy about their various occupations till the fifth,
> The sixth is siesta for the weary, the seventh ends it,
> From the eight to the ninth it's exercise time,
> And the ninth then tells us to take our couches for dinner ...
>
> Martial, *Epigrams* 4.8

The legion

The Roman army originally consisted of Greek-style phalanxes. But these were shown to lack flexibility, and in the fourth century BC Rome completely reorganised its army around legions. The principle of the new organisation was that each legion consisted of three lines of men, one line behind the other, each line of men consisting of a series of smaller units called *manipuli*, 'handfuls' or maniples, which had some flexibility of action within the overall structure. Each legionary was equipped with a throwing spear, a shield and a sword. The enemy was softened up by a volley of spears, behind which the legionaries charged in to get to work with the sword. This formed the basis of the Roman citizen army that was to conquer the Mediterranean.

- In the second century BC, one legion consisted of 4,200-5,000 men, divided into three lines: *hastati* ('spearmen') and *principes* ('first men') in the front two lines, and the most experienced soldiers (*triarii*, 'third-rank men') in the last.
- Each line was made up of maniples, commanded by a centurion. There were ten maniples of 120 men in each of the first two lines, and ten maniples of 60 men in the last. So the legion lined up ten-ten-ten, the spaces between maniples in the first line being covered by those in the second, and the spaces between them covered by those in the third.
- In addition there were 1,200 or more *velites*, inexperienced light-armed troops, evenly distributed among the lines.
- Each legion was supported by 300 cavalry.
- Men were recruited by a call-up, the annual selection process which all men aged 17-46 were summoned to attend, for acceptance or rejection. They normally served for six years, receiving a daily allowance of just over a *sestertius*.

The Roman general Marius (157-86 BC) reorganised the legion round the cohort:

- The basic unit of the new legion was now the cohort, 480 men per cohort, ten cohorts per legion.
- A cohort consisted of three new maniples of 160 men each (=six new centuries of 80 men per century). Each maniple consisted of a mix of men from each of the three old lines, increasing its tactical flexibility. *Velites* and cavalry were absorbed into the new maniples. So the new maniple was a microcosm of the old legion.
- The new legion in battle formation lined its ten cohorts up four-three-three.
- The *aquila*, eagle, now became the legion's chief standard (previously other animals had been included – wolf, horse, boar – though the eagle had always held first place).

Augustus (first emperor, 27 BC – AD 14) created a professional, standing army which in AD 14 consisted of twenty-five legions of 5,400 men each. Each had its own number and honorific title, e.g. *Legio I adiutrix* ('helper'), *Legio V Alaudae* ('Larks'), *Legio VI Ferrata* ('Ironclad'). Legionaries were recruited from Roman citizens and provincials, and locally when legions acquired permanent bases. They served for 25 years and were paid 1,200 sesterces a year, with various supplements (including a pension on retirement).[5] Auxiliaries doubled the legionary force to make a total of about 300,000 soldiers in all.

Sources of information

See the general Reading List on p. 8, especially the *Oxford Classical Dictionary* (third edition).

Latin Dictionary: James Morwood, *The Pocket Oxford Latin Dictionary* (Oxford 1995).

Latin Grammar: James Morwood, *A Latin Grammar* (Oxford 1999).

Latin Quotations: James Morwood, *A Dictionary of Latin Words and Phrases* (Oxford 1998).

Latin reference: J.R. Stone, *Latin for the Illiterati* (Routledge 1996).

Classical Myth: Pierre Grimal, *The Penguin Dictionary of Classical Mythology* (Penguin 1991).

Comparative and absolute dating of events: W.R. Biers, *Art, Artefact and Chronology in Classical Archaeology* (Routledge 1992).

Public classical organisations:

The Classical Association: Dr Jenny March, PO Box 38, Alresford, Hants SO24 0ZQ.

Friends of Classics: Jeannie Cohen, 51 Achilles Road, London NW6 1DZ.

Notes

1. Greeks in a Roman World

1. We have about 300 quotations from some 60 plays of Aeschylus, plus about 200 quotations 'from Aeschylus' which cannot be assigned to a specific play; about 650 quotations from about 100 plays of Sophocles, plus about 300 quotations unassignable; over 800 quotations from *c.* 60 plays of Euripides, about 200 quotations unassignable. Some of these 'quotations' amount to but a single word – e.g. from the ancient dictionary of rare words by Hesychius (fifth century AD).

2. I repeat here that, where e.g. Penguin, World's Classics and Wordsworth Classics fail, almost all classical literature is available in translation in the Harvard-Heinemann Loeb editions (Latin and Greek on the facing page).

3. See N.G. Wilson, *Photius: The Bibliotheca* (Duckworth 1994) for a discussion and selected translation.

4. They also act as a check on readings in manuscripts that do survive. It is comforting that in most cases, a quotation of e.g. Sophocles in one of these earlier sources will square with our medieval manuscripts.

5. This is a complex, and fascinating, study. I here gloss over some of the differences between what happened in the Latin West after the end of the western Roman empire in the fifth century AD, and the Greek East, where the Roman empire survived in its Byzantine form till the fifteenth century. For a superb account, see L.D. Reynolds and N.G. Wilson, *Scribes and Scholars* (Oxford 1974).

6. The reason why we have seven (or six + one) plays by Aeschylus and seven by Sophocles is that these were the plays selected by the educational establishment for general reading. Indeed, we would have had only eight by Euripides, had not the fourteenth-century Greek scholar Demetrius Triclinius nosed out nine more in some Byzantine library.

7. Papyrus was manufactured in Egypt from *c.* 3000 BC from a marsh plant *Cyperus papyrus*, especially common in the Nile delta ('papyrus' is thought to derive from 'that of Pharaoh', as if its production was a royal monopoly). Its manufacture is described in detail in Pliny, *Natural History* 13.74-82 – essentially a matter of laying the pith of the plant in strips side by side vertically, and then a similar layer of strips on top horizontally, and pressing them together. A 'roll' of papyrus would run from twenty to twenty-six feet long, and take e.g. a book of Thucydides or a Greek play 1,500 lines long. See *Oxford Classical Dictionary* (third edition, 1996), 'books, Greek and Roman'.

8. A means of photographing a manuscript with a camera through various filters, covering the complete spectra, that will cut out some colours and sharpen others. By this means it is possible, by tweaking, to produce pictures that bring up the ink on the text you wish to read, however faint.

9. The book as we know it, pages folded vertically down the middle and stitched together down the fold or spine, was called a codex and was in use by the first century AD as a notebook. The codex became common after the second century AD, as a result of Christians adopting the format for their scriptures (because of the ease of reference?).

10. E.G. Turner, *Greek Papyri* (Oxford 1968) makes an excellent introduction.

11. In all about 30,000 papyrus texts have been edited, and a huge number still await investigation in libraries in Europe, Egypt and North America.

12. *Oxford Classical Dictionary* (third edition, 1996), under 'papyrology, Greek'.

13. See Richard Janko's thrilling account in *The Council of University Classics Departments Bulletin* no. 26 (1997), 3-19.

14. *Moralia* VIII, 718c.

2. The Classical Period

1. Lord Macaulay's poem about how Horatius kept the bridge is the story of the aftermath of that incident, when Lars Porsena came with his army to try to reclaim Rome for the Etruscans.

2. See Appendix 4.

3. See Elizabeth Rawson, 'Roman tradition and the Greek world' in *Rome and the Mediterranean* (Cambridge Ancient History vol. VIII, second edition, Cambridge 1989), 434ff.

4. See J. Paterson in P. Jones and K. Sidwell, *The World of Rome* (CUP 1997), 22ff. As a growing Mediterranean power, Rome had in fact been attracting Greek *literati* from the third century BC. See note 6.

5. As we have seen, there had been interaction between Greeks and Romans before Greece became a province. The act of provincialisation was simply a convenient marker for Horace's comment.

6. The first Latin literature we know of was composed by a Greek, Livius Andronicus, from Tarentum, in 240 BC. Twenty-one fragments of his translation of Homer's *Odyssey* into Latin survive. He translated closely, but freely changed Greek names into Latin (the Greek Muse, *Mousa*, becomes Latin *Camena*, Odysseus becomes Ulixes, and so on) and toned down Homeric 'indignities' (so 'Odysseus' knees were loosed' became 'Ulysses' heart froze').

7. L.D. Reynolds and N.G. Wilson, *Scribes and Scholars* (second edition, Oxford 1974), 18ff.

8. In imperial times, largely owing to the huge number of Greek-speaking slaves there, the language of the common people of Rome was Greek rather than Roman (N. Purcell in Jones and Sidwell, 169) – one of the reasons why the early Church liturgy was in Greek.

9. The point being that Roman historians were not above a little spin.

10. The situation in the West from the fourth century AD onwards is extraordinarily complex. I offer a very generalised account.

11. The Roman empire traditionally defined its northern limits as around the Rhine-Danube frontier. Romans knew how far they could go. Migrating German tribes had been giving Rome trouble since the late second century BC.

12. This sent shock-waves round the known world. 'In one city, the whole world perished', cried St Jerome. St Augustine wrote his *City of God* to try to explain why God should allow such a thing to happen to an apparently Christian city.

13. The Roman empire in the Greek-speaking East (its capital Byzantium= Constantinople=Istanbul), eventually to be known as the Byzantine empire, largely survived these incursions.

14. It was one of Christianity's great strengths as a religion that it was tolerant of secular government. This relaxed attitude presumably had something to do with early Christians' beliefs that the world was about to end anyway.

15. Briefly, Islam, invented in the seventh century AD, swept east and west with tremendous rapidity. In (modern) Iraq, Syria and Egypt, Arabs came across translations of Greek mathematical, astronomical, philosophical and medical texts in Syriac (for Christian use). They were deeply impressed, and Arabic scholars began translating these works from Syriac (and, eventually, Greek) into Arabic, and writing commentaries on them. Plato, Aristotle, Hippocrates, Galen, Euclid, and Archimedes, among many others, were treated in this way. These were subsequently translated into Latin, and thus made accessible to the West (Spain, which the Arabs conquered in the eighth century AD, was an important conduit). One of the main figures here is the eleventh-century African translator Constantine, who travelled to the east before settling in Salerno with the main works of Arabian doctors, all based on Hippocrates. These he translated into Latin, causing a great stir and a demand for more translations. Thomas Aquinas (1224-1274) knew Aristotle in a Latin version, translated from Arabic. At this time one or two original Greek texts had arrived in the West and been translated, but it was the fourteenth century before Greek texts and Greek teachers in any numbers arrived in Italy from Byzantium, brought by Greek scholars fleeing the Ottoman Turks, and Greek became widely known again from the original sources. Arabic numerals, incidentally, became known in Europe in the ninth century AD via the Latin translation of Al-Kuwarizmi's book on algebra (al-jabr, 'reunion of broken parts'). Latin scholars turned his name into Algorismus, whence algorism, the Arab, or decimal, system of numeration. The Arab contribution to the intellectual debates these translations raised in the West was considerable. W. Montgomery Watt, *The Influence of Islam on Medieval Europe* (Edinburgh 1972) is a fine little introduction to the subject.

16. Reynolds and Wilson, 34f.

17. Classicists too easily forget that the New Testament, being in Greek, is at one level a classical text, though the Jewish thought-processes are in many ways rather alien, and the Graeco-Roman world is marginal to its concerns (in this respect the New Testament is a very important document for classical historians).

18. The language of the Church was Greek till *c*. AD 250. Many Latin Christians at first were slow to accept Jerome's version, preferring the Old Latin versions they were familiar with, and St Augustine was concerned that it should not alienate Greek Christians by replacing the Septuagint. This was the third-century BC Greek version of the Old Testament and Apocrypha and regarded as 'inspired': *septuaginta* is Latin for seventy, the claimed number of translators. By the eighth century Jerome's version had become standard in the West, and in 1546 the Council of Trent called it the 'authentic' text for use in the Roman church.

19. 'What has Athens to do with Jerusalem, or the university with the Church?' he once exclaimed.

20. H.I. Marrou, *The History of Education in Antiquity* (New York 1956), 439ff.

21. N.G. Wilson, *Scholars of Byzantium* (Duckworth 1983), 153-4.

22. It is not surprising that the languages are not learned as thoroughly today as they were a hundred years ago. There was no such thing as a compulsory National Curriculum a hundred years ago, let alone IT, PSE, Citizenship, business studies, vocational training, and so on. One is not comparing like with like. Nowadays one can study for a Classics degree at Oxford without having learned either language at school.

3. Excavating the Past

1. Guides were a feature of ancient sites too: see Peter Jones, *Ancient & Modern* (Duckworth 1999), 24. My favourite modern guide was an Italian who urged us in a church in Ravenna to look in the Virgin's knickers. It finally emerged that she meant niches.

2. Ancient literature, written for the most part by the educated élite, tells one very little about anyone else. Archaeology, however, is no respecter of persons and can be as informative about the poor as it is about the rich.

3. The original temple had been built *c.* 560 BC but was burnt down by a madman called Herostratus in 356 BC because he wanted to become famous. It was rebuilt to the same massive size as the original.

4. *Acts* 19.23-41.

5. If occupation of the site has been continuous, the ancient name will often have survived in some form or other. For example, ancient Smyrna survives in Izmir.

6. This account is based on Wood's *Discoveries at Ephesus* (1877). A brilliant book telling the exciting stories behind a large number of similar excavations of ancient Greek sites is Richard Stoneman's *Land of Lost Gods* (Hutchinson 1987).

7. It was ironical that Wood had already read an ancient source saying that a rich Roman, Damianus, had joined the temple to the city with a covered roadway via the Magnesian gate, 'so that the priests should not be kept away from the temple whenever it rained'. He had chosen to ignore it.

8. Pliny the elder had warned about this: 'it was built on marshy soil so that it might not be subject to earthquakes or threatened by subsidence. To ensure the foundations of so massive a building would not be laid on shifting, unstable ground, they were underpinned with a layer of closely trodden charcoal, and then with another of sheepskins with their fleeces unshorn.'

9. Since 1895 Austrian archaeologists have been excavating and in part reconstructing Ephesus itself.

4. Greeks and the Near East

1. 'As far as we can tell' applies more than ever to claims for 'firsts' in this chapter.

2. On their failure to experiment, see Chapter 14.

3. Cloning, gene mutation and so on may present all sorts of ethical and moral dilemmas, but they surely present no theological ones. I remain baffled by assertions that scientific views of the world have any bearing on the existence (or otherwise) of a deity.

4. Here I draw on P.V. Jones, 'The independent heroes of the *Iliad*', *Journal of Hellenic Studies* vol. cxvi (1996), 108-18. I have now modified the views expressed there about the extent to which Homeric epic anticipates sixth-century Greek rationalism.

5. Homer presents the gods as numinous and terrifying in his third-person narrative, of course: it is the way heroes *talk* about them that interests me here. Likewise, Homer occasionally introduces the concept of ineluctable fate, but fate is the will of the poet: it is a literary card, which Homer plays or not, as he chooses (he is not a theologian). But it is never allowed to reduce the heroes to puppets.

6. The modern mind is shocked by this, but not the ancient. Gods help only winners: far from demeaning Achilles, Athene's help is a sign that he is worth helping.

7. This all occurs in speech. Homer virtually never comments on the action in such a way in his third-person narrative. He merely reports what is happening, without interposing personal observations on it. It is the characters who make the judgements and establish the moral framework within which the epic is constructed. The contrast with the modern novelist, who uses the authorial voice in the narrative to explore, reveal and define the interior and most intimate thoughts of everyone, on every subject, in minutest detail, all the time, could not be more distressing.

8. See my discussion of Homer's hellenisation of universal folk-tales in the *Odyssey* in P.V. Jones and G.M. Wright, *Homer: German Scholarship in Translation* (Clarendon 1997), 29-34.

9. Translated by M.L. West. Cf. S. Dalley, *Myths from Mesopotamia* (Oxford 1989), VI v.

10. The conclusions about Greek and Near East connections that M. Bernal draws in Chapter 1 of his *Black Athena* (London 1987), 'The ancient model in antiquity', are absurdly exaggerated, but much of his general picture is sound. An early researcher into such a connection was Clement of Alexandria, who was seeking parallels between the Bible and Homer in the second century AD. William Gladstone produced three volumes arguing that the God of the Old Testament was the very God worshipped by Homeric heroes. Zachary Bogan, a fellow of Corpus Christi, Oxford, compared Homer and Hesiod with the Old Testament scriptures in 1658. Since the nineteenth century, the pace has been hotting up. M. Krenkel's 'Biblische Parallelen zur Homeros' appeared in 1888; V. Bérard's *Les Phoeniciens et l'Odyssée* in 1902-3; H. Wirth's *Homer und Babylon* in 1921; A. Ungnad's *Gilgamesch-Epos und Odyssee* in 1923.

11. We are talking here of Sumerian and Akkadian (Babylonian languages, Sumerian literature starting *c.* 2600 BC and the language moribund by *c.* 1600 BC but continuing to be studied; and semitic Akkadian, most of whose surviving literary texts date from the seventh century BC); Ugaritic, a west Semitic language, whose surviving literary texts are found on the coast of modern Syria opposite Cyprus – a major ancient entrepôt – dating to *c.* 1400 BC; Hebrew, from the twelfth century BC; Phoenician, its documents surviving but its literature entirely lost, having been written on perishable materials; and non-Semitic Hurrian and Hittite, these speakers living to the north of Syria and stretching into Asia Minor (i.e. modern Turkey), their surviving literature dating from the twelfth century BC.

12. As West admits, a lot of the book consists in gathering together observations already made on the matter. But there is a very great deal too that is new, and the sheer weight of comparisons is overwhelming. Interestingly, West omits Egypt from his survey, finding its influence on Greek poetry and myth 'vanishingly small'. Bernal's *Black Athena*, of course, places enormous emphasis on the Egyptian/African influence on Greece.

13. See in general W. Burkert, *Greek Religion* (Blackwell 1985).

14. Ken Dowden, *The Uses of Greek Mythology* (Routledge 1992) and Richard Buxton, *Imaginary Greece* (Cambridge 1994) are clear-headed introductions to the subject.

15. The *Marmor Parium* ('Marble from Paros') is a record of events from the first king of Athens to the year it was composed (264 BC). It moves without a tremor from myth (Deucalion's flood and Athene and Poseidon's contest over Athens through the Amazons and Orestes) to history (Homer, Sappho and the battle of Marathon, etc.).

16. Deliciously elucidated by Jasper Griffin, with other examples, in his *Homer on Life and Death* (Oxford 1980), 174ff.

17. Anthropologists anthropologise it, psychiatrists place it on the couch,

French structuralists and deconstructionists frankly structure and deconstruct it – and that is just the academics. Myth generously welcomes all-comers, as writers and artists down the ages have discovered.

18. *Antigones* (Oxford 1984), 231.

19. Lowell Edmunds, *Oedipus: The Ancient Legend and its Later Analogues* (Johns Hopkins 1985), 61-2.

5. Democracy's Brief Day

1. The figures show that, while democracy survived, on average two out of ten *stratêgoi* a year were condemned to death by the Assembly after the annual review. The wise ones, of course, left or did not return to Athens if they felt such a judgement might be passed.

2. Though it should be noted that they did not change their original resolution that the thousand leaders of the rebellion should be executed.

3. Nor, incidentally, is our system especially English. Our 'mother of parliaments' was invented by the French overlords of this country after William Duke of Normandy took us over in 1066. Simon de Montfort, that well-known Englishman who first summoned an embryo parliament in the thirteenth century, was born in Gascony. No wonder it was called a parliament (Fr. *parler* 'to speak'). English was not spoken in it till 1362.

4. See John Richardson's 'Governing Rome' in P. Jones and K. Sidwell (eds.), *The World of Rome* (CUP 1997), ch. 4.

5. See in particular Jennifer Roberts, *Athens on Trial* (Princeton 1994), a brilliant history of the anti-democratic tradition in the West.

6. I do not attack or question it either. I just wish we called it what it was. I know words change their meaning. But in the case of democracy, we lose important distinctions by ignoring its original force.

7. Plato, *Protagoras* 319B-D.

8. Polybius, *Histories* VI.43-4.

9. Pliny, *Natural History* XXXV, 69.

10. See Frank Turner in G.W. Clarke (ed.), *Rediscovering Hellenism* (Cambridge, 1989), ch. 4, 'Why the Greeks and not the Romans?'

6. Rhetoric: Persuasion for All

1. *Iliad* 9.443.

2. JACT, *The World of Athens* (Cambridge 1984), 292.

3. Two of the Greek language's favourite particles are *men* 'on the one hand' and *de* 'on the other hand'. The search for oppositions is structured into the heart of the language.

4. E.g. in his *Gorgias*.

5. Interestingly, Aphrodite, goddess of sex, was often depicted in company with Peitho, goddess of persuasion.

6. One would not think so to witness the hysterical trumpetings of newspapers and television stations when they change the studio-set of a news programme or the typeface of a paper, as if this made the slightest difference to what they actually contained. Nice things are, it is true, probably nicer than nasty things, but one does not read a paper to admire its typeface or watch a news programme to prostrate oneself in front of its colour scheme.

7. See Malcolm Heath, *Hermogenes, On Issues* (Clarendon 1995), 20-1.

8. Freud did not help matters either, with his bizarre views about the supreme importance of the unconscious mind.

7. Men on Women

1. A.R.W. Harrison, *The Law of Athens: the Family and Property* (Oxford 1968), 346.

2. With a very few, very specifically limited, exceptions, e.g. Sappho. See the weighty source books and analyses in M.R. Lefkowitz and M.B. Fant (edd.), *Women's Life in Greece and Rome* (Duckworth 1982) and E. Fantham, H.P. Foley (etc., edd.), *Women in the Classical World* (Oxford 1994). An excellent, brilliantly concise account is provided by G. Clark, *Women in the Ancient World* (Greece and Rome: new surveys in the Classics no. 21, Oxford 1989, with supplement 1993).

3. The first Greek philosopher Thales (sixth century BC) expressed gratitude to Fortune for three blessings: 'That I was born human (*anthrôpos*) and not animal, man and not woman, Greek and not non-Greek (*barbaros*).'

4. *Metaphysics* 1.5, 986a22-6.

5. See Plutarch's *Life of Pericles* 24, 32 for the fullest account of Aspasia's life, if you can believe a word of it.

6. Square brackets indicate that there is doubt over the authorship to which the speech was assigned in the manuscript.

7. The comparative liberation of women over the past forty years is due to desirable but unprecedented social and economic conditions. I do not think we learn anything by imagining that those conditions could have applied two thousand years ago. The historian tries hard not to impose contemporary values on past worlds.

8. Emperor and Empire

1. The Athenians also, for all their pride in their achievements, did not spare their institutions. Plato, essentially a pessimist, had no time for democracy or the arts or much else – indeed, everything on this earth is second-rate compared with his perfect world out there somewhere; Aristotle, essentially an optimist, took a teleological view, saw everything working towards a better state and asked how far this or that institution promoted this improvement. The good life, in other words, is not 'out there' but could be discovered and led. From Xenophanes, attacking the immorality of the literary Greek gods and highlighting the pointlessness of praying to a statue ('as well pray to a house'), through the unrelenting political and cultural satire of Aristophanes, to Socrates' relentless attacks on false values, and tragedians' intensive questioning of moral and religious assumptions, Athenians did not live in complacent times.

2. *Pro lege Manilia* 65.

3. For the whole of Calgacus' devastating critique, see Tacitus, *Agricola* 30-2.

4. The crunch for the system would come when Augustus died: only if power was automatically transferred to his successor could this quasi-monarchy be said to work. It was, in the peaceful accession of his nominee Tiberius in AD 14. Augustus was, of course, far too intelligent to write any rules of succession into his political settlements.

5. See J.S. Richardson in P. Jones and K. Sidwell (edd.), *The World of Rome* (Cambridge 1997), 84, 109-11.

6. Paul Zanker, *The Power of Images in the Age of Augustus* (Michigan 1988) brilliantly describes how Augustus negotiated his visual image, or caused it to be negotiated, among those whom he ruled.

7. Thus the eastern provinces were under the control of Antony and declared for him and his Egyptian queen Cleopatra in the final conflict with Octavian-Augustus. It was no empty gesture when, Antony defeated, Octavian immediately made Egypt a province under his personal control in 30 BC.

8. From 167 BC Roman citizens in Italy did not pay tax. This was the result of the revenues accruing from the acquisition of overseas territory.

9. Romans were a bloodthirsty people (it was no coincidence that Mars, god of war, was father of Romulus) and throughout the imperial period emperors felt it important to show that they were up to the business of killing.

10. A *forum* is best thought of as a large, lavish, ornate, public space for shopping, business and general daily intercourse.

11. Since Romans did not know about bacteria, baths had more to do with the 'feelgood' factor than with cleanliness. They were the equivalent of clubs, meeting places for leisure activities, sporting and cultural. They could contain shops, dentists, lawyers, whores, massage parlours and libraries. High and low, great and good, made use of them: they made the life of the rich accessible to all. As Trevor Hodge points out in his wonderful *Roman Aqueducts and Water Supply* (Duckworth 1992), the main purpose of aqueducts was to supply water for baths. They were the great Roman leisure facility, demanded by troops wherever they were stationed.

12. 'Slave' to us connotes a beaten, maltreated human. This is not necessarily the rule. Anyone in the ancient world could be turned into a slave overnight at any time, by conquest or piracy, and have their value then realised on the open market. An owner who bought (say) an Aristotle or (to make a modern comparison) a Rothschild would not fail to put their particular skills to use in his own interests. Only the most brilliant slaves would find themselves in high position with the emperor. The great advantage for an emperor of hiring slaves, and freed slaves, was that their loyalty could be guaranteed: they owed their position in life and what security they had to no one else.

13. Elagabalus is a fine example.

14. The key text here is Fergus Millar's brilliant *The Emperor in the Roman World* (Duckworth 1977).

15. Betty Radice's *The Letters of the Younger Pliny* (Penguin 1969) is the handiest selection.

16. *The Legacy of Rome* (Oxford 1992), 7.

17. The European Community provides a more difficult – or, as we have to say now, 'problematic' – case.

18. Since this is not a letter to or from Cicero, it presumably found its way into his collection as a letter 'for information' sent by the conspirators, to whose cause Cicero was sympathetic. Cicero's *c.* 800 letters are a goldmine for the history of the late republic, as for the man himself.

9. The English Vocabulary

1. On all this, see David Crystal, *The English Language* (Cambridge 1995), 123, 126. I use Crystal extensively in this chapter, but draw more attention to Greek than he does.

2. David Corson, *The Lexical Bar* (Pergamon 1985), 26.

3. See in general J.G.F. Powell, *Introduction to Philology for Classicists* (Joint Association of Classical Teachers 1988). Our sources for this early period include e.g. Latin texts from monastic centres that sprang up when St Augustine came to Kent in AD 597 to convert the Anglo-Saxons (Christianity had already been preached to the Celts under the Roman Empire), vocabulary lists of Latin words translated into Old English *c*. AD 700, *Beowulf* (*c*. AD 750) and the translations from Latin into Old English made by King Alfred (AD 849-899). The total number of words surviving from Old English texts is about 3.5 million (Crystal, 10).

4. See S. Keynes and M. Lapidge, *Alfred the Great* (Penguin 1983), 125-6.

5. Ranulf Higden (1352) reports the teaching of languages as follows: 'Children in school ... are compelled to abandon their own language and to carry on their lessons and affairs in French, and have done since the Normans first came to England.' His translator, John of Trevisa, reports that, now in 1387, the situation has changed: 'in all the grammar schools of England children abandon French and compose and learn in English.' The language was clearly in a rapid state of flux at this time. See Crystal, 35.

6. Powell, 11-12.

7. See Corson, *passim*.

8. For a brilliant text-book for 11-12 year olds about words of Graeco-Latin origin, see Adrian Spooner, *Lingo* (Bristol 1988). Barbara Bell, *Minimus* (Cambridge 1999) is a very simple Latin course aimed at primary school children.

10. The Language of Grammar

1. *Poetics* xx.

2. P.H. Matthews in G. Lepschy (ed.), *History of Linguistics vol. II: Classical and Medieval Linguistics* (Longman 1994), 11ff. I use Matthews widely in this chapter. Stoics (their founder was the Cypriot Zeno, 335-263 BC) divided philosophy into logic, ethics and physics. The study of language came under 'logic'. But how far is language 'logical'?

3. The date of Dionysius is disputed. He may well be first century AD.

4. E.g. Varro *de lingua Latina* x.30.

5. H.I. Marrou, *A History of Education in Antiquity* 371.

6. Lepschy, 45. I give a simplified explanation of a disputed subject.

7. 'Oblique' cases are those that 'lean away' from the nominative, Latin *obliquus* (Varro, *de lingua Latina* viii.49, contrasting the oblique cases with the 'upright' ones, *rectus*).

8. Quintilian's *Institutio Oratoria* discusses in twelve books the training of an orator from boy to finished article – a 'good man skilled in speaking', whose eloquence is matched by his moral force.

9. Here it is worth observing that what we know as syntax (sentence construction) did not receive a full treatment till Priscian in the fifth/sixth century AD. These early grammarians were interested primarily in words and word-formation (accidence – Latin *accidentia*, 'variable properties').

10. E. Rawson, *Intellectual Life in the Late Roman Republic* (Duckworth 1985), 118ff.

11. Homer *Iliad* 6.402-3.

12. David Sedley, 'The etymologies in Plato's Cratylus', *Journal of Hellenic Studies* 118 (1998). Sedley argues that, however bizarre these etymologies are, Plato believes that words can be decoded to reveal important philosophical insights.

13. Aulus Gellius, *Noctes Atticae* x.7.

14. Rawson, 122-23. Caesar's work survives only in quotation. He argued, for example, that the genitive singular of words like *Pompeius* must be *Pompeii* (to distinguish it, presumably, from the vocative *Pompei* and nominative plural *Pompeii*). *Harena*, sand, must not be used in the plural, nor *quadrigae*, a four-horse chariot, in the singular. Caesar may even have proposed the introduction of a present participle for the verb 'to be', *ens* (*ent-*) 'being', by analogy with Greek *ôn* (*ont-*, cf. 'ontology').

15. Grammarians like Varro and Quintilian adopted conflicting principles to adjudicate different cases, calling on current usage, analogy, educated agreement, ancient practice, etymology, the usage of approved authors, and so on. See Holford-Strevens, *Aulus Gellius* (Duckworth 1988), 127.

16. Ancient anomalists, with their belief in language as an irregular series of 'signs' controlled by some underlying system that would explain everything, resemble modern linguisticians for whom 'natural language is an autonomous object of investigation, to be studied in its own right, as a phenomenon connected with human nature' (P.M. Seuren, *Western Linguistics* [Blackwell 1998]). One is reminded of Chomsky's 'deep structures', though Chomsky's assertion that all languages are at heart uniform argues that he is more of a formalist than has seemed to be the case. For analogists, however, language was simply a convention, neither 'true' nor given by nature, to be rendered as logically as possible by any means. Their counterparts today are the 'formal semanticists', for whom logic and model theory, often depending on computer analyses, provide the best means of understanding language. See Seuren, 26-7.

17. Greeks tended to be monoglot, looking down on anyone who did not speak Greek as 'barbarian'.

18. See under 'Translation' in *Oxford Classical Dictionary* (third edition, Oxford 1996).

19. R.A. Kaster, *Suetonius: de grammaticis et rhetoribus* (Oxford 1995), section 23. Suetonius makes it clear that Palaemon favoured cunnilingus and fellatio, both signs of dissolution to Romans who thought males should be in the penetration business.

20. Quintilian, *Institutio Oratoria* I.iv.5 '[the study of literature is] necessary for boys, a delight for the old, the sweet companion of our privacy and the only branch of learning that has more substance than show.'

21. Marrou, 376-7.

22. To sound a personal note: when I was compelled to analyse English through English in my first year at secondary school, I was completely at sea. When I had to do it through Latin, it all made perfect sense.

11. Epic Influence

1. The first word of western literature. I have tried to keep the translation as close to the Greek as possible. Words in square brackets are not there in the Greek, but inserted to help the meaning along.

2. Hesiod *Theogony* 53ff.

3. Also treated by A.D. Nuttall in his *Openings: Narrative Beginnings from the Epic to the Novel* (Oxford 1992), 1-32.

4. I do not pretend to pursue the full range of sources Milton may have had at his disposal. My interest is restricted to the Homeric and Virgilian connections. See Nuttall, 74-113.

5. *Theogony* 1-52.

6. E.g. J. Carey and A. Fowler, *Poems of John Milton* (Longman 1980); J. Leonard, *John Milton: The Complete Poems* (Penguin 1998). This is not to deny that these generally excellent commentaries are rewarding in many other ways.

7. In *Georgics* 4.67ff, Virgil himself offers a delicious parody of epic battle when he describes how bees fight each other. He concludes 'A handful of dust will end it all'.

12. Standing on Orders

1. The origins of the stone-built Greek temple in the seventh century BC are obscure. There are certainly near eastern connections, and Greeks learnt monumental stone-working techniques from the Egyptians. The idea of a surrounding colonnade seems uniquely Greek.

2. Roofs were made of tiles – marble, in the case of the Parthenon – and supported by wooden beams and rafters. These either decayed or were set on fire, bringing the whole structure down. Some temples, however, were re-roofed when they were turned into churches. (Ancient temples were designed to hold not worshippers, but a statue of the god: worship went on outside, at the altar. Christians put roofs on to create a space for the congregation.) This had happened to the shoe-box element of the Parthenon when in 1687 a Venetian mortar lobbed into it. Since at the time the *cella* was being used as an ammunition dump by Turks defending Athens against Venetian attack, the whole lot blew up, taking much of the Parthenon with it. Fortunately Lord Elgin was on hand a hundred years later to prevent an even greater disaster and rescue much of what had survived, in which neither Greeks nor the ruling Turks had shown a great deal of interest.

3. There are two other styles: Tuscan, which is like Doric minus the flutes, triglyphs and metopes, and 'composite', a combination of Ionic and Corinthian (i.e. the capital combines the Ionic volute at the top with the Corinthian acanthus leaves below). The composite may well have been a Roman invention.

4. Sir John Summerson's excellent little *The Classical Language of Architecture* (Thames and Hudson 1980), to which the Renaissance sections of this chapter are much indebted, also begins like this. J.S. Curl, *Classical Architecture* (Batsford 1992) is another superb introduction.

5. The temple of Aphaia on Aegina is the last to have monolithic columns. The fact that three are made of drums may suggest construction was delayed.

6. To cut down weight and thus save on transport costs. One example. Four pieces of limestone were cut in Corinth for the temple of Apollo at Delphi. Cost – 244 drachmas. To ship them the forty miles from Corinth to Delphi – 896 drs. To carry them ten miles from the port (Kirrha) up to Delphi (a climb of 2,000 feet) – 1680 drs. In other words, the cost of transport was ten times that of quarrying. The Parthenon required 22,000 tons of marble from Mt Pentelicus ten miles away, pulled by oxen on carts whose axles had no roller- or ball-bearings. A contract tells us each block had to be of uniform colour, and free from natural flaws and accidental damage. See B. Ashmole, *Architect and Sculptor in Classical Greece* (Phaidon 1972), 17, 94.

7. The temples and their sculpture were originally highly coloured.

8. Interestingly, there seems to have been no forward planning in temple design. So a temple was built outside in: in other words, after the foundations and base were laid, the diameter and spacing of the columns were worked out; they were then constructed; then the entablature was put up to fit the columns; and only then did work start on the shoe-box (because you then knew how high the internal walls had to be) and only then, on the roof. It all seems to have been pretty rule-of-thumb.

9. Martin Thorpe, *Roman Architecture* (Bristol Classical Press 1995) is an excellent, slim introduction to the subject.

10. The ancients greatly preferred architecture to nature.

11. It used to be said that Romans invented the arch. This is not true. They first occur in Macedonian tombs of the fourth century BC, and Hellenistic arched gateways appear occasionally after that. But arches were never a rival to other techniques of construction in the Greek world. The Romans put them at the heart of their building technique.

12. Free-standing Roman columns were sometimes made of brick and then faced. Where coloured marble was used, Romans often preferred monolithic columns to exploit the veining in the stones.

13. The Schools in Oxford illustrates all five orders up the building.

14. On the technical problems see e.g. D.S. Robertson, *Greek and Roman Architecture* (second edition, Cambridge 1969), 231-66. Greeks had experimented with curved space in the construction of round buildings (*tholoi*).

15. Nero was among the first to introduce these new developments into private architecture. The remains of his notorious 'Golden House' (*domus aurea*), built on 200 acres of confiscated land in the middle of Rome after the great fire of AD 64 – which some accused him of starting – bear witness to brilliant use of the new vaulted ceilings.

16. See e.g. J. Onians, *Bearers of Meaning* (Princeton 1988), 59-129. It is worth pointing out here that Islamic architects immediately saw the possibilities of the Roman rounded style and adopted it e.g. for their mosques.

17. Onians, 36-40.

18. E.g. Alberti, *de re aedificatoria* (1452), who started it all, Sebastiano Serlio's six books on architecture published between 1545 and 1575, which became the standard handbooks for the next hundred years, Andrea Palladio, *I Quattro Libri dell' Architettura* (1570), Philibet de l' Orme, *Architecture* (1567), James Gibbs, *Rules for Drawing the Several Parts of Architecture* (1732).

19. Or in the previous colonial lands of the West.

20. Palladio is a nickname based on (Athene) Pallas, goddess of wisdom. His real name was Andrea di Pietro dalla Gondola.

21. The temple front was left by Hadrian with its original dedication to Marcus Agrippa (27-25 BC).

13. Stoics and Epicureans

1. Since virtually none of the work of the early Greek Stoics survives, we have to construct the details of Stoic philosophy largely from later writers, especially Romans like the philosopher-politician Cicero, Nero's adviser Seneca, the Greek philosopher Epictetus, and the emperor Marcus Aurelius.

2. Epicurus' will, three letters and one collection of forty maxims are recorded for us by Diogenes Laertius, the third-century AD biographer of the ancient philosophers (who also has much to say about Stoicism). The great Roman poet Lucretius is a vital source for Epicureanism: he wrote his *On the Nature of the Universe* in an effort to recommend Epicurus' teachings to the Romans.

3. Much of this account of Stoics and Epicureans is based on the excellent introduction by R.W. Sharples, *Stoics and Epicureans* (Routledge 1996). There is a huge scholarly literature on all the issues I discuss. I do not pretend to have done more than present an outline of some of the two philosophies' most influential main ideas.

4. The logic behind this may go something like: if you die you stop breathing. Therefore breath is essential to life. Therefore it must reach all parts of the body. If breath is a life-principle, and the source of life is God, then God must be a special sort of life-principle. Fire is associated with the heavens (the sun). God is therefore a sort of heavenly fiery breath.

5. The philosopher Heraclitus from Ephesus (*fl.* 500 BC) had already connected the soul with fire.

6. Stoics had trouble explaining the presence of evil in a god-filled universe.

7. For Stoic views on language, see Chapter 10.

8. The ancient philosopher Carneades put this argument in its place. To say 'That X will occur is true' is merely a way of defining truth. It does not tell one anything about the likelihood or not of X occurring.

9. Ancients, being on the whole deeply results-conscious, would have found this very hard to swallow.

10. As a social doctrine, this does not exactly commend itself. As a voluntarily adopted personal doctrine, it provided considerable comfort to US Vice-Admiral James Stockdale as he tried to maintain inner strength as a POW in Vietnam 1965-73. He found it to be a considerable help to treat all life's externals – his status, his body, his possessions, reputation and so on – with Stoic indifference. What he would not compromise was his internal moral purpose and will power. See C. Gill (ed.), *The Discourses of Epictetus* (Everyman 1995), xxiv n. 17.

11. This would have been anathema to Greeks, who defined citizenship very narrowly.

12. Except in places like Alexandria (see p. 17), thinking or research was not a state subsidised activity. Only those of independent means, or professionals like doctors or teachers, could carry it out. Plato founded his Academy and Aristotle his Lyceum as private educational and research institutes, funded from student fees.

13. Parmenides' problem is essentially a linguistic one, a matter of defining what we mean by 'is'. Since 'is' can be both existential ('X exists') and descriptive/predicative ('X is something or other'), there is no problem in saying 'X is a tree now and not-tree in the future': we are merely shifting from one use of 'is' to another. But Greek philosophers had not yet got a grip on the problem of the relationship between language and the world (to that extent, Parmenides is an important pioneer). See G.S. Kirk, J.E. Raven and M. Schofield, *The Presocratic Philosophers* (second edition, Cambridge 1983), 245-6 for other possible analyses.

14. So, the universe has to be infinite otherwise the atoms would all pile up in a heap somewhere. As the universe is infinite, there must therefore be an indefinite number of other worlds, past, present and future.

15. For Lucretius' twenty-nine arguments for the mortality of the soul, see *On the Nature of the Universe*, 3.417ff. For Lucretius and Epicurus, see note 2.

16. Lucretius 5.195ff.

17. On all this, see H. Jones, *The Epicurean Tradition* (Routledge 1989), 53-4.

18. Greeks for whom the competitive life was all would have found this difficult to take.

19. Given the dramatic medical advances of the last century, we would have to add 'unnatural and necessary' to Epicurus' list.

20. Plutarch, *One cannot enjoy a pleasant life following Epicurus* (*Moralia* 1097A).

21. But is it not selfish to help others when all you are doing is bringing pleasure to yourself? No. An act which serves other is not tainted because it also serves oneself. See Matt Ridley, *The Origins of Virtue* (Penguin 1997): 'Our minds have been built by selfish genes, but they have been built to be social, trustworthy and cooperative' (249).

22. See H. Jones (note 17), *passim*.

23. See A.H. Armstrong's essay in ed. M.I. Finley, *The Legacy of Greece* (Oxford 1984).

24. By the sixth century AD, however, Christians had thrown off Judaic restraint in this respect and were no longer averse to the concept.

25. Let alone how Plato's thought was developed by disciples after Plato. It must be said here that in the West Plato and other Greek writers were known only through those who wrote about them in Latin. Thus St Augustine was a major source for Platonic thought. See next note.

26. Plato's *Timaeus* was a key text here. It was translated into Latin by Chalcidius in about AD 400, and was the only Platonic dialogue to circulate in the West in Latin until the twelfth century.

27. Translations from Epictetus are found in Gill (see note 10).

28. *Meditations* is a modern title. The sixteenth century manuscript from which the first printed edition was made was entitled *To himself*. Marcus Aurelius was Roman emperor AD 161-180, and his *Meditations* record (in Greek) his private, daily thoughts, probably in later life. There is no thematic organisation by topic or anything of that sort. Working in the Stoic tradition as he was, he examines his own conduct in these reflections and advises himself. See Hard and Gill, *Marcus Aurelius: Meditations* (Wordsworth Classics 1997).

14. Breaking the Ancient Stranglehold

1. See G.E.R. Lloyd, *Analogy and Polarity* (Cambridge 1966) for these two very early forms of argument, with their attendant problems of the extent to which things claimed to be absolutely identical or opposite are so.

2. In other words, while one can discuss rationally the historical background to and argument of a text like the New Testament, there is (as Wittgenstein saw) a limit to which one can talk rationally about religious faith itself.

3. The first experiment in the West, one used to be told, was the demonstration by Anaximenes (sixth century BC) that air could be the basic substance because, if one blew onto the palms of the hand with the mouth open, the air felt hot, if with lips pursed, it felt cold. This proved – as indeed it does – that air could be hot or cold, and the deduction 'therefore' followed that it could turn into anything. Other exceptions can be found in e.g. optics (refraction, by Ptolemy), vivisection of animals (by Galen, showing peristalsis of the stomach and the nervous system in pigs), and harmonics (by Pythagoras, the numerical relationships of octaves, fourths and fifths). But even these were not true experiments, i.e. tests designed to demonstrate the truth of competing, plausible hypotheses, but rather evidence to support one's own theories. See G.E.R. Lloyd, *Methods and Problems in Greek Science* (Cambridge 1992).

4. See P.R.S. Moorey, *Ancient Mesopotamian Materials and Industries* (Oxford 1994).

5. See R.S. Brumbaugh, *Ancient Greek Gadgets and Machines* (Greenwood, 1966).

6. The invention of the vacuum pump was crucial. It demonstrated that gases could expand vastly and contract minutely. An atomic model of the world, in which the atoms in the gas separated out or closed together, explained this phenomenon far more neatly than any other model.

7. Sir Isaac Newton represented new model science admirably. Not averse himself to speculation, he nevertheless drew a rigid value-distinction between mere hypothesis and experiment controlled by rigorous testing.

8. Hippocrates came from Cos and lived in the fifth century BC. That is all we can say for sure about him: he is 'a name without a work'. Or rather, a name with thousands of works. It was not till the time of the emperor Hadrian (second century AD), 500 years after Hippocrates' death, that the corpus of his work became finally stabilised. Any medical treatise written during that five-hundred-year period had a good chance of being called 'Hippocratic' – such was his reputation.

9. I call it 'Galen's' because Galen was the source. It was Hippocratic in origin. These groups of fours were also squared with earth, air, fire and water to produce a neatly holistic synthesis.

10. Has any single person been more of a benefactor to the human race than Louis Pasteur? Pasteurisation, anthrax, germ theory, vaccination, rabies, fermentation – there was scarcely a problem he touched which he did not solve.

11. Roy Porter, *The Greatest Benefit to Mankind* (HarperCollins 1997), 171.

12. Porter, 215-16.

13. See in general Anthony Grafton, *New Worlds, Ancient Texts* (Harvard 1992).

14. If we are amazed that astrology, messages from the dead, aliens, crop-circles – the whole panoply of paranormal piffle promising crocks of gold where the rainbow ends – are still with us, so they were with the Greeks. Sophocles was entertaining holy Asclepian snakes at home at the height of the enlightenment. Recently it was reported that the bones of St Luke might have turned up in Padua.

Appendix 1

1. *The Sunday Telegraph* 17 September – 24 December 1995, *The Daily Telegraph* 19 October 1996 – 1 March 1997. See Reading List.

2. It is worth saying here that Latin had no letters 'v' or 'j' – only 'u' and 'i'. The use of 'v' and 'j' in texts is an English convention.

3. Romans introduced *y* to replicate Greek *u* in the first century BC. Y was used only in words adopted from Greek. The same is true of Latin *z*. Neither is a 'natural' Roman letter.

4. To fit the patterns of Latin declension of noun.

Appendix 2

1. Adapted from my introduction to *Classics in the Curriculum* (QCA Publications 1997).

2. M. Beard and J. Henderson, *Classics: A Very Short Introduction* (Oxford 1995).

3. The Joint Association of Classical Teachers, Institute of Classical Studies, Senate House, Malet Street, London WC1E 7HU (phone 0207-862-8706) has details.

4. 'A white paper on Latin and the Classics in urban schools', *Classical Outlook* 55.2 (1977), 26-30, illustrates the benefits that even a little Latin can bring to deprived children. The sample tested for five months in Indianapolis, for example, showed a one year gain in reading, four months in spelling, seven to nine months in various forms of mathematics and five months in science over the control group.

Appendix 3

1. Ascherson may be misguided on this issue, but his *Black Sea* (Random House 1995) is superb.

2. 'Modern' derives from *modernus*, a Latin formation based on *modo*, 'just now, recently'. It is first attested in the sixth century AD. The term *modernus* was used in the middle ages not of the rejection but of the reworking of the classical world to suit the modern age. *Renovatio* was another term for the same process. The greatest *renovatio* of them all was the Renaissance.

3. I am ashamed to admit that I prefer virtue, self-abnegation and balance to vice, self-indulgence and intolerance.

4. Abuse of innocent geographers is an unavoidable ritual in any educational debate.

5. If 'élitism' means 'producing the best', I am all in favour of it. But in association with classics, it always means 'snobbery'. People, however, are snobs, not languages.

6. A Council of Industry and Higher Education report for 1995 demonstrated that graduates in classics (which was defined as study of the languages or history or culture of the ancient world from prehistoric to Byzantine times) enjoyed a higher employment rate than any other group. I have to say I regard such statistics with suspicion, but do not see any other way of counteracting the rubbish that is put out about the unemployability of classicists. See p. 143.

7. See R.M. Ogilvie, *Latin and Greek* (Oxford 1964).

8. Only our enclosed, secretive, cabalistic parliamentary 'democracy' is intent on keeping the lid on things.

Appendix 4

1. See O.A.W. Dilke, *Mathematics and Measurement* (British Museum 1987).

2. For the full, very complex story, see *Oxford Classical Dictionary* under 'names'.

3. See E.J. Bickerman, *The Chronology of the Ancient World* (Thames and Hudson 1968).

4. When hangers-on paid court to the Great and Good in the hope of a handout.

5. See L. Keppie, *The Making of the Roman Army* (Batsford 1984).

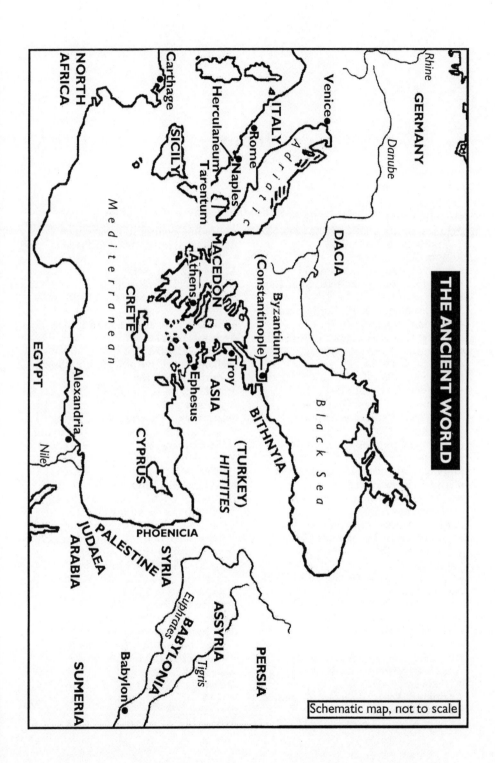

THE ANCIENT WORLD

Schematic map, not to scale

Index

absolute values (and rhetoric), 56

Achilles, in the *Iliad* 34-9, as hero 55, in proem to *Iliad* 103-9

Actium, 21

adjectives, defined as nouns 94

Aeschylus, *Philoctetes* 9-10, Near East 37

Africa, colonisation 16, Punic wars 18, Roman empire 21-3, 78, 135

afterlife, Epicurean views 124-6

aithêr, 133

Alaric the Hun, 22

alchemists, 131

Alexander the Great, 16-17, 19, Ephesus 30, Attic Greek 96-7

Alexandria, research centre 17, language 95

Alfred the Great, 89

allegorisation of myth, 23

alphabet, invention 16, teaching 99

altruism, Epicurean 127

American revolution, discussions of democracy 54

analogy, grammar 94, regularity 98, architecture 119, stoicism 122, argument 132

anaphora, 111

anathema, against teaching Greek 24

Andromache, and Hector 67-9

Anglo-Saxon, and English 87-92

anomaly, and grammar 98

Anticythera machine, 132

Antigone, 44, 67

Antipater (poet), on Ephesus 29

Antipater (general), destroys democracy 46

Antipater (Aristotle's executor), 69-70

antithesis, 111

Antony, Marc, Cleopatra 17, 21, 78, son 24, Ephesus 30, Caesar 85

Aphrodite, near eastern origins 41

Apollo, in Homer 34-7, *Iliad* proem 103-4

Apollonius, conics 17

Apollonius Dyscolus, 97-8

Arabic translations of Greek, 23, 155 note 15

arches, Roman architecture 116-18

Archimedes, 17

architrave, 115-19

archons, executive officials 45, 48-9, dating years 150

argument, rhetorical 56-63

Aristarchus, 17

aristocracy, democracy 45-6, voting 51, sources 65, Augustus 78, satisfying 84, Roman 150

Aristophanes, *Acharnians* 48, 66, *Clouds* 55

Aristophanes of Byzantium, 17, 95

Aristotle, *Constitution of Athens* 12, inventions 33, voting 51, rhetoric 56, 58-63, will 69-70, language 93-4, behaviour 122, altruism 127, renaissance 132-5

army, Roman citizen 18, end of republic 21-2, Augustus reforms 79, organisation 151-2

arranged marriages, 74

Artemis, 5, 27, 29, 31

Asia Minor, in Roman empire 9, 18, 22, 27-8, ruling 77-8, Pliny 83, Columbus 135

Aspasia, 66, 145

Assembly (*ekklêsia*), 46-55, Macaulay 145

ataraxia, 126

Athenaeus, 11, 144